A Library of Modern Religious Thought

ROMAN CATHOLIC MODERNISM

A LIBRARY OF
MODERN RELIGIOUS THOUGHT
General Editor: Henry Chadwick, D.D.

S. T. COLERIDGE
CONFESSIONS OF AN INQUIRING SPIRIT
Edited by H. St. J. Hart

LESSING'S THEOLOGICAL WRITINGS
Selected and translated by Henry Chadwick

DAVID HUME
THE NATURAL HISTORY OF RELIGION
Edited by H. E. Root

S. KIERKEGAARD
JOHANNES CLIMACUS
Translated and edited by T. H. Croxall

JOHN LOCKE
THE REASONABLENESS OF CHRISTIANITY
Edited and abridged by I. T. Ramsey

THE MIND OF
THE OXFORD MOVEMENT
Edited by Owen Chadwick

LIBERAL PROTESTANTISM
Edited by Bernard M. G. Reardon

ROMAN CATHOLIC MODERNISM
Edited by Bernard M. G. Reardon

ROMAN CATHOLIC MODERNISM

EDITED AND INTRODUCED

BY

BERNARD M. G. REARDON

SENIOR LECTURER IN RELIGIOUS STUDIES
UNIVERSITY OF NEWCASTLE UPON TYNE

STANFORD UNIVERSITY PRESS
STANFORD CALIFORNIA

FIRST PUBLISHED 1970

© 1970 A. AND C. BLACK LTD

ISBN 0 8047 0750 2

LIBRARY OF CONGRESS CATALOG CARD NUMBER

77-130825

PRINTED IN GREAT BRITAIN BY

T. AND A. CONSTABLE LTD

HOPETOUN STREET, EDINBURGH

CONTENTS

	PAGE
INTRODUCTION	9
1. The Modernist Aim	9
2. Loisy	16
3. Tyrrell and Von Hügel	36
4. Philosophical Modernism	52
5. The Movement in Italy	59
6. Condemnation	63
7. The Significance of Modernism	65

PART I. LOISY

What *is* the Essence of Christianity?	69
The Church	75
Christian Dogma	82
Catholic Worship	89
"Autour d'un petit livre"	98
L'Évangile et l'Église in Retrospect	107

PART II. TYRRELL

Revelation	111
Belief and Truth	119
1. The Truth of Beliefs	119
2. Belief in God	121
3. The Incarnation	126
4. Belief and Historical Fact	133
The Nature of Christian Doctrine	137
Dogma and Development	145
Catholicism	150
Medievalism and Modernism	164

5

PART III. VON HÜGEL

The Historical Element in Religion 173
Freedom in the Church 180
The Modernist Crisis 184

PART IV. BLONDEL, LABERTHONNIÈRE AND LE ROY

MAURICE BLONDEL 187
The Problem of Apologetics 187
1. Natural and Supernatural 187
2. Philosophy and Christianity 191
Concerning *L'Action* 195

LUCIEN LABERTHONNIÈRE 196
Knowledge of Being and Knowledge of the Self 196
The God of the Greeks and the God of the Christian 198

ÉDOUARD LE ROY 199
What is a Dogma? 199

PART V. BUONAIUTI AND OTHERS

What Modernists Want 207
The Programme of Modernism 211
1. The True Presupposition of Modernism 211
2. Criticism and the Development of Christianity 217
3. Agnosticism and Immanentism 228
The Future of Catholicism 233

APPENDIX. The Papal Condemnation 237
1. *Pascendi Dominici Gregis:* September 8, 1907 237
2. *Lamentabili Sane Exitu:* July 3, 1907 242

INDEX OF PERSONS 249

INDEX OF SUBJECTS 251

ACKNOWLEDGEMENTS

Thanks are due to the following for permission to print extracts from the books mentioned: Librairie J. Vrin, Paris, for permission to translate from Alfred Loisy's *Autour d'un petit livre* and from Laberthonnière's *Essais de philosophie religieuse* and *Le réalisme chrétien et l'idéalisme grec*; J. M. Dent & Sons Ltd, London, and E. P. Dutton & Co., Inc., New York, for Baron Friedrich von Hügel's *Essays and Addresses on the Philosophy of Religion* and for his *Selected Letters*; The Harvill Press Ltd, London, and Holt, Rinehart and Winston, Inc., New York, for Alexander Dru and Illtyd Trethowan's translation of Maurice Blondel's *Lettre sur les exigences de la pensée contemporaine en matière d'apologétique* (English title: *A Letter on the Requirements of Contemporary Thought and on Philosophical Method in the study of the Religious Problem*; American title: *The Letter on Apologetics and History and Dogma*); Presses universitaires de France, Paris, for permission to translate from "Lettre-préface pour une réédition de *L'Action*" by Maurice Blondel in *Études blondéliennes*, i; Librairie Bloud & Gay, Paris, for permission to translate from Edouard Le Roy's *Dogme et Critique*; John Murray (Publishers) Ltd, London, for Ernesto Buonaiuti's *What We Want* in A. L. Lilley's translation; and James Nisbet and Company Ltd, London, for *Pilgrim of Rome: An introduction to the life and work of Ernesto Buonaiuti*: edited by Claud Nelson and Norman Pittenger.

INTRODUCTION

1. The Modernist Aim

The word *modernism*, even in a religious context, has more than one connotation. Today indeed its use is less common than a generation or so ago; but broadly speaking, and for those who employ it in an approbative sense, it means that the modern mind is entitled to judge what is true or right in accordance with its own experience, regardless of whether or not its conclusions run counter to tradition and custom.[1] In this sense, therefore, Modernism could fairly be defined as the attempt to synthesize the basic truths of religion and the methods and assumptions of modern thought, using the latter as necessary and proper criteria. Hence a "modernist" interpretation of Christianity, be it Protestant or Catholic, will be one which seeks to reconcile the essentials of doctrine with the scientific outlook characteristic of the modern world. And since Christianity is an historical religion, claiming that certain alleged historical events are of vital significance for the relations of God and men, a special problem will be that of determining the historicity of its original traditions by the light of historical criticism. Further, it is obvious that from correlating old beliefs with new knowledge a wide variety of views is likely to result, depending partly on what is held to be fundamental in religion and partly on what is taken as valid in the modern standpoint. Hence we have some modernisms which are more "advanced" than others, in so far as they are ready to concede more to criticism when it happens to conflict with tradition, as well as modernisms identifiable in terms of one or another of the historic Christian divisions. For Modernism, like Liberalism, connotes an attitude of mind which is not necessarily tied to a single inheritance of faith or practice.

The present volume is concerned with Modernism in the Roman Catholic Church, although not in so broad a sense as to include relatively "progressive" Catholic opinion in all ages.[2] On the contrary,

[1] Cf. H. D. A. Major, *English Modernism* (*1927*), p. *8.*
[2] Cf. H. L. Stewart, *Modernism, Past and Present* (*1932*), which deals with "modernist" tendencies in the setting of Christian history as a whole.

9

its proper subject is the movement of thought within that Church which began about *1890*, during the liberalizing pontificate of Leo XIII, and was suppressed by his successor, Pius X—of peasant birth—some twenty years later. To denote this more restricted meaning of the term it will be convenient to employ an initial capital letter, as is nowadays usual.[1]

Nevertheless it would be highly misleading to suggest that Modernism, understood in even this limited way, can be looked on as a single coherent doctrine. As was often said at the time, *il y autant de modernismes que de modernistes*,[2] and the remark, as any student of the movement quickly becomes aware, is by no means an exaggeration. Yet to present Modernist teachings in the guise of a consistently thought-out system was the deliberate intent of the papal document—the encyclical letter *Pascendi dominici gregis*—by which Modernism was formally condemned. On the very morrow of its appearance this account of their aims was, for all its gravity, wholly repudiated by Modernists and their sympathizers as a travesty of the facts. Loisy, himself the most distinguished of them, refused to accept any description of the movement's adherents as "a homogeneous and united group". Tyrrell, scarcely less prominent as a leader of *avant-garde* thinking among Catholics, declared that, with all due respect to the pope's utterance, "Modernists wear no uniform nor are they sworn to the defence of any system: still less of that which His Holiness has fabricated for them".[3] Baron Friedrich von Hügel, a close friend of both Loisy and Tyrrell, and a man firmly attached to the Modernist aim of securing freedom for scholarship in the Church, likewise objected that the Vatican account of the movement entirely misrepresented it.[4] Indeed, upon this the Modernists were at one, Loisy going so far as to call the pope's exposition of their doctrines "a fantasy of the theological imagination" and "a system conceived after the manner of the

---

[1] It is still not clear exactly when or how application of the word to Roman Catholic thinkers originated. The earlier use of *modernismo* by ecclesiastical authority seems to have been in a pastoral letter of the bishops of Turin and Verceil, published on Christmas Day, *1905*. Even so, with the reference there given to it, the expression was no novelty, having made an appearance at least a year previously. Cf. J. Rivière, *Le Modernisme dans l'Église* (*1929*), pp. *13–34*.

[2] Cf. A. Loisy, *Mémoires pour servir à l'histoire religieuse du notre temps* (*1930–31*), iii, p. *212*.

[3] *Mediaevalism*, p. *106*.

[4] Cf. Loisy, *op. cit.*, ii, pp. *569* f.

scholastic theories, where not one of them will recognize himself".[1] An anonymous Italian reply to the encyclical, bearing the title *Il programma dei Modernisti*, whilst in general deploring "so deliberate" an attempt to show Modernist views to the public under a false and unfavourable light, rejected in particular the papal thesis that "our zeal to reconcile the doctrines of Catholic tradition with the conclusions of positive science springs really from some theoretical apriorism which we defend through our ignorance of scholasticism and the rebellious pride of our reason".[2]

If, then, in Modernist eyes this official portrait had no resemblance to the truth, how, on the other hand, did they see themselves? The most evident fact about them is surely their insistence that they did not constitute a sect or ecclesiastical party or even a school of thought. They certainly had no formal association, did not meet in regular conference and possessed no official organ, although there were of course journals like *Il Rinnovamento* and *Annales de philosophie chrétienne* which were well known to reflect Modernist opinion. Moreover their range of interests was wide. Some were theologians, others biblical critics and historians, whilst others again were more concerned with social theory and liberalism in politics. As Loisy noted at the time, if they found themselves "in agreement on certain points, and in the first instance on the necessity of a reform of Catholic teaching", it was because they had "entered by different routes into the current of contemporary thought" and "through varied experiences" had reached the same conclusions.[3] The movement was also cosmopolitan. Numerically indeed its supporters were chiefly French and Italian;[4] but Tyrrell was an Anglo-Irishman and von Hügel an anglicized Austrian; whilst Modernist tendencies, at any rate in the

---

[1] Loisy, *Simples réflexions sur le décret du Saint-Office "Lamentabili sane exitu" et sur l'encyclique "Pascendi dominici gregis"* (*1908*), pp. *14.*, *149.*

[2] *The Programme of Modernism*, translated from the Italian, with an introduction by A. L. Lilley (*1908*), pp. *1*, *15*. The English translator was Fr Tyrrell himself. The accusation of "ignorance of scholasticism" may have had some truth in respect of Blondel and Laberthonnière, not to mention Loisy, who never claimed to be a philosopher at all, but it certainly did not apply to Tyrrell.

[3] *Op. cit.*, p. *52*.

[4] Cf. Alfred Fawkes, *Studies in Modernism* (*1913*), p. *375*: "Modernism proper is a movement of the Latin mind. . . . Its home is in the Latin countries—France and Italy; and at the head of every department of its activity stands a man of Latin race." But the generalization, although plausible, is not unexceptionable.

shape of the *Reformkatholizismus* associated with F.-X. Kraus (*1840–1901*) and Hermann Schell (*1850–1906*), were not lacking in Germany.[1] Again, although most Modernists were priests—Mgr Mignot, one of the movement's strongest sympathizers ("the Erasmus of Modernism", he has been called), was an archbishop, occupying the see of Albi in the south of France—some, like von Hügel or Le Roy of Fogazzaro, were laymen. But whatever the diversity which Modernists displayed amongst themselves they were united in their deep longing for and determination to promote such an intellectual renewal of Catholicism as would equip it for the task of confronting the twentieth-century world, not with suspicion or open hostility, as in Pio Nono's notorious *Syllabus of Errors (1864)*, but with a genuine understanding of its needs and problems.

That Catholicism and the Catholic Church, were they effectively to meet the challenge of an increasingly secular civilization, would have to abandon many of the attitudes of the Counter-Reformation—attitudes, furthermore, which the growth during the preceding century of a reckless ultramontanism had served only to render the more grotesque—was with the Catholic Modernists a basic conviction. They were troubled because they were themselves Catholics and thus seemingly committed to the ways of the past, and yet men also of their own age, sharing its aspirations, aware of its problems and participating in its knowledge. Could a really critical intelligence, they had to ask themselves, any longer in conscience submit to the authority of a Church which tacitly ignored or even overtly denied much that the modern mind finds it impossible to disown, save by forfeiting its own integrity? They—and very many others, they felt assured, whose views were not publicized—were as Catholics in a grave dilemma. On the one hand, they could not bring themselves to abandon their religious heritage, the cardinal values of which were proven, nor, on the other, were they able to opt out of the cultural conditions which any educated man of their age took for granted. The seriousness of the problem was of course no new discovery. A generation earlier the English liberal

---

[1] On Schell in particular see J. B. Pett, "Un théologien novateur en Allemagne", *Revue du clergé français*, Jan. *15, 1898*, pp. *310–326*. It is arguable that the United States of America too had a native Modernist in the person of William L. Sullivan (*1872–1935*), a Paulist who eventually left the Church to become a Unitarian minister. Cf. John Ratté, *Three Modernists: Alfred Loisy, George Tyrrell, William L. Sullivan (1968)*.

Catholic, Lord Acton, had suggested that the Church "in her zeal for the prevention of error, represses that intellectual freedom which is essential to the progress of truth" and that in the supposed interest of safeguarding the faith "she claims a right to restrain the growth of knowledge and to justify an acquiescence in ignorance".[1] The whole tendency of Vatican policy during the preceding century had been to exclude the very idea that (in the words of the *Syllabus*) "the Roman Pontiff can and should reconcile himself with, and accommodate himself to, progress, liberalism, and modern civilization".

Towards the century's end, however, it was becoming only too obvious to Catholic scholars, awake now to the nature and extent of modern Protestant research in the field of the Bible and early Christianity, that the narrowly traditionalist standpoint upon these matters, rigidly upheld in the seminaries, was likely to involve all Catholic teaching and apologetic in increasing discredit. The "biblical question" had in fact become for the modern believer a crucial issue.[2] Not only did the old dispute as to the relations of scripture and tradition assume a new aspect, but the critical approach to what Trent had declared to be the twin sources of divine revelation had come to focus the entire problem of the relations of faith and knowledge, religion and science, which the nineteenth century had already posed at other levels. Scientific biblical study was proving a tough enough morsel for traditional Protestantism to digest—as witness, in their day, the *Essays and Reviews* and Colenso controversies in this country; in Catholicism it was bound to challenge the very basis on which the Church's own infallible authority and divine mission were alleged to rest. Yet if the Catholic Church were to sustain its claim on modern men's allegiance it could not continue to evade the questions which, for the educated intelligence, called insistently for answer. Not only was there need for a new apologetic; the good name of Catholicism as the friend and patron of intellectual freedom—whatever its past record may have been—was now finally at stake.

The accession of Leo XIII on the death in *1878* of Pius IX held, as it seemed to many, all the promise of a new and more liberal era in Vatican policy, both politically and intellectually. The new pontiff

---

[1] "Conflicts with Rome", in *Essays on Freedom and Power* (ed. G. Himmelfarb), p. *244*. The essay here cited was first published in *1864*.
[2] Cf. A. Houtin. *La question biblique au XIXe siècle* (*1902*).

differed markedly in character from his benign but purblind predecessor. Leo was reminiscent less of a Counter-Reformation than a Renaissance pope—the vices, needless to say, excepted: "a lettered Italian of an almost extinct type", it was then observed.[1] An aristocrat by birth, he possessed intellectual and literary tastes, but above all an instinct for diplomacy. In contrast to Pius he had the appearance of being a liberal, turning his back on the political intransigence with which Vatican policy had long come to be associated. The appearance nevertheless was to prove largely illusory, since he was scarcely in fact less of an ultramontanist than the man he had succeeded. His ends, in other words, remained those of his predecessor, but he sought them by other means. Aware that the international reputation of the papacy had suffered under Pius, whose dominant aim in a seemingly hostile world had been to consolidate the Church and his own authority behind defensive dogmatic barriers, Leo sought to restore that reputation by deliberately fostering good relations in the international field. Accordingly the Vatican's façade of intransigence had to be modified. The substance of policy would continue unaltered, but its methods were to be adjusted to the changed conditions. As Wilfrid Ward afterwards expressed it, the pope's attitude in effect was: We must use the modern liberties—our ultimate ideal being largely to get rid of them.[2] However, back in the eighties Leo's true mind was not yet known and even his subsequent official acts, such as the encyclicals *Rerum novarum* (*1891*), on social questions, and *Providentissimus Deus* (*1893*), on the Scriptures—not to mention the early letter, *Aeterni Patris* (*1879*), urging renewed study of the Thomist philosophy—seemed to be at last encouraging more adventurous ways of thought in the Church. Further, the new pontiff had in *1880* opened the Vatican archives for the first time to the world's scholars, and the later international Catholic congresses held in Paris (*1888, 1891*), Brussels (*1894*), Fribourg (*1897*) and Munich (*1900*) were widely taken as evidence of a fresh spirit in the Vatican.[3] It thus looked, on the surface at least, as if the liberal Catholic movements, in France, Germany, England and even Italy, which under Pius (or in the case of Lamennais

---

[1] Fawkes, *op. cit.*, p. *81*.

[2] *Ten Personal Studies* (*1908*), p. *192*.

[3] The Biblical Commission was established in September *1902*, with an apparently liberal membership, von Hügel being among those offered a place on it. Cf. M. de la Bedoyère, *The Life of Baron von Hügel* (*1951*), pp. *136* f.

and Montalembert Gregory XVI) had met with little but opposition
and by this time had virtually petered out, might possibly revive. At
all events the intellectual climate of Rome when the final decade of
the century opened was felt to be in no wise unfavourable to a new
liberty both in scholarship and in philosophical speculation. Loisy,
then at the Institut Catholique of Paris, declined to be pessimistic
about *Providentissimus Deus*—although von Hügel was less sanguine—
and men like Léon Ollé-Laprune and his young disciple, Maurice
Blondel, were confident that any officially-sponsored break with the
arid textbook metaphysics of the seminaries was sign enough that
Catholic philosophy was at last free to take a modern direction.[1]

The Modernist movement, with its faith in the possibility of a
synthesis of Catholicism and modernity, can fairly be said to have
been the creation of the new pontifical reign. To the older liberal
Catholicism it owed little directly, except to Newman and perhaps
Montalembert.[2] The problems which had troubled the Liberals still
awaited solution, being intrinsic to the age, while any overt attempt
to link fresh endeavours in thought and scholarship to theirs would,
in view of their predecessors' fate, have been undiplomatic, to say
no more. Loisy quite certainly believed himself, in his own critical
research, to be making a completely new start, with only Renan's
example to guide him. When in *1889* he was appointed to a professorship in Holy Scripture at the Institut he was conscious of beginning not
only his own life-work but a task never before undertaken by a
Catholic scholar.

> I had conceived [he afterwards wrote] a programme of very
> simple, but vast and logical teaching, which would have filled my
> life had I been left to fulfil it. My fundamental thought, which I did

---

[1] Wilfrid Ward, writing in *1893*, went so far as to state that the pope "had
notoriously encouraged historical studies and encouraged their pursuit in the most
absolutely candid and critical spirit" (*William George Ward and the Catholic
Revival*, p. *425*).

[2] It has been argued that Modernism was a conscious attempt to resume the
work of Johann Adam Möhler and the Catholic Tübingen theologians of the
period *1815–1840*. See E. Vermeil, *Jean-Adam Möhler et l'école catholique de Tübingue.
Étude sur la théologie romantique en Würtemberg et les origines germaniques du
modernisme (1913)*. Loisy however denied the truth of this as far as he himself was
concerned, and there is no evidence that either von Hügel or Tyrrell or any other
Modernist deliberately took his cue from Möhler and his school.

not utter too clearly, was that there was no scientific study of the Bible in the Catholic Church, and that it had to be created by shifting . . . questions of biblical introduction and exegesis from the theological and dogmatic spheres into the sphere of history for rational and critical study![1]

And he adds:

> In taking possession of the chair of Holy Scripture at the Institut Catholique . . . I had no undue confidence in my youth [he was by then 32] and my limited science; but I was confident in the goodness of my cause, in the legitimacy of my enterprise, in the rightness of my action, notwithstanding the ambiguity which would inevitably result from the contact that had to be maintained with theology and the official teaching of the Church.[2]

2. Loisy

Ambiguity—*équivoque* is his word—was thenceforward indeed to be the mark of Loisy's work until his eventual excommunication in *1908*. In historical retrospect he remains the most impressive, because the most learned, subtle and eloquent, of the Modernist leaders. As a biblical scholar he was among the most brilliant of his day, and although he always insisted that his *métier* was exclusively that of historian and exegete, the long series of publications bearing his name—for he was an exceedingly prolific as well as elegant writer— cover a wide range of subjects, historical, exegetical, theological and philosophical.[3] Over the last thirty years or so of his life, however, he had no religious affiliations of any kind and was content to be known as a humanist. But even in his final phase as a Catholic he had to all intents ceased to regard Modernism as anything other than a defeated cause to which he no longer felt himself committed. For to Loisy's logical intelligence a modern *rationale* of Catholicism was available to the individual Catholic only so long as the Church itself was willing

---

[1] *Mémoires*, i, p. *172*.
[2] *Ibid.*, p. *179*.
[3] For a complete bibliography of Loisy's writings, published and unpublished, see A. Houtin and F. Sartiaux (ed. E. Poulat), *Alfred Loisy, sa vie, son œuvre (1960)*, pp. *303–324*.

to countenance it. A Catholic whom the Church disowned, on whatever ground, had no title to speak on its behalf. For, as Loisy saw it, Modernism was not and could not be merely the expression of an idiosyncratic or a sectarian viewpoint. It either was Catholicism renovated in a modern style or it was nothing at all. Tyrrell, Loisy's English *confrère*, was less logical; but his personal conviction as a Christian went far deeper.

Alfred Firmin Loisy was born at Ambrières (Marne) in February *1857*. As the son of a small farmer he would have been brought up to his father's work had it not been for his physical weakliness; nevertheless, to embrace the priesthood was his personal decision, not dictated by parental wishes. In *1874* he entered the *grand séminaire* at Châlons, with his faith in the traditional Catholic system so far quite undisturbed. "No least cloud of doubt," he tells us, "yet troubled my relations with the divine world."[1] The Church he took to be "a great school of holiness and truth" whose officers, in possession of clear and certain teaching, "laboured with one accord to keep their charges in the way of salvation".[2] Even so, he was old enough for his intellectual precocity to begin to assert itself. Between his religious devotion and his rational curiosity, tension was very soon to grow, and before many years had passed—he was ordained priest in *1879*— he was wide awake to the difficulties of reconciling the doctrines in which he had been instructed in boyhood with the conclusions to which his studies in the theological faculty at the Catholic university of Paris had already led him.

Almost from the first, in fact, his career as a student had brought him intellectual stress, and he gained no comfort from his spiritual directors. Moreover in December *1882* he began to attend Renan's lectures at the Collège de France, and it was from these that his sense of vocation as a scientific biblical scholar may be said to have sprung.[3] Yet although he admired Renan as a teacher he did not make his personal acquaintance and indeed never spoke to him. He still thought Renan's general position false and that he was wrong to have left the Church. "So I instructed myself at his school, hoping to prove to him that all that was true in his science was compatible with Catholicism sanely understood."[4] It also was during his course at the Institut that

---

[1] Loisy, *op. cit.*, i, p. *35*.　　　　　　　[2] *Ibid.*, p. *44*.
[3] Cf. *Mémoires*, iii, pp. *99, 437*.　　　　[4] *Ibid.*, i, p. *118*.

B

he came under the influence of the historian, Louis Duchesne (*1843–1922*), whom he later spoke of as having done "more than anyone to initiate a scientific movement in French Catholicism".[1] But an interesting pointer to the way his mind was shaping at this time is the imaginary dialogue he composed as taking place between a young scholar—himself presumably—and the Church. The latter he represents as saying:

> I must allow that my teaching, immutable in its principles and in its end, can and ought to be modified in its form, to be perfected in its exposition, in order that it may better respond to the needs of the generations which it must bring to God. Perhaps my doctors in this century have been inferior to their task and have not understood that it is permissible for them to abandon the old formulas, that they ought almost to forget them, in order to preserve for the world the very substance of the truth which is entrusted to me. God will give me, I hope, men apt for this work, and you will no longer be able to accuse me of ignorance.

To which the young scholar replies:

> It is not your formulas that you must translate for us into a speech intelligible to the men of our age; it is rather your ideas themselves, your absolute affirmations, your theory of the universe, the conception you have of your own history, that you must renew, rectify, and reconstruct.[2]

A parochial ministry—and for a short while he was a village *curé*—might have deflected his thoughts away from such difficulties and speculations, but his return to Paris and academic work compelled him to face the intellectual problem of Catholicism in its full bearing.

---

[1] *Ibid.*, p. *164*. At first, however, he felt a certain coolness towards Duchesne. "I knew well," he wrote, "that he had much yet to teach me in the order of science; but my life was consecrated not to science but to the service of the Church through science." He was also embarrassed—surprisingly, in view of the ironical style which he himself was afterwards to assume virtually as a habit—by Duchesne's "Voltairean tone". "Nor," he adds, "did I inwardly appreciate his Rabelaisian jokes." *Ibid.*, pp. *105* f. He also considered him to be at heart a sceptic. On Duchesne as scholar and churchman see C. d'Habloville, *Grandes figures de l'Église contemporaine (1925)*.

[2] The whole dialogue is given in *Mémoires*, i, pp. *118–125*. See also *Choses Passées (1913)*, pp. *95* f.

By *1892* he was in no doubt that "what we have to do is to renew theology from top to bottom, to substitute the religious for the dogmatic spirit, to seek the soul of theological truth and leave reason free under the control of conscience".[1] In the meantime he was prosecuting his critical studies with, as events were to show, a fatal assiduity.

The first crisis in Loisy's affairs occurred in *1893*. The rector of the Institut Catholique, Mgr D'Hulst, a man of what were then considered broad views, was prompted by the recent death of Renan to contribute an article to the liberal Catholic periodical, *Le Correspondant*, on "The Biblical Question". His aim was the very laudable one of helping to create in the Church a climate of opinion favourable to scientific biblical study. Unfortunately he had himself little first-hand knowledge in this field, and in any case his attempt to distinguish the terrain of science and history, in which the biblical writers may very well have gone astray, from that of faith and morals, as to which the divine inspiration would have preserved them from error, was not kindly received and set off an acrimonious controversy. His colleague Loisy was not mentioned by name in the article but the latter's teaching had already come in for criticism at the famous seminary of Saint Sulpice, and it was widely assumed that D'Hulst was trying obliquely to defend both the soundness of his Hebrew professor's reputation and the good name of the Institut itself—as indeed he was, in a way. But *qui s'excuse s'accuse*, and thus Loisy found himself implicated in a dispute not of his own choosing, a fact from his point of view all the more embarrassing since his good-natured rector had also, in the process, seriously misrepresented him. For Loisy did not now accept any of the theories of inspiration current in the Church, whether "conservative" or "broad". The issue, for him, was not the *area* of inspiration at all. Rather did he see the whole idea of inspiration as a purely theological one and of no relevance to criticism as such. Historical documents— and the Bible was no exception—required in the first place to be studied by the historical method, inasmuch as their content had been conditioned and limited by their time and place of origin. Criticism necessarily preceded theology and edification, and might show that in certain respects ancient scriptures were unsuited to the purposes to which later piety had adapted them. Hence "il ne s'agit plus de savoir

[1] *Mémoires*, i, p. *210*.

si la Bible contient des erreurs, mais bien de savoir ce que la Bible contient de vérité".[1] "I had found", he said,

> a clear and advantageous distinction, in my principle of the truth of the Scriptures. There was the historical sense of the texts and their traditional one; the first appertaining to them in virtue of their origin and true nature, the second that which has been grafted on to them by the work of faith in the later evolution of Judaism and Christianity. For the critical historian only the first is to be considered as the meaning of the biblical text; the second regards the history of exegesis and belief.[2]

The controversy was brought to a finish however by a sudden papal pronouncement in the shape in the aforesaid encyclical *Providentissimus Deus*, reaffirming the doctrine of inspiration as laid down by Trent and the Vatican Council of *1870*. This document, after the manner of such utterances, was not free from ambiguity, and Loisy, as we have seen, was not dismayed by it, but the general inference at the time was that liberal ideas on this subject could henceforth expect no official encouragement and men like the young Institut professor had better take care. D'Hulst submitted at once, as indeed did Loisy himself, whose compliance nevertheless did not save him from dismissal.

After an interval of some months the former university teacher was appointed chaplain to a girls' school run by Dominican nuns in the Paris suburb of Neuilly. His unexacting duties left him time to study and during the five years he spent there his interests widened considerably. More and more clearly did he see his task to be nothing less than that of "adapting Catholic doctrine to the exigencies of contemporary thought".[3] "I did not", he subsequently recorded, "accept any article of the Catholic creed, except that Jesus had been 'crucified under Pontius Pilate'." The rest presumably he interpreted only in a figurative or symbolical sense. But what he did not question was that religion is "an immense power, which had dominated, which dominated still, and which promised to dominate always, the history of humanity". Admittedly its historic forms had had their limitations, faults and abuses, "but they represented almost the whole moral life of the human race". Christianity was distinguished from all other religions by

[1] *Études bibliques* (3rd ed., *1903*), p. *146*.
[2] *Mémoires*, i, p. *178*.   [3] *Ibid.*, p. *358*.

its lofty moral idealism, whilst the Catholic Church was "the mother of the European peoples". A queen whose power had declined, she yet had great influence, and did she but know how to speak to the peoples "no adverse power could withstand her". "To this Church, in spite of all she had made me suffer already, I remained", he says, "sincerely devoted". In no way did its service seem to him incompatible with that of truth or humanity. The intellectual blindness and moral shortcomings of contemporary ecclesiastics were only too obvious, but he was not in the dilemma of having either to endorse the obscurantist teaching with which Catholicism was usually associated or else to repudiate the Church altogether. On the contrary, the Church's moral action deserved support, "and the possibility of a reform which would modify Catholicism without destroying it seemed to me all the more admissible since in all directions many people, on one point or another, more or less timidly or courageously according to their character, appeared to welcome it".[1]

Thus by the autumn of *1894* Loisy had already reached what in essence was to be the standpoint of his later, distinctively Modernist writings. His sincerity is not to be impugned, as it sometimes has been.[2] It was simply that Loisy's whole idea of Catholicism, as he viewed it in the light of history, now differed profoundly from that commonly presented to the faithful, and that he likewise was convinced that this much revised version would have to be publicly adopted if Catholicism were to retain any credibility among the educated. And this was to remain his *locus standi* as a Modernist. When in the end the course of events carried him outside the Roman communion he also found himself outside Christianity. The non-Catholic Christian will probably fail to see the logic of this, but at no time did Loisy envisage the possibility of some Protestant *tertium quid*. He was a Catholic first and last, and when he ceased to be a Catholic he likewise ceased to be a Christian. But he was content to regard himself as a Catholic so long as the Church itself tolerated him.

His critical and apologetic aims were further stimulated by his friendship not only with Mignot but with Baron von Hügel, whom he had met in the previous November. Von Hügel was always to stay singularly loyal to him, even when he could no longer share

---

[1] *Ibid.*, pp. *363* f.
[2] Cf., *e.g.*, Rivière, *op. cit.*, p. *98*, and de la Bedoyère, *op. cit.*, p. *73*.

his views or approve his actions. It was to the baron that, in September *1896*, Loisy first disclosed the fact that he was engaged in writing what he intended to be a major work, in the shape of a general exposition of Catholic doctrine as adapted to the times and for the benefit of non-Catholics as well as Catholics; and he was particularly concerned to inquire whether the writings of Newman might be of assistance to him in the preparation of it.[1] He was not yet familiar with Newman's works apart from extracts from the *Essay on Development,* but these had aroused his curiosity. When later he came to read Newman more extensively he was deeply impressed: "Ce doit être", he wrote to von Hügel, "le théologien le plus ouvert qui ait existé dans la sainte Eglise depuis Origène."[2] The theory of development as stated by Newman he thought especially valuable, superior to Harnack's or Sabatier's. "La théologie catholique", he advised readers of the *Revue du clergé français,* "a eu de nos jours le grand docteur dont elle avait besoin".[3] At the same time it would be a mistake to suppose any great influence from Newman's side on the substance of Loisy's thought. The cardinal's work helped him in so far as it confirmed ideas already well shaped in his mind. Moreover he could hardly have failed to see the advantage of claiming for his own views the authority of so eminent a figure in the Church.[4] But Loisy's personal conception of the development of doctrine was by this time assuming a much more radical form than in Newman's *ad hominem* argument. Of historical criticism the English divine, back in *1845,* had known nothing and his essay takes no account of it. Loisy realized that doctrinal development—to the historian an unquestionable fact—needs to be studied in its widest context and with a clear understanding of its implications.

These ideas were to be set out in the *livre inédit* referred to above, but they had a public *début* in a series of articles which Loisy wrote about this time for the *Revue du clergé français* under the pseudonym of A. Firmin.[5] The *livre inédit* had taken note of certain "postulates"

---

[1] This undertaking was never published, but Loisy himself provides a detailed account of it in his *Mémoires,* i, ch. xvi.

[2] *Mémoires,* i, p. *426.*

[3] December *1, 1899,* p. *20.*

[4] Cf. P. Desjardins, *Catholicisme et critique (1905),* p. *117* and Bernard Holland (ed.), *Select Letters of Baron von Hügel (1927),* p. *16.*

[5] See "Le développement chrétien d'après le cardinal Newman", December *1, 1898,* pp. *5–20;* "La définition de la religion", February *15, 1899,* pp. *193–209;* 'L'idée de la révélation", January *1, 1900,* pp. *250–271;* and "Les preuves et

which were basic to Catholicism as traditionally taught but which modern science had plainly rendered untenable. The first of them was the Old Testament idea of God and creation, supposedly integral to Christian theism. The second was the belief that the Old Testament, again, had predicted Christ and the Church under the guise of the Messiah and his Kingdom; and the third, that Catholicism in its actual historic evolution, complete with hierarchy, dogma and sacraments, was of Christ's direct institution. Loisy's contention was that these obsolete notions would have to give way to principles which science and criticism could endorse. But this in turn entailed a thorough revision of the concept of revelation itself. Revelation in traditional teaching was an absolute, unalterably fixed; but the historian as such knows nothing of absolutes, only relativities. Hence in a properly historical perspective revelation must be seen rather as "a kind of divine education proportioned to the intellectual conditions of the men for whom it was destined". In other words, it can be intelligibly discussed only in terms of human experience, subject as this always has been to the particular conditions obtaining. Dogma, which is the outcome and articulation of this experience, lies under the same relativity and in its attempt to describe the ineffable falls back on "a species of algebraic notation" composed of symbols and metaphors. These symbols and metaphors, in relation to the experiences to which they give utterance, are a creative stimulus, but they are not wholly adequate or final and their utility varies with its dependence on man's intellectual and moral progress. The fault of the traditional teaching was in having so fastened its attention upon the forms of the symbols themselves as almost to have forgotten the reality for which they stand.

But Loisy's criticism was directed not only against the familiar visage of Catholic theology; he also had liberal Protestantism in mind, more particularly as represented by his own fellow-countryman, Auguste Sabatier, whose *Esquisse d'une Philosophie de la religion*, had then recently been published.[1] The liberal Protestant viewpoint was by

---

l'économie de la révélation", March 5, 1900, pp. 126–153. Cf. E. Poulat, *Histoire, dogme et critique dans la crise moderniste* (1962), pp. 779–794.

[1] 1897. His *Religions d'autorité et la religion de l'Esprit* appeared posthumously in 1904.

now well known: Catholicism, with its massive accretions of hierarchy, dogma and sacramentalism, had, it was maintained, stifled the original gospel of Jesus, while in the modern world its authoritarianism was anachronistic. It was indicted, that is, at the bar of both criticism and history, and of their verdict there could be no doubt. Loisy, however, judged all this to be too hasty. Modern Protestantism was one thing, but Christianity in its primitive form another. The former was purely individualistic, whereas to the latter mere individualism in religion would have been unintelligible. Man is related to God in and through his relation to his fellows. But if religion, historically viewed, is basically social it will inevitably demand social expression; institutions are of its nature. Religious faith is individual, but it arises within a community of belief. Christianity therefore, as a communal religion, is more than the original teaching of Jesus: the gospel had been its primary phase, but that now lies in the distant past. Christian experience, as history proves, transcends the consciousness of Jesus himself inasmuch as it is always meeting new conditions and assimilating fresh elements. What the Bible speaks of is the Kingdom of God, "not some psychological experiences from which posterity might gain profit". Christianity is identifiable not in terms merely of one or two residual beliefs to which all else is at best only accessory, but by its living action and its power to influence souls. As for the Catholic conception of authority, it is by no means the static thing liberal Protestantism imagines. Dogmas are not immutable; Catholic teaching is adaptable and has been adapted. "It has been forced in the past, is forced every day, to complete them, explain them, make them more precise, and to clarify and improve them by additions, explications and refinements." In so far as the liberal objection has substance it is because, contrary to Catholicism's true character, Catholics themselves tend to ossify tradition into traditionalism, to mistake formula for faith and to confuse the interests of religion with the temporal advantage of the hierarchy. Hence if liberal Protestantism is fallacious, Catholicism needs also to take fresh account of itself. Loisy's argument was a dress rehearsal of what was to come later, in amplified form, in L'Évangile et l'Église. Meantime he returned to what he regarded as his proper employment, biblical study. His first book, published in *1890*, had been a history of the canon of the Old Testament to which a subsequent volume, dealing with the canon of the New, was added in *1891*.

Two more, histories of the biblical text and versions, had appeared in *1892* and *1893* respectively. These all dealt with "safe" subjects. Now, in October *1900*, he contributed a further article to the *Revue du clergé français* on the religion of Israel.[1] This was offered to readers as a brief introduction to the modern critical view of the Old Testament. Traditional notions were quietly dismissed; Hebrew religion was to be seen as a process of development, the documentation of which varied widely in date and historical value. Thus the period of the monarchy was in outline clear, but between Samuel and Moses it could only be glimpsed, and from Moses back to Abraham "all is darkest night". The opening chapters of Genesis were mythological, their significance being religious not scientific.[2] Placing the religion of Israel within the larger context of world religions generally, however, he claimed for it a perfection "as near as is possible for the human condition". And the author had strictures also for the positivistic approach of Frazer and his like. The category of evolution, as applied to religious phenomena, required to be used with caution. It was a useful hypothesis, not a demonstrable law. Again, one could not assume that "primitive" religion as known in modern times affords any exact parallel with that of remote antiquity. In any case the forms of religion are one thing, the ineffable reality which they seek to represent another. The idea of God may have been humble enough in origin "without religion automatically ceasing to be a great thing". Even fetishism is "a sign of the divine presence". Yet for the same reason the most exalted concept of deity remains an image, "an *idol* in the root meaning of the word", in which man tries to fix the infinite.

Thus, in a short space, Loisy had contrived to say much for the benefit of Catholic readers (and the clergy especially) which to liberal-minded Protestants was already so familiar as to be commonplace. But the archbishop of Paris, Cardinal Richard, censured the article and forbade publication of those that were to follow. In the meanwhile Loisy had resigned his chaplaincy at Neuilly—the last

---

[1] The essay was published as a brochure in *1901*. The articles originally intended as its sequel, although at first suspended, were later (*1906*) added to it to make up the volume, *La religion d'Israël*, the final, enlarged edition of which appeared in *1933*.

[2] A volume entitled *Les mythes babyloniens et les premiers chapitres de la Génèse* dates from *1901*.

ecclesiastical office he was ever to hold—and in the November of that
year was appointed to a lectureship at the École des Hautes Études, a
post which gave him both a salary and academic status independent
of the Church. This he was to occupy for the next four years. In the
circumstances it was of no small interest to his friends to learn that
he had permitted his candidature to be canvassed for one or the other
of two bishoprics then vacant, those of Monaco and Tarentaise. Not
that Loisy himself seriously expected the elevation: "Il est trop
probable", he wrote to von Hügel, "que je resterai, entre mes deux
trônes, assis par terre." But he took care nevertheless to be a little
more circumspect in venting his opinions.

Loisy's views on the biblical question were summarized in the second
edition of *Études bibliques*—a collection of previously published
articles—which he brought out in *1901*.[1] The first chapter discusses
the principle of the critical method as applied to the Scriptures: the
Church's doctrine relates only to their theological interpretation and is
not directly concerned with problems of historicity. The provinces of
the theologian and the historical critic are thus distinct—a point on
which Loisy was emphatic.[2] The inspiration of scripture, the writer
contends, did not involve verbal dictation, but simply guidance in
religious and moral matters, and as between divine and human there
can be no unequivocal distinction. Hence if the biblical author's
"science" is at odds with modern knowledge there is no need for
concern. As Loisy put it in his suppressed introductory chapter, the
Church's presentation of her essential truths—"the attitude of faith
notwithstanding"—can only be "relative and imperfect, wrapped up
as it is in symbols which depict these truths merely by analogy, without
affording them adequate expression".[3] In view of this intrinsic limitation
it is dangerous for the Church to propound doctrines which on many

---

[1] The first edition made an unobtrusive appearance in *1894*. The original
introduction to the second edition was however suppressed, although the third
edition (*1903*) did carry it. But it was missing from some copies even of this. In
fact those which included it were advertised as "hors de commerce"!

[2] "De même que le critique ne peut ni ne doit définir la portée dogmatique
d'un texte, le théologien ne peut ni ne doit en définir la signification historique.
Le principe du critique ne lui permet pas de formuler des conclusions de foi.
Nul principe du théologien ne l'autorise à formuler des conclusions d'histoire"
(*Études bibliques*, 3rd ed., p. *36*).

[3] *Ibid.*, p. *17*.

points can be shown to be false by an impartial science.[1] The rest of the book Loisy devotes to specific critical questions, including such matters as the first eleven chapters of Genesis ("not history but a religious philosophy thereof"), the alleged Mosaic authorship of the Pentateuch, the messianic idea—the essential value of which depends not on its particular form but on "the invincible spirit which impels it forward, especially when events appear certain to overwhelm it"— and the "symbolical" character of the fourth gospel.[2]

But the signal literary event of *1902*, for its author, was the publication of *L'Évangile et l'Église*, his best-known work and one which Tyrrell was to salute, in his own final publication, as "the classical exposition of Catholic Modernism".[3] It served the immediate end of refuting liberal Protestantism as represented by the eminent German scholar, Adolf Harnack, in a course of popular lectures given at Berlin university a couple of years previously. These had lately been published under the title *Das Wesen des Christentums* and were being widely read and praised.[4] Harnack had claimed that the conception of Christianity which he here put forward rested upon a critical estimate of the historical evidence. That evidence, he maintained, was supplied by the synoptic gospels alone, so far as they could be relied on for an authentic record of Jesus' mission and fundamental teaching, which in Harnack's view could be reduced to two simple principles: "God as Father and the human soul so ennobled that it can and does unite with him." Jesus assuredly taught the coming Kingdom of God, but the

---

[1] *Ibid.*, p. *24*. But Loisy had said much the same many years previously in his (unsubmitted) doctoral thesis *De divina bibliorum inspiratione tractatio dogmatica* of *1883*, which although never published, was afterwards summarized by the author in *Choses passées*. He had come to see even at that date that if revelation were contained in the Bible without error, as had been stated by the Vatican Council, it must be in relative form, proportionate to the time and circumstances under which the books appeared and to the general knowledge of the time and of those circumstances. "Les Livres saints étaient des livres écrits commes les autres, avec moins d'exactitude et de soin que beaucoup d'autres. Si le Saint Esprit s'en était mêlé, ce ne pouvait être pour en faire des sources historique de premier ordre" (p. *58*). Cf. J. T. Burtchaell, *Catholic Theories of Biblical Inspiration since 1810* (*1969*), pp. *221* ff.

[2] In his introduction Loisy had written: "Ce qui fait depuis longtemps obstacle à l'intelligence de ce chef-d'oeuvre de théologie mystique c'est qu'on l'interprète à la fois comme une histoire et comme un traité de théologie scolastique" (p. *95*).

[3] *Christianity at the Cross-Roads*, p. *92*.

[4] An English translation, *The Gospel and the Church*, by T. B. Saunders, appeared in *1901*.

apocalyptic trappings in which the announcement was made were merely "the whole Jewish limitations which necessarily attached to the message in its original form". But these limitations—the "husk", as Harnack chose to call them—have to be dispensed with by the modern Bible reader seeking the "kernel" of ageless truth which they enclose: namely, that "the Kingdom of God comes by coming to the individual, by entering into his soul and laying hold of it". Individual religious life alone indeed was what Jesus aimed to kindle. He "never had anyone but the individual in mind, and the abiding disposition of the heart in love". The conclusions to be drawn from this, as touching historic Catholicism, were obvious. The metaphysical theories of Christ's person evolved by the early church Fathers and laid down in the creeds and conciliar definitions have no legitimacy. "The Gospel, as Jesus proclaimed it, has to do with the Father only and not with the Son." Dogma, with its centuries of theological elaboration, along with the whole outward and visible institution of a Church claiming divine dignity" has no foundation whatever in the gospel. It is a case not just of distortion but of total perversion. If Christianity is to meet the needs of modern man its message must be restated in its pristine simplicity, free of the "vast and monstrous fabric" by which it has so long been encumbered.

In Loisy's judgment, however, Harnack was profoundly mistaken. Both he and Sabatier sought to achieve their desiderated reconciliation of Christian faith with "the claims of science and the scientific spirit of our time" by reducing Christianity to a single sentiment. Thus science and religion could not conflict because they never really encountered each other. Moreover, Harnack's appeal to history as the basis of his reconstruction was so narrowly conceived as to be useless. "Is the definition of Christianity put forward by Herr Harnack", he asked, "that of a historian or merely that of a theologian who takes from history as much as suits his theology?"[1] Harnack had swept tradition away, yet if the "essence" of Christianity is to be disclosed it can only be from *within* this same tradition.

Whatever we think, theologically, of tradition, whether we trust it or regard it with suspicion, we know Christ only by the tradition, across the tradition, and in the tradition of the primitive Christians.[2]

[1] *L'Évangile et l'Église* (E.T.), p. 4.   [2] *Op. cit.*, p. 13.

The very idea of the gospel apart from tradition is in "flagrant contradiction with the facts submitted by criticism". The essence of Christianity lies in the work of Jesus and its whole outcome, or else nowhere,
and is vainly to be looked for in the scattered fragments of his discourse.

It has always to be kept in mind, says Loisy, that the role of the
historical critic is that of investigator, not of judge. "Criticism has not
to decide if Jesus is or is not the Lord Incarnate", or whether the idea
of the Messiah "in its earliest form, and in its successive transformations,
is a truth". As beliefs these are addressed to *faith*—to the man, that is,
"judging with all his soul the worth of the religious doctrine presented
to him"; whereas the historian knows them simply as conceptions or
forces "whose antecedents, central manifestation and indefinite progress
he can analyse up to a point, but whose deep meaning and secret
power are not things that can be deduced from simple analysis or
critical discussion of texts and facts". Thus the historian recognizes at
once, on the evidence of the gospels, that what really was central to
the preaching of Jesus was the Kingdom of God, the necessary preparation for which was penitence.[1] But the agent or mediator of the
Kingdom is the Messiah, an apocalyptic figure with whom Jesus
apparently identified himself.[2] Hence if he is the Son of God it is not
simply because he "knows" God in any especially intense or ultimate
way but because he has himself a divine function to fulfil. This
conviction was shared by the apostles also, for whom the experience of
his resurrection confirmed his status as Christ and Lord, although the
resurrection itself was not an event that could have been objectively
established: "The entry of a man into immortal life escapes our powers
of observation". What mattered was the faith, not the "fact", which
may be variously explained. For it was out of the faith that the Church
was born.

In this sense the Church was the necessary consequence of the work
of Jesus.

It was a community having as its basis a belief in the "good
news" of the resurrection of Jesus; as its law, charity; as its end, the

[1] It is only fair however to point out that Harnack assigned to Jesus' preaching
of the Kingdom a more prominent place than Loisy implies. But Loisy, unlike
Harnack, regarded the eschatological imagery in the gospels as integral to Jesus'
message. What signifies from the historian's angle is not whether *we* can accept it
but whether Jesus and his disciples did so.   [2] *L'Évangile et l'Église*, p. *104*.

propagation of a great hope; as its form of government, the distinction between the apostolic college and the ordinary disciples.[1]

Harnack's notion of an "individualist" gospel has no foundation in the New Testament. Jesus himself did not think of the Kingdom after that manner, nor did his disciples. Jesus did not expressly found the Church, as history knows it, but the idea of an "invisible society formed for ever of those who have in their hearts faith in the goodness of God" was something as foreign to his mind as to those of his followers. He himself indeed foretold the Kingdom, but it was the Church that came;[2] and the Church as an historical institution could not but submit to the principles of historical development and hence reveal "a continual effort of adaptation to conditions always new and perpetually changing". The Church can therefore fairly say that "in order to be at all times what Jesus desired the society of his friends to be, it had to become what it has become; for it has become what it had to be to save the gospel by saving itself".[3] Thus the Church today resembles the community of the first disciples neither more nor less than a grown man resembles the child he once was.

> The identity of the Church or of the man is not determined by the permanent immobility of external forms, but by continuity of existence and consciousness of life through the perpetual transformations which are life's condition and manifestation.

The power of adaptation recognizable in the Roman Church is that Church's best title to the admiration of the impartial observer. It is not that she alters the gospel or tradition, but that "she knows how to understand the needs of the time".

In line with his argument that the growth of the Church's institutional structure has been legitimized by its very necessity is Loisy's view of the development of dogma. Such development, he allows with Harnack, was not *in* the gospel and could not have been there. But neither does it follow that, as Harnack also supposed, the dogma does not proceed *from* the gospel or that the gospel does not "live" in dogma as well as in the Church. For the fact is that dogma is already present in the New Testament itself as the expression of the spiritual experience of the primitive Church. Philosophy, however, was

---

[1] *Ibid.*, p. *147*.   [2] P. *166*.   [3] P. *150*.

necessary for its further development; and the alliance of philosophy with faith enabled the Church to link its own tradition with the science of the age, so transforming both into an erudite theology which believed itself to possess the knowledge both of the world and of God. "Philosophy could become Christian without being obliged to deny itself, and yet Christianity had not ceased to be a religion, the religion of Christ."[1] The result of course must not be judged as a scientific achievement; the concern of the early Church was for souls, not mere learning. But "from the moment the gospel is believed, it is impossible not to think of the belief, not to work at the thought, and so produce a theology of faith".[2] To decry theology, therefore, is idle. The faith would not have been preserved without transmission, which in turn would not have been feasible without a positive teaching. Equally has it to be realized that the Church's conceptions are not truths fallen from heaven and maintained by theological tradition in precisely their original form. They are the outcome of human need, and they register changes in the human outlook. What the historian sees in them, that is, is simply an interpretation of the facts of religious experience. It is not to be conceived therefore that their future should not correspond with their past. New ideas are bound to lead to fresh understanding. The letter killeth, the spirit giveth life.

Finally, as with hierarchy and dogma, so with the cult. History knows no instances of a religion without a ritual.

> The Christian spirit gave life, and still gives it, to practices apparently trivial and easily becoming superstitious; but the point at issue is whether those who follow them do not find Christ therein, and whether they would be capable of finding him more readily elsewhere.[3]

On the liberal Protestant view—a conclusion neither rational nor evangelical—corporate worship would be impossible.

Loisy's "petit livre rouge"—the first of a series bound in light red wrappers—ended with the reflection that all churches, orthodoxies and forms of worship are caught up in a religious crisis brought about by the political, intellectual and economic evolution of the contemporary world—in short, by the modern spirit. The best means of meeting it, however, is not the suppression of all ecclesiastical organization,

[1] P. *191*.   [2] P. *222*.   [3] P. *270*.

orthodoxy and traditional worship—"a process that would thrust Christianity out of life and humanity"—but to take advantage of what *is*, in view of what should be, to repudiate nothing of the heritage left to the present age by former centuries, to recognize how necessary and useful has been the immense development that has taken place within the Church and hence "to gather the fruits of it and continue it, since the adaptation of the gospel to the changing conditions of humanity is as pressing a need today as it ever was or ever will be".[1]

The initial impression left by *L'Évangile et l'Église* upon Catholic readers was by no means unfavourable. As polemic against liberal Protestantism it appeared highly successful.[2] Von Hügel was warm in his praise of it—"Just simply superb"—and appreciation was voiced not only by men like Blondel or Wilfrid Ward or Pierre Batiffol; even Cardinal Sarto, the future Pius X, spoke well of it, if with reservations. The archbishop of Albi, who alone of the author's friends had seen the work in manuscript, declared that he (Loisy) had never written anything "as complete and objective". More than a mere refutation of Harnack, its publication would put its author "at the top of the Christian critics".[3] Here, indeed, Mignot glimpsed the book's real significance, for what Loisy had to say was intended even more as a critique of traditionalist Catholicism than as an anti-Protestant polemic. The author, moreover, did not deny the critical method on which Harnack had based his views, mistaken though he judged these to be. On the contrary, he himself applied the same methods with greater rigour and to the point of a radical historical scepticism much beyond anything the German scholar envisaged. To Loisy, Christianity had no fixed "essence" or nucleus above time and change. Once the ship of faith had cut loose from her moorings in history the exact course followed would have to be determined by the winds and tides of circumstance. Catholicism would be justified, if at all, not by dubious claims deriving from documents or traditions incapable of

---

[1] P. 276.

[2] Loisy himself always remained convinced of the validity of his argument as against Harnack's reduced conception of Christianity. "La critique du protestantisme libéral est de tout le petit livre, ce a qui l'auteur n'aurait rien à changer, ou si peu que rien. Il lui est toujours impossible, au point de vue historique, de reconnaître en cette forme du christianisme, l'expression exacte du passé chrétien" (*L'Évangile et l'Église*, 5th ed., p. 6).

[3] Loisy, *Mémoires*, ii, p. 133.

verification or precise interpretation, but on actual experience, on the recurring needs of generations of baptized believers owing allegiance to a great historic institution. "Reprocher à l'Église catholique tout le développement de sa constitution, c'est donc lui reprocher d'avoir vécu." This, certainly, was apologetic in a new key, and Abbot Cuthbert Butler of Downside, although he found much to admire in it, guessed at once that Loisy "had put the fat in the fire with a vengeance". The question that must immediately have entered the minds of even the author's liberal sympathizers was whether, in proving so much, he had not proved too much, and that an argument as effective against modern Protestantism might turn out to be no less a dissolvent of Catholicism. In any case the finger pointed by Loisy at official Catholic teaching was so obvious that a reply from traditionalist theologians, if not from Herr Harnack—who in fact did not answer it—was expected. Within a few weeks the book had become a matter of public controversy. It was attacked by the ultramontane periodicals, *L'Univers* and *La vérité française*—Loisy, it was being said, was "worse than Renan"—though it was criticized also by such a moderate as Batiffol. In January *1903*, Cardinal Richard formally condemned it, and seven other French bishops followed suit. Loisy at once indicated his submission, but the hostile reaction to his views continued, although no censure came from Rome itself.[1] In the autumn, and mainly at the instance of friends who advised him to do something to clarify his position, he published a sequel, *Autour d'un petit livre*, in the shape of a series of letters (never actually sent) to a number of eminent churchmen, clerical and lay. The writer's explanations, however, far from qualifying the opinions previously stated, gave them a sharper polemical edge, whilst the tone adopted was hardly conciliatory. The central theme is Christology, the subject of the letter addressed to Archbishop Mignot. Here Loisy draws a clear distinction between the Jesus of history and the Christ of Catholic faith, but argues also that nothing which can be said of the former need contradict what is believed of the latter. The one is simply the man of Nazareth in his human aspect, subject to the conditions, material, intellectual and moral, of all historical existence; whereas the other is the object of a religious devotion beyond the reach of critical investigation and thus not to be denied

[1] For contemporary criticisms of *L'Évangile et l'Église* see Poulat, *op. cit.*, pp. *125–153*.

C

on critical grounds. Nevertheless, historically speaking, it can be affirmed that Jesus was not conscious of himself as a divine being, although the messianic idea contains at least the seed of the Church's subsequent doctrine. The process was developmental. First, Christ's death on the cross had to be accounted for, in a manner consonant with the messianic claim. Then, with the Gentile mission, fresh categories had to be found to render the idea intelligible in a cultural ambience very different from that of the original disciples. Finally, it achieved expression in the Platonist-Stoic Logos concept, although the rationalizing movement was not complete until the decrees of the general councils. All the same, once admit the necessity and nature of the development and it becomes evident that it must continue. The terms variously employed have a temporary utility, but their adequacy is limited since they can never be commensurate with the mystery they are intended to convey. In fact, all theological language is symbolic and its meaning in the end is elusive. For what pertains to dogma pertains to divine revelation itself, the latter being understood as man's consciousness of his relationship with God—a dynamic not a static thing. Hence "the evolution of faith cannot fail to be co-ordinated with the moral and intellectual evolution of man".[1]

In his second letter, addressed to Cardinal Perraud of Autun, Loisy reverts to the biblical question, underlining views already stated in the "Firmin" articles. Many facts make it evident, he points out, that the books of the Bible have not come down to us without undergoing variations such as raise considerable historical problems; problems, furthermore, to which the theological tradition has no ready answer, for the simple reason that it has never really confronted them. This task now devolves upon the critic, without aid from the theologian. The third letter, to the bishop of La Rochelle, concerns, in particular, the study of the gospels, which to the historian reveal "a work of progressive idealisation, of symbolic and dogmatic interpretation".[2] Elsewhere, Loisy returns to the question of whether or in what sense the Church was founded by Christ. The purpose of L'Évangile et l'Église, he explains, was to demonstrate the continuity between the

---

[1] *Autour d'un petit livre*, p. *195*. But concerning revelation itself Loisy adds: "C'est l'homme qui cherche, mais c'est Dieu qui l'excite; c'est l'homme qui voit, mais c'est Dieu qui l'éclaire. La révélation se réalise dans l'homme, mais elle est l'œuvre de Dieu en lui, avec lui et par lui" (pp. *197* f.). [2] *Ibid.*, p. *83*.

Church and the Gospel, but that the former was divinely instituted is an affirmation of faith, not an assignable event in history.[1] Lastly, regarding the sacraments, it has to be understood that the decrees of Trent relate, again, not to history but to theology. The dominical institution of the sacraments, like that of the Church itself, is essentially a matter of faith in the glorified Lord.[2]

Such, then, in outline was the proposed Modernist re-interpretation of Catholicism, at least according to Loisy's terms. The question was whether ecclesiastical authority would or would not countenance it. Loisy himself certainly professed to hope so, but it is clear from his own subsequent statements that by this time his confidence in the possibility of a Catholic *rinnovamento* of the kind he looked for was fast ebbing. But was he indeed any longer himself a Catholic, or even a Christian, by belief? "Christ", he confessed in his journal, "has even less importance in my religion than he has in that of the liberal Protestants; for I attach little importance to the revelation of God the Father for which they honour Jesus. If I am anything in religion, it is more pantheist-positivist-humanitarian than Christian."[3] It was a strange admission for a man who still was a priest of the Church saying his daily mass and seeking publicly to vindicate historic Catholicism in the eyes of the non-believing intelligentsia. No doubt he could defend the Church with sincerity as a great and on the whole beneficent force in history; but as to its supernatural credentials his answer even then was noticeably equivocal.

Pope Leo XIII died on July *20, 1903*; his successor, Pius X, elected not many days later, was to prove himself a man of very different stamp and outlook. It became apparent from the outset of his reign that his attitude towards doctrinal innovation and reformism would be unsympathetic. Not two months passed before he warned the clergy against "the insidious manœuvres of a certain new science which adorns itself with the mark of truth"[4]. But still no express condemnation was voiced at Rome.[5] Before the year was out, however—and despite the efforts of friends on his behalf—five of Loisy's works, including *L'Évangile et l'Église* and *Autour d'un petit livre*, were placed on the

[1] P. *161*. He is addressing a fellow-liberal, the abbé Félix Klein.
[2] *Ibid.*, p. *227*.
[3] *Mémoires*, ii, p. *397*. Cf. Houtin and Sartiaux, op. cit., pp. *121–129*.
[4] A. R. Vidler, *The Modernist Movement in the Roman Church* (*1934*), p. *133*.
[5] Cf. J. Rivière, *op. cit.*, p. *190*.

Index as containing "very grave errors" in regard to the primitive revelation, the authenticity of the gospel history and teaching, Christ's divinity and knowledge, his resurrection and the divine institution of the Church and the sacraments. Loisy, correct as ever in his clerical behaviour, again submitted, but in words of characteristic ambiguity. Yet as a token of good faith he offered to resign his lectureship at the École des Hautes Études and even to suspend publication of the critical studies on which he was then working. What he was not able to do, on the other hand, was to comply with the pope's demand that he should confess his errors and subject himself "fully and without restriction" to the judgment of the Holy Office on his writings. To have done that would have been to retract his most sincere belief, namely, that science is autonomous and cannot allow its rights to be inhibited by external authority, even in the name of divine revelation. Thus to all intents his role as a Modernist, *i.e.* a reforming Catholic, was ended. All that he afterwards wrote about the movement was merely by way of analysis and comment; no longer was he a protagonist,[1] or even an adherent. But the expected excommunication was not pronounced. He went into retirement in the country in order to pursue his exegetical work, of which the monumental but destructively radical commentary on the synoptic gospels was the principal outcome.[2] The papal acts condemning Modernism were delayed—rather surprisingly—until *1907*. When, thereafter, Loisy refused to render any further submission he was excommunicated by name, on March 7, *1908*. A year later he was appointed to the chair of the history of religions at the Collège de France, an office once held by Renan—a fact the irony of which would not have escaped its new occupant.[3]

3. *Tyrrell and Von Hügel*

Loisy pre-eminently was the critic and historical scholar among the Modernists; his role as theologian and apologist, although significant,

[1] See, in addition to the *Mémoires* and *Choses passées*, *Quelques lettres sur des questions actuelles et sur des événements récents* and *Simples réfléxions sur le décret du Saint-Office* Lamentabili sane exitu *et sur l'encyclique* Pascendi dominici gregis, both published in *1908*.

[2] *Les Evangiles synoptiques, 1907–1908.*

[3] The last of Loisy's "little red books" bore the title *La Crise morale des temps présents et l'éducation humaine* (*1937*). He died in the spring of *1940*, as the German armies were invading France.

was secondary, at least in his own estimation. In the case of George Tyrrell the truth is rather the reverse of this. Tyrrell was not a scholar, in the pure sense, and never aspired to be. He was not perhaps even a theologian, according to the conventional pattern of the schools. But an apologist he certainly was: the opening chapter of *Through Scylla and Charybdis* (*1908*) is as able a defence of Catholicism as may anywhere be found. Yet he also was much more—a truly religious thinker, with something, one feels, of the spirit of Luther in him. For Tyrrell was Modernism's prophet, apostle and most conspicuous martyr. Unlike Loisy, who seems never to have given himself heart and soul to the priestly vocation and in whose mind a germ of fundamental doubt was present from the very beginning, Tyrrell was an ardent Catholic who in his earlier days displayed all the aggressiveness often associated with the convert. From the start of his career in the Roman Church he was confident that as far as he was concerned to be a Catholic was to be a priest, and to be a priest was to be also a Jesuit. Keenly intelligent, imaginative and mercurial to the point of recklessness, he was never the man for half-measures or discreet adjustments. An Irishman from Dublin, he was a born fighter whose pugnacity sometimes disturbed his best friends and well-wishers.

The death of his father, only a couple of months before his own birth in February *1861*, meant that he was brought up, the youngest of three children, by his mother alone, in circumstances of genteel poverty. The family belonged to the Church of Ireland and looked on Roman Catholics as intellectually and socially inferior. But George became attracted to High Church Anglicanism and made friends with Robert Dolling, who at the time was still a layman. In March *1879*, at the age of *18*, he left Dublin for London to assist Dolling with his social work, but before long he was in contact with the Farm Street Jesuits with a view to his conversion to the faith.[1] His instruction—penny-catechism treatment—was quickly got through and in a few weeks he was "received". He at once set about the business of becoming a Jesuit himself, a calling of which he had already formed the most idealistic expectations. After a year's probation as a teacher in Jesuit

---

[1] "I went, almost from the first, to St George's, Southwark, for Mass and other services; and I looked up all the Catholic churches in London, with a sort of morbid curiosity, like that which draws a moth to a candle" (*Autobiography and Life of George Tyrrell*, ed. M. D. Petre, *1912*, i, p. *155*).

schools, first in Cyprus and then in Malta, he entered on his novitiate in the autumn of *1880*. His philosophical and theological training were acquired at Stonyhurst, and following a spell of parish work after his ordination in *1891* he was appointed to a professorship in philosophy at St Mary's Hall, Stonyhurst, a post he held until *1896*, when he joined the staff at Farm Street. These years were, in fact, those of his greatest assurance as a Catholic and as a priest. He was almost militantly orthodox. Yet they also witnessed the first signs of his difficulties not only with the Society but with official Catholicism at large. For his original Thomist fervour had now turned him into a critic of the way in which the scholastic philosophy was usually taught in Jesuit establishments, *i.e.*, in its Suarezian rather than its original form. "Aquinas", he afterwards wrote, "was essentially liberal-minded and sympathetic. . . . This was what I fought for, for two years. . . ." He wanted, in short, to use the neo-scholastic movement to defeat "the narrow spirit" which animated too many of its promoters.[1]

Tyrrell's first book, *Nova et Vetera*, a work mainly of a devotional character, appeared in *1897*, the year in which he made the acquaintance of Baron Friedrich von Hügel (*1852–1925*), who was to become the closest of friends and to exercise profound influence in the shaping of his mind. Von Hügel, an Anglo-Austrian, was at once a devout believer and a man of penetrating intelligence and wide learning. As Tyrrell's biographer, Maude Petre, remarks: "In this friend Tyrrell found the kind of critic he most needed; one who could appreciate his strength and correct his deficiencies."[2] The elder man soon introduced him to the writings of Catholic thinkers like Blondel and Laberthonnière who had already broken with the scholastic tradition and were working out a philosophy on activist or voluntarist lines. Indeed, at this period, the baron was a good deal more "advanced" in his opinions than was the Jesuit. "Every time I meet you or hear from you", the latter wrote to him in *1901*, "I am poked on a little further."[3]

---

[1] Tyrrell remained cognisant of his debt to his Thomist training. "Whatever order or method there is in my thought," he wrote in *1900*, "whatever real faculty of reasoning and distinguishing I have acquired, I owe it to St Thomas. He first started me on the inevitable, impossible, and yet not all-fruitless quest of a complete and harmonious system of thought" (Petre, *op. cit.*, ii, p. *248*).

[2] *Ibid.*, ii, p. *87*.

[3] A year later he again was writing: "All the vast help you have given me— and surely I have grown from a boy to a man since I knew you—has been in

But although in the early stages of their friendship von Hügel's influence tended to stimulate Tyrrell's advance, later on the position was reversed and, as Miss Petre says, "we find him endeavouring to check the rapidity of one to whom quick movement was all too natural". In fact Tyrrell's own outlook at this time (*1897-1900*) could be described as—the term is his own—a "mediating liberalism", a standpoint much akin to that of Wilfrid Ward and illustrated, in Tyrrell's case, by the volume, *External Religion: its Use and Abuse* (*1899*) and several of the essays (as, for example, that on "Liberal Catholicism") reprinted in *The Faith of the Millions*.[1] His former enthusiasm for St Thomas was now cooling off; in its stead he felt the attraction of Newman, an influence, however, which itself quickly declined with the first impact of the critical studies into which von Hügel had been guiding him.

The commencement of the distinctively Modernist phase of Tyrrell's thinking was marked by an article called "The Relation of Theology to Devotion", first published in *The Month* in November *1899* and subsequently reprinted in *The Faith of the Millions*[2] and again in *Through Scylla and Charybdis*, where it appeared under the title "Lex Orandi, Lex Credendi".[3] Of this, Tyrrell himself declared that it contained the essence of the views expressed in his later writings.[4] He employs the word "theology" in a broad sense to include not only speculative doctrine but dogma itself. Similarly by "devotion" he means not simply a conscious disposition of the will towards God but the ordinary day-to-day life of the believer. The distinction he seeks to make, that is, is one between religion in the abstract, or in its scientific aspect, and as it really is, as *lived*. A like distinction, he points out, is obviously applicable in other spheres. Nature, for instance, can

---

opening up my eyes to an ever fuller and deeper knowledge of the data of the great problem of life" (Petre, *op. cit.*, ii, p. *96*). Cf. F. von Hügel, *Selected Letters* (*1896-1924*) (ed. Bernard Holland), p. *12*.

[1] In two volumes, *1901*.

[2] i, pp. *228-252*.

[3] Pp. *85-105*.

[4] "On re-reading it carefully I am amazed to see how little I have really advanced since I wrote it; how I have simply eddied round and round the same point. It is all here—all that follows—not in germ but in explicit statement—as it were in a brief compendium or analytical index" (*Through Scylla and Charybdis*, p. *85*).

be classified as in a museum, "but the world at large refuses to be harnessed to our categories, and goes its own rude, unscientific way".[1] Unity and order are artificial; life, which is real, does not disclose them so readily. Hence what is scientifically true in the abstract may be practically false in the concrete. And what applies so evidently to the natural is likely to be even more true of the supernatural. Philosophy itself ought to be a warning of this, for such "non-analogous" ideas as it may form of the other world are only very meagre descriptions indeed. "Whatever shred of truth they convey to us may, or rather must, like all half-evidence, get an entirely different complexion from the additional mass of truth that is hid from us." Theology's statements, on the other hand, are "analogous", but even they do not take us much farther, since the infinite necessarily eludes the grasp of language. The danger for theology arises when this truth is overlooked, as it commonly has been. The mistake of anthropomorphism lies "not so much in thinking and speaking of God humanwise—for that we are constrained to do by the structure of our minds—as in forgetting that such a mode of conception is analogous". The value of natural theology is that it brings home to us the inevitable shortcomings of all human conceptions of the divine. This truth is only disguised by the tendency of theology and metaphysics to represent their conclusions as scientifically factual. Popular anthropomorphism, as in the Old Testament, brings us nearer to the reality.

> God has revealed himself, not to the wise and prudent, not to the theologian or the philosopher, but to babes, to fishermen, to peasants, to the *profanum vulgus*, and therefore He has spoken their language.

The Church's responsibility is to preserve, not to develop, the exact ideas which such simple utterance was able to convey to its first hearers.

> This "deposit of faith", this concrete, coloured, imaginative expression of Divine mysteries, as it lay in the mind of the first recipients, is both the *lex orandi* and the *lex credendi*; it is the rule and corrective, both of popular devotion and of rational theology.[2]

[1] *Op. cit.*, p. *82*.   [2] P. *95*.

Accordingly, theology needs constantly to be checked by it—corrected and guided by experience. If and when it begins to contradict the facts of the spiritual life it forfeits its claim to acceptance. It will have to be reminded that, like science, its hypotheses, theories and explanations must square with the facts, by which is meant the Christian religion as lived by its consistent professors.

Tyrrell's opposition to theological rationalism was further disclosed in an article he contributed to *The Weekly Register* in December *1899* entitled "A Perverted Devotion". This concerned the doctrine of hell, upon which subject he here called for a "temperate agnosticism". Attempts to qualify the doctrine or to whittle away its meaning by rationalizing arguments are mistaken, inasmuch as the real objections to it are moral. What needs to be recognized is the inadequacy of all human conceptions in face of so great a mystery. Taking the widest view, Tyrrell concludes that because "God's spirit working outside the Church is preparing for himself an acceptable people", those within should meet that movement "by purging out of our midst any remnant of the leaven of rationalism that we may have carried with us from earlier and cruder days, when faith needed the rein more than the spur".[1] Such statements may today seem trite, but, as Tyrrell's biographer observes, "in the history of this article we have the beginning of the end" of the writer's career as a Catholic priest. The discussion it aroused led in fact to Tyrrell's voluntary retirement from Farm Street, and for the next few years—until *1905*—his home was the Jesuit "holiday house" at Richmond in Yorkshire.

Here, however, he had abundant leisure for writing, and among the literary fruits of this Richmond period were two pseudonymous publications, *Religion as a Factor of Life*, by "Dr Ernest Engels",[2] and *The Church and the Future*, by "Hilaire Bourdon",[3] and a volume under his own name entitled *Lex Orandi; or, Prayer and Creed*. Published in 1903, this last, which bore the *imprimatur* of Cardinal Bourne of Westminster, was in fact a revised and enlarged version of the "Engels" book. Its argument, as the title suggests, is the relation of faith to prayer. A religious belief, Tyrrell holds, is to be judged by its prayer-value.

[1] Petre, *op. cit.*, ii, p. *118*.
[2] A brochure of *78* pages, it was published by Pollard of Exeter in *1902*.
[3] Printed "for private circulation only" in *1903*.

Beliefs that have been found by continuous and invariable experience to foster and promote the spiritual life of the soul must so far be in accord with the nature and laws of that will-world with which it is the aim of religion to bring us into harmony; their practical value results from, and is founded in, their representative value.[1]

Not that the world of spiritual reality can be properly represented in terms of the natural; but we can be sure that between it and the formulation of Christian truth in the creed an analogy exists the precise nature of which is hidden from us. This is demonstrated by the universally proved value of the creed as "a practical guide to the eternal life of the soul"—a proof which is based on the experience not of any individual, however wise or holy, but on that of the whole tradition of Christian faith and piety—"of the Church of the Saints in all ages and nations, or the consensus of the ethical and religious *orbis terrarum*".[2] The real basis of dogma is the need of the human soul; it lies in devotion rather than in metaphysics, or indeed in history simply as such:

> Certain concrete historical facts enter into our creed as matters of faith. Precisely as historical facts they concern the historian and must be criticized by his methods. But as matters of faith they must be determined by the criterion of faith, *i.e.* by their proved religious values.[3]

Thus the distinction so firmly drawn by Loisy in the interest of historical science is maintained by Tyrrell in that of religious belief itself. But in

---

[1] *Lex Orandi*, pp. 57 f.

[2] *Ibid.*, p. 58. At this time, Tyrrell still adhered to the Thomist doctrine of analogy, which he considered afforded ample cover for his own theory of dogma. It steered, he thought, "successfully between the Scylla of illegitimate dogmatism and the Charybdis of Spencerian agnosticism" (*op. cit.*, p. 83). Thus it may be said that, "though we know God's kind of being only in terms of our own, the Infinite only in terms of the finite, yet He is not therefore unknowable or unknown; nor is our action void of all effect in the order of Eternity. Confusion as to this fundamental point is at the root of nearly all the difficulties we experience in endeavouring to reconcile the chief mysteries of faith with our natural understanding" (p. 80). His later writings, however, contain statements indicative, rather, of that (agnostic) "dogmatic symbolism" with which he is charged by, *e.g.*, M.T.-L. Penido (*Le rôle d'analogie en théologie dogmatique, 1931*).

[3] P. 169.

this, Tyrrell's thinking, though basically his own, reveals also the influence of the current philosophy of pragmatism, the chief exponents of which were C. S. Peirce and William James. Truth in any sphere, he contends, is substantiated in practice. The truths even of history and physical science are accepted "only because they explain and fit in with the life that we live, and offer means of its expansion". Had they no bearing on the concerns of temporal life they would be "merely curious riddles awaiting solution". The same applies *a fortiori* to the truths of religion. Not only must the apologist connect the latter with the truths of history and science; he will go on to relate the vitalities of religion to life in general and show that the one demands the other.

Lex Orandi is a sketch for a philosophy of dogma.[1] Its sequel, *Lex Credendi*—which was to bear no *imprimatur*—did not follow until *1907*. Neither work is polemical in tone. *The Church and the Future*, however, was deliberately provocative and may be said to occupy a place in Tyrrell's writings comparable with that of *Autour d'un petit livre* in Loisy's. That Tyrrell had imbibed Loisy's doctrines is obvious. The whole purpose of the book is to contrast "official" Catholicism with the liberalized version of it which the author now believed to be not only feasible but necessary. Official Catholicism adheres to the theory that Christ and his apostles delivered the complete *depositum fidei*—*i.e.* the dogmas, sacraments and other essential institutions of the Catholic Church as it exists today—to St Linus (who followed St Peter in the Holy See) and the episcopate united with him, who in turn transmitted it infallibly to their successors, without substantial increment though more fully"explicated", illustrated and systematized.[2]

---

[1] It has been surmised that Tyrrell was a good deal indebted for his view of dogma to Matthew Arnold and especially to *Literature and Dogma*. Thus Henri Bremond, who knew Tyrrell personally and was himself well read in English literature, wrote in *1913* to Loisy: "Pour Tyrrell, vous l'avez façonné, ainsi que Laberthonnière; et les grands libéraux anglais ont fait le reste, Mat. Arnold, Literature and dogma—un tiers de Tyrrell est là-dedans—Jowett, etc." (Loisy, *Mémoires*, iii, p. *268*). Occasional references to Arnold may be found in Tyrrell's writings, but Bremond exaggerates. Certainly Miss Petre reveals no such special influence. Vidler, on the other hand, thinks Bremond's estimate sound, although the aim of Tyrrell's own works was "to show that the criterion of experience justifies not Arnold's vague liberalism but a full and rich Catholicism". Arnold's opinions really are more akin to Harnack's, as Vidler allows. See *The Modernist Movement in the Roman Church*, pp. *159–162*.

[2] *Lex Orandi*, p. *29*.

It is a notion which the historical facts as known to modern scholarship totally disallow, and no serious historian of early Christianity would attempt to maintain it. Is, then, Catholicism itself discredited? Tyrrell does not think so; but the Church of the future will have to produce a new account of itself and in terms of an ecclesiology which will be at once social, evolutionary and mystical. The juridical-authoritarian conception will surely have to go; instead, the Church must be seen as "an art-school of Divine majesty". Institutionally she brings together all who profess a desire to be schooled in the art of divine love as revealed in Christ, in order that by their collective study, experience and endeavour they may not only keep the art alive but bring it to ever greater perfection.[1]

> Outside such a society the isolated individual is cut off from the corporate life of Christ; he is deprived of the heritage of the gathered experience and reflections of multitudes of generations from which, as from a starting capital, he may set forth in search of further gains; he is cut off from the stimulus, the infection of enthusiasm, that is yielded by co-operation with others who are animated by the same spirit, who live for the same ideals as himself.

But the old theory of ecclesiastical infallibility must give way to a new and much broader one, with the real nature of dogmatic truth at last properly understood. For the creed is "a guide to life as expressed in speech and action", not a set of theoretical propositions. A body of "symbolized eternal realities", it should be presented by the Church "to the mind and understanding of her children as a means of waking, forming, and educating in them that same spirit which gave birth to these conceptions".[2] No modification of doctrine, therefore, which is not life-giving and which does not foster and develop charity can survive. As for the claim of Catholicism to be of divine institution, that can be conceded only in so far as it is "the creation of that Spirit which created both Christ and the Church to be different phases of the same movement".[3] The Church indeed is a divine institution only in the same sense that the Bible is a divine book possessing divine authority: "The modifications that criticism has enforced upon the

---

[1] *The Church and the Future* (ed. *1910*), p. *73*.
[2] *Ibid.*, pp. *84* ff.
[3] P. *64*.

latter conception must be applied to the former."[1] The author concludes with the not very surprising observation that the heterodoxy of his views from the "official" standpoint was not open to question.

It was at this stage of his theological development that Tyrrell may be said to have shed his Newmanism, which in any case was little more than skin-deep.[2] The idea of the *depositum fidei* as "a divinely communicated 'Credo' or theological summary", which Newman's *Essay on Development* appeared in the main to assume, was one which critical historical study rendered untenable. A true conception of development would have to be an evolutionary one.[3] But this in turn implied a new conception of revelation, displacing the traditional propositional view. Revelation, that is, was not in origin a body of doctrines but rather an idea or spiritual impulse which is perpetually fructifying in Christian experience and of which the theological formulation is therefore subject to constant change and improvement.[4] The criterion of theological truth, accordingly, is fidelity to experience, not identity with the past—a principle to be given unequivocal expression in another of Tyrrell's anonymous writings of this period, his

[1] "The notion of a complete ecclesiastical organism produced abruptly by a divine *fiat* on the day of Pentecost belongs to the same sort of philosophy as the Mosaic cosmogony" (p. 65). Cf. Petre, *op. cit.*, ii, p. 187.

[2] In May 1906, Tyrrell confessed to a French correspondent that he "had never read [Newman] very much, but he had read the 'Grammar of Assent' three times and the 'Essay on Development' about as often". "The former did effect a profound revolution in my way of thinking, in the year 1885, just when I had begun to feel the limits of scholasticism rather painfully." He adds: "Personally, I do not think his effort to unite the conception of development with the Catholic conception of tradition was successful or coherent; but it has given an impulse to thought which may issue in some more successful effort" (Petre, *op. cit.*, ii, p. 209).

[3] In June 1900, Tyrrell wrote to von Hügel: "I have been reading Harnack . . . and have been impressed with the madness of supposing that we can go on ignoring so plain a fact as the growth of Catholicism out of a germ as unlike Catholicism as a wall-nut [sic] is unlike a wall-nut tree. It will take all our wits and more learning than at present, alas! . . . to show that the outgrowth is a real and legitimate development; and yet our theologians go on dreaming and romancing about a full-fledged apostolic Catholicism, and are anxious to anathematize the very notion of development by putting Newman's Essay on the Index" (British Museum Add. mss 44927).

[4] As Tyrrell wrote in a paper that has remained unpublished: "What man needs primarily is not theological information, but that inward stimulus and attraction towards the divine which forms the subject matter of theological reflection, and is fostered by such reflection to a certain extent" (British Museum Add. mss 52369).

"Confidential Letter to a Friend who is a Professor of Anthropology" (*1904*). The professor whose religious doubts Tyrrell endeavours to meet was fictitious, but the invention was a convenient device of the author's for the purpose of showing how acceptance of the truths of science and history is no necessary obstacle to the holding of the Catholic faith, rightly interpreted. The professor's difficulty—whether or not he ought to remain a member of the Church—stemmed from the fact that he had equated belief with "theologism", or mental assent to a system of ideas grounded in the rational understanding. On the latter view his position would, in all honesty, be impossible; but not if Catholicism be "primarily a life and the Church a spiritual organism in whose life we participate, and if the theology be but an attempt of that life to formulate and understand itself—an attempt which may fail wholly or in part without affecting the value and reality of the said life".[1] True Catholicism is a religion of ideal and intention rather than of any existing institutions, a power of the spirit rather than of the letter. As a man's conscious self is not the whole or even possibly the real self, so "the self-conscious, self-formulating Catholicism of the thinking, talking, and governing minority is not the whole Church but only an element (however important) in its constitution".[2] The theologian naturally is tempted to reduce faith to a detailed system and, by ignoring the differences between the actual facts of religious experience and their analysis and expression, to make out that no man can live the life of faith without first accepting the preliminary theological analyses. But such a view is at variance not only with reason and experience but with "the whole character of that Gospel which was preached to the simple and hidden from the sophists". On the other hand, spiritual experience is enhanced and deepened by the life of society, which "makes us heirs of its own collective experience in the past". The social and institutional element is thus not only an advantage, it is a necessity:

> In all ways . . . communion with the visible Church is an effectual sacrament of communion with the invisible, a condition greatly favouring the supernatural life of Faith, Hope, and Charity.[3]

[1] *A Much-Abused Letter*, p. *51*.
[2] *Op. cit.*, p. *59*.
[3] *Ibid.*, p, *83*.

His correspondent's real quarrel, says Tyrrell, is not with the Church but with the theologians, who no doubt are as sincere and convinced in their way as were the Pharisees of old. But like them their spiritual perception is blunted by their own dogmatism. Hence, "may not Catholicism like Judaism have to die in order that it may live again in a greater and grander form?"

Meanwhile, Tyrrell was making efforts to secure his release from the Society, hoping that this could be brought about by amicable arrangement. Unfortunately for him, passages from the "Letter" were quoted anonymously and in a garbled translation in the Milan newspaper, *Il Corriere della Sera*, in December *1905*. Tyrrell, when questioned, acknowledged the authorship of these to the General of the Society, but stressed that his essay, taken as whole, should be regarded as "medicine for extreme cases" only. To the General's demand for its public repudiation, however, his answer was to publish the entire document along with an explanatory introduction under the title *A Much-Abused Letter* (*1906*). The upshot was his dismissal from the Society without regularization of his position as a secular priest.[1] Over the next year or so he moved from place to place, staying with friends, before finally settling at Storrington in Sussex, in accommodation made available to him by the ever-loyal Miss Petre. But the *celebret*, or authorization to say mass, was not forthcoming despite lengthy negotiations, and when on the appearance of *Pascendi* he attacked the encyclical in two articles in *The Times* (Sept. *30* and Oct. *1, 1907*) all hope that such authorization would ever be granted was extinguished. Three weeks later he was deprived of the sacraments on instructions from the Holy See.

Yet whatever the Church might say or do, Tyrrell still felt himself to be a Catholic, with a work of reform to strive for in whatever way he could.[2] He continued therefore to write and to publish: *Through Scylla and Charybdis*, a collection of essays most of which had already been printed in different periodicals was the product of *1907*; *Medievalism*, a reply in the form of an open letter to a reference to himself

[1] On the whole matter of Tyrrell's break with the Society of Jesus see Petre, *op. cit.*, ii, chs. X to XIV.

[2] As he wrote to an Anglican friend at the time: "I feel that my work is to hammer away at the great unwieldy carcase of the Roman Communion and wake it up from its mediaeval dreams. Not that I shall succeed, but that my failure and many another may pave the way for eventual success" *ibid.*, ii, p. *373*.

in a Lenten pastoral of Cardinal Mercier's, appeared in the following year; and his best-known book of all, the posthumous *Christianity at the Cross-Roads*, in 1909.[1]

Through Scylla and Charybdis; or, The Old Theology and the New, derived its title from the author's intention to avoid both "the rock of tradition" and the "whirlpool of progress".[2] Tyrrell here argues that the *depositum fidei* itself is unchanging, but that it does not consist, as the old orthodoxy holds, of a set of theological propositions, an idea he dismisses as "theologism". Fundamentally, revelation is incapable of development, whereas liberal Protestantism—from which Catholic Modernism must be carefully distinguished—defaults on the principle of *semper idem*. Furthermore, though revelation is not a body of statements but an experience, the latter "is rightly and profitably made the subject-matter of theological reflection".[3] And in its aspect of "science", theology must develop freely and under no other limitations than are imposed by its subject-matter and the laws of thought, the Church's teaching-office being "simply to guard the Apostolic Revelation identically for all ages and capacities", with the result that "her dogmatic decisions possess a protective but not a scientific or philosophical infallibility". To speak of revealed truth as "prophetic" is simply to make the point that it views the world and history *sub specie aeternitatis*.

As the poet or dramatist manipulates history and philosophy in the interests of a higher ideal, that finds but an imperfect expression in the actual; or as the artist corrects "the trembling hand of Nature" and gives forth in its purity the thought she stumbles over; so the prophet sees and expresses the religious meaning of the world and life.[4]

But if the prophet's work is essentially that of "getting at the more inward and deeper truth through the husk of the phenomenal and relative", then "his reading of past history is as little historical as his reading of future history". He sees "fact" indeed, but fact transfigured and rearranged always to a practical end, that of the spiritual life of man.

---

[1] Reprinted, with a foreword by A. R. Vidler, in *1963*.
[2] Petre, *op. cit.*, ii, p. *318*.
[3] *Through Scylla and Charybdis*, p. *353*.
[4] *Ibid.*, p. *302*.

Medievalism is a purely polemical work, somewhat verbose and strident in tone, but also fearlessly outspoken and clear-sighted. Written in haste and under pressure of strong feeling, it is not among Tyrrell's best efforts, as he himself was aware. *Christianity at the Cross-Roads*, on the other hand, although its author was by now a mortally sick man, is generally considered his masterpiece.[1] As Vidler justly observes, it is "a declaration of faith, and not of scepticism", despite the fact that its standpoint is far removed from that of Tyrrell's early Jesuit writings. His conviction that Roman Catholicism, whatever its accretions and perversions, is the only really authentic form of Christianity, remains unshaken. On the contrary, he sees it as of all religions the truest and most characteristic expression of man's abiding spiritual need. No doubt of existing Catholicism, he says, "the various phases of the religious Idea, each with its particular alloy and limitation, are somewhat violently held together by a continual synthetic effort"; nevertheless there is "good reason to think that Catholic Christianity is more capable of conforming itself to the exigencies of a historical science of religion than any of those forms that have narrowed themselves to the development of some particular element of Catholicism, even though it be the highest. In fact, the science of religion would, in some sense, be a science of Catholicism, of a microcosm in which the whole religious process of the world is represented."[2] But at the same time Modernists "are not such utopian dreamers as to imagine that those, whose temporal interests are vested in existing Catholicism and its worst corruptions, will ever open their arms to welcome such a science". The whole Modernist hope, rather, is in "the irresistible tide of truth and knowledge, which must at last surround and surmount the barriers of ignorance, buttressed up by untruthfulness; and, above all, in such inward and living Christianity as may still be left in a rapidly dying Church".[3] The spirit of Christianity, however, has

---

[1] It was prompted, in part at least, by an article highly critical of Modernism from the pen of the Anglican liberal, W. R. Inge, afterwards dean of St Paul's. (The article was subsequently reprinted in the latter's *Outspoken Essays*, First Series (*1919*), ch. VI, under the title "Roman Catholic Modernism".) In essence Tyrrell's reply to Inge is contained in a sentence or two: "Whatever Jesus was, He was in no sense a Liberal Protestant. All that makes Catholicism most repugnant to present modes of thought derives from Him" (*Christianity at the Cross-Roads*, p. xxi).

[2] *Christianity at the Cross-Roads*, pp. *278* f.   [3] *Op. cit.*, p. *280*.

D

repeatedly saved the Church from the hands of its worldly oppressors within as well as without, and may yet do so again.

By the time *Christianity at the Cross-Roads* reached the public, Tyrrell was dead, and with his death Modernism lost its most forceful personality.

This was certainly felt to be so by Tyrrell's principal friend and confidant, Baron von Hügel, who himself in after years drew further away from the Modernist position, with which at the time of the crisis he had been closely associated. Von Hügel's own interest had lain mainly in the field of biblical studies, and it was for freedom in this regard that he consistently strove. His friendship with Loisy, the essential soundness of whose opinions he believed in for as long as he possibly could, rested largely upon their shared concern for the autonomy of historical science. As he put it to Tyrrell: "The Church, *i.e.* ecclesiastical officials, has a right to many, even great sacrifices on our part, but not simply to anything and everything."[1] In so far, then, as Modernism meant complete liberty to adopt the objective and critical approach to Christian history and to the Bible in its historical aspect, von Hügel was completely at one with the movement. Where he had less sympathy with it was on its philosophical side, with its strong immanentist and pragmatist tendencies. By contrast his own deep-rooted sense of the transcendence and "otherness" of the divine, later to receive powerful stimulus from the writings of Ernst Troeltsch, came in time, along with his interest in mysticism, to dominate his whole theological outlook. His earlier philosophy, of an idealist type, thus fell away and was eventually repudiated by him, although his personal regard and respect for both Blondel and Laberthonnière, in whom the *méthode d'immanence* had its chief exponents, continued undimmed.[2] Nevertheless, any attempt to minimize the baron's faith in the general cause for which the Modernists fought, or the encouragement he was always ready to give them, would be to present a false picture. He was ever their friend,

---

[1] *Selected Letters*, p. *136*.

[2] As he wrote to a Swiss correspondent in July *1921*: "Je me trouve forcé, en simple loyauté, d'aller, ou de rester, encore plus à droite. J'admire encore beaucoup telles pages de mes (toujours bien-aimés) amis *Maurice Blondel* et *Louis* [sic] *Laberthonnière*; mais je dois avouer que mon intérêt pleinement vivant est maintenant donné aux penseurs . . . qui, sont en train de nous constituer une *epistémologie critico-réaliste*" (*op. cit.*, p. *334*).

whether in England, France or Italy, and the patron of their enterprises. Paul Sabatier went so far as to call him "the bishop of Modernism". In any case it has been well said that Modernism played the same part in von Hügel's development as Quietism in Fénelon's and Jansenism in Pascal's. But although for long under a cloud of ecclesiastical suspicion he was never disciplined, thanks no doubt to his rank and social influence and to the fact that he was a layman.

Von Hügel was not by nature a polemist and in his published writings he for the most part avoided controversy. At the height of the Modernist crisis he brought out the book on which his reputation as a theologian mainly rests, *The Mystical Element in Religion* (*1908*), described years later by William Temple as arguably "the most important theological work written in the English language during the last half-century", both "a penetrating piece of psychological analysis" and "a great achievement in constructive philosophy".[1] The first series of his collected *Essays and Addresses on the Philosophy of Religion* was published in *1921*, the second posthumously in *1926*.[2] Perhaps the most noteworthy of his public statements at the time of the Loisy affair, however, was his article in the Paris *Quinzaine* for June *1*, *1904*, "Du Christ éternel et de nos christologies successives", in which he defended the legitimacy of the Christian and Catholic act of faith against radical historical scepticism. His own position he summarizes thus:

> Although the act of Christian faith necessarily goes beyond the historic facts—the object, each one for itself, of historic-critical proof—it nevertheless demands facts of that nature. It demands them because that is a condition of all human assent, since our souls are only awakened to the presence of spiritual realities when a contingent and historic stimulus from without excites them. It demands them because all complete and deep religion calls for a factor of this nature. The more complete and profound a religion is, the more

---

[1] Cf. M. de la Bedoyère, *op. cit.*, p. *223*. But *Eternal Life: a Study of its Implications and Applications*, first published in *1912*, is as important as any of von Hügel's works for the understanding of his thought.

[2] The unfinished Gifford lectures, intended for delivery at Edinburgh university *1924–1926*, form part of the volume *The Reality of God and Religion and Agnosticism*, edited by Edmund G. Gardner and published in *1931*.

it will present this paradox of the permanent seized through the transitory, the eternal manifested in time.

It was a conviction he never relinquished or qualified.

4. Philosophical Modernism

According to *Pascendi* Modernism was a close-knit intellectual scheme the basis of which was a philosophy of agnosticism. This however the Modernists themselves consistently denied, urging that their dominant concern was with historical criticism, especially as applied to the scriptures. Yet their movement certainly came to be associated with a philosophy, and one that readily lent itself to their apologetic purposes. Philosophical Modernism, moreover, was principally a French phenomenon, represented by three distinguished thinkers, two of whom—Blondel and Le Roy—were laymen, the third, Lucien Laberthonnière, being a priest of the Oratory. Unlike Loisy, all three remained loyal Catholics, submitting to authority, although the last-named, as a cleric, was disciplined.

Maurice Blondel (*1861–1949*) won early fame with his doctoral thesis, published in *1893* under the title *L'Action: essai d'une critique de la vie et d'une science de la pratique*.[1] Begun when the author was only *21*, it is a work of outstanding originality despite the notorious density of its style. Even as a student at the École Normale Supérieure, Blondel was well aware of the shortcomings of the traditional type of apologetic, with its arid rationalism and failure to understand the real difficulties of the modern mind. What was needed, he realized, was a genuinely philosophical approach, grounded in what he terms a "logic of action". "My original intention", he long afterwards wrote, "was to establish a philosophy which was autonomous and which from a rational point of view nevertheless complied with the most minute and rigorous demands of Catholicism." But the substance of this philosophy would no longer be the familiar idealist game of ideas.

---

[1] The first edition was not reprinted in Blondel's lifetime and so became something of a bibliographical rarity. It was republished in *1950*. The second and much revised edition in two volumes which the author himself brought out in *1936–1937* is regarded by most students of his work as less satisfactory than the original.

My primary aim was to discover by studying human activity and thought the points of intersection which not only make it possible for Christianity to strike roots deep in our consciences, but also for it to make demands in the name of inner integrity as well as in the name of divine authority and of the outward manifestations which authenticate revealed truths and prescriptions. . . .

Human action seemed to me to be in fact that point on which the powers of Nature, the light of intelligence, the strength of the will, and even the benefits of grace, converge . . . .[1]

The apologetic problem was raised specifically in his subsequent *Lettre sur les exigences de la pensée contemporaine en matière d'apologétique* (*1896*),[2] a work which especially impressed von Hügel, whom Blondel had met in the spring of *1895*. Blondel's objection to the scholastic method was that it tries first to establish revelation as an *a priori* possibility before going on to demonstrate its actuality in Christianity, an implausible procedure that might perhaps appeal to believers but scarcely to the sort of person to whom such apologetic was supposed to be addressed. A truer method would be to adopt the Pascalian approach of *Quelle chimère est-ce donc que l'homme*—to show that for all men revelation is an inescapable issue and that moral responsibility is incurred in its acceptance or rejection.[3] Blondel's whole argument is that at the deepest level of his being, man longs for something "uniquely necessary" (*l'unique nécessaire*) which at the same time remains inaccessible to his own striving. The search itself is demanded by the very fact of "action", this being understood in the broadest sense as man's total experience of life. For in acting we do not act merely for action's sake, but rather for what transcends each and every particular act. Thus human activity, however limited, has a wealth of latent significance which it is the task of the reflective understanding to discover. For this reason Blondel always insisted that his philosophy was not irrationalist. On the contrary, "the progress of action causes the progress of thought,

---

[1] "Lettre-préface pour une réédition de l'Action", in *Études blondéliennes*, i, (*1951*), pp. *16* f.

[2] An English translation is included in A. Dru and I. Trethowan (edd.), *Maurice Blondel: The Letter on Apologetics and History and Dogma (1964)*.

[3] On the influence of Pascal upon Modernist thought, see D. M. Eastwood, *The Revival of Pascal (1936)*.

as the progress of thought conditions and determines the progress of action".[1]

According to Blondel, man is dichotomized at the very root of his being into a boundless will to achieve and an ever restricted power of achievement. From this he concludes that transcendent Being is immanent in every form of human experience. There is, that is to say, something within us which is also not of us, something both antecedent and ulterior to us, and apart from which our existence is an enigma. The point of Blondel's apologetic is therefore that "supernature" is not simply a possible *explanation* of human experience, it belongs to its very essence. Man's life is oriented towards God not at certain levels or moments only but continuously and through every potentiality of his being.

This thesis, worked out step by step in *L'action*, is shown in the *Lettre* in its bearings on contemporary thought. Blondel draws attention, on the one hand, to the modern sensitiveness to the distinction between concept and reality, and on the other to the principle that nothing can enter into a man which does not in some sense proceed from him: the notion of a heteronomous truth is alien to the modern outlook. But whereas the traditional, scholastic apologetic is unacceptable on both counts, a "method of immanence" removes the difficulty by discovering the vital connection—one not in idea only but in action—between nature and supernature.

Some years later Blondel contributed to the current debate—provoked by Loisy—on the question of faith and history with a long article entitled *Histoire et Dogme: Les lacunes philosophiques de l'éxégèse moderne (1904)*.[2] Here he distinguishes between what he calls "extrinsicism", by which dogma determines the reading of history, and "historicism", by which history determines the interpretation of dogma—Loisy's position—and goes on to state, if somewhat obscurely, an alternative position of his own depending on a re-appraisal of the whole idea of tradition. This last he describes as a "preserving" or "conquering" power. "It discovers and formulates truths which the past lived, without being able to articulate them or define them explicitly." It is founded upon authoritative texts, but its strength comes from a living experience such as enables it eventually to trans-

[1] *Bulletin de la Société française de Philosophie, 1902, p. 100.*
[2] There is an English translation by Dru and Trethowan. See note 2, p. 53 above.

cend these instead of remaining subservient to them.[1] Facts, in short, "do not suffice for dogma" except through the "screen" of faith; but by the same token the believer cannot be content— with Loisy—to regard biblical criticism as a completely autonomous science.

For the greater part of his academic career, Blondel held the chair of philosophy at the university of Aix-Marseille, the loss of his sight obliging him to retire in *1927*. But with the development of the Modernist crisis he gave up further publication, apart from one or two works of a non-controversial nature, until *1934*, when the first of the series of volumes made its appearance which represent his final position in philosophy as it relates to Christianity.[2]

Blondel has been called "the spiritual father of Modernism".[3] This is altogether an overstatement; nevertheless, much Modernist writing reveals his inspiration. The man most obviously his disciple was Lucien Laberthonnière (*1860–1932*), professor of philosophy at the Oratorian college at Juilly. Laberthonnière's work could fitly be characterized as Blondel simplified and creatively interpreted. His first book was a collection of essays on religious philosophy,[4] the most important of which bore the title, "Le dogmatisme moral", a phrase that may be taken to indicate his general standpoint. Basically his contention is that philosophy is not simply a method of procedure with no proper subject-matter of its own, but a view of life demanding a moral no less than an intellectual conversion.

[1] Cf. W. Scott, S.J., "The Notion of Tradition in Maurice Blondel", in *Theological Studies*, September *1966*, pp. *384–400*. Von Hügel, however, on this issue, found himself on the side of Loisy. As he afterwards (*1912*) wrote to Maude Petre: "B[londel] wrote as one with little sense or knowledge of historical method and the precise historical documents and facts; and my mind and hand were and are nearly as much in those things as L[oisy]'s own" (British Museum Add. mss *45362*. Cited by A. R. Vidler, *A Variety of Catholic Modernists* (*1970*), pp. *120* f.).

[2] *La Pensée* (*2* vols.) was followed in *1935* by *L'Étre et les êtres. La Philosophie et l'esprit chrétien* (*2* vols.) appeared between *1944* and *1949*, and *Les exigences philosophiques du Christianisme* in *1950*. These all were dictated to an amanuensis, often from a sick-bed. To the end of his life Blondel was unusually devout, hearing mass daily, so long as health permitted. At his funeral the archbishop of Aix declared: "C'est en voyant Maurice Blondel que j'ai compris ce que c'est qu'être à l'Eglise." Cf. *La Vie intellectuelle*, July *1949*, pp. *53* f.

[3] G. de Ruggiero, *Modern Philosophy* (trans. A. Hannay H. and R. G. Collingwood), p. *213*.

[4] *Essais de Philosophie religieuse* (*1903*).

The aim of my philosophical doctrine [he wrote] is to give sense to life, to human existence, so that every doctrine is a *moral work.* ... Its truth is to be viable.[1]

Here he went rather beyond Blondel, who claimed for his philosophy of action that it was a metaphysic in its own right and not, as many of his critics objected, a thinly-disguised apologetic. Laberthonnière, however, stresses the Augustinian view that since *Deus est veritas* Christianity must itself be the true philosophy. But if Laberthonnière's is essentially a religious philosophy it is not because he derives his conclusions from fixed dogmatic principles but because he attempts to define in philosophical terms a religious experience of which dogma has been the historic expression. His starting-point therefore is not an ecclesiastical formulary but a spiritual fact. "The affirmation of God, like our own self-affirmation, is a living action."[2] Further, the degree of our personal self-fulfilment is the measure of our understanding of God's nature and purposes, an understanding which in turn depends on our recognition of others as themselves *subjects,* like us.[3] He goes on:

> It seems as though the God who wills and loves us were, so to speak, enlarged by us in his own being. In loving him we help him to rediscover himself in us as we rediscover ourselves in him. He comports himself in us as if he had need of us in order to be. Just as we affirm ourselves freely by him, so he by us freely affirms himself.

The immanentism of such a statement might seem extreme but for the added qualification: "We, if we willed to affirm ourselves without him, would lose ourselves, while he could affirm himself without us and yet lose nothing of the fullness of his being." Thus Laberthonnière's doctrine, like Blondel's, is strictly a *method* of immanence, a rationale of how "supernature" is actually encountered in life. Putting it in more familiar theological language, supernature is nature permeated through and through by grace. "If, in a sense, it is neither legitimate nor even possible to hold to a 'separate' philosophy it is because, in fact, there is no 'separate' nature."[4]

Laberthonnière's central theme is the Divine love, both for man and

---

[1] *Op. cit.,* p. *288.*   [2] *Ibid.,* p. *76.*
[3] Pp. *87* f.   [4] P. *172.*

within man. God is not an immutable "essence", as in the tradition of Hellenic thought, but a living Being the dynamism of whose personality is symbolized by the dogma of the Trinity. Herein lies the difference between Greek idealism and Christian realism.[1] The former conceives reality as a hierarchy of ideas falling within the ultimate unity of a supreme Idea, fixed, final and determined, which may be called indifferently either God or Nature. The Christian view, by contrast, is dynamic, concrete and individualizing. God here is no impersonal Absolute, but personal being at its highest—"un Dieu-personne qui est une puissance d'agir". Christian doctrine, accordingly, is not a body of abstract theory, not a philosophical *Weltanschauung*, but an interpretation of a sequence of events in which the purpose of God is spiritually discerned. Thus any sharp distinction between an event and its "meaning"—as was made, for example, by Loisy—is mistaken. If approached in a merely external way a religious truth is without significance; it must be appropriated by the inner self and become a vital experience. Christ, for the believer, is not simply a fact of history but a present reality.

In *1905*, Laberthonnière assumed the editorship of *Annales de Philosophie chrétienne*, an organ of liberal Catholic thought, for which he himself now supplied a good deal of the matter, carrying it on until *1913*, when its suppression was ordered by the authorities. At the same time two further works of his own were refused the *imprimatur*. Thereafter he published no more.[2]

But the philosophy most characteristic of the Modernist viewpoint, with its stress on the primacy of action, was that of Édouard Le Roy (*1870–1954*), a professor of mathematics at the Lycée Hoche and subsequently Bergson's successor at the Collège de France. His discussion of the nature and function of dogma in *Dogme et Critique* (*1907*) is indeed as important in its way as the apologetic of *L'Evangile et l'Eglise*. The nucleus of the book consists of an article, "Qu'est-ce qu'un dogme?", which he wrote for the *Quinzaine* in April *1905*, the rest of it being made up of criticisms and replies. Le Roy's philosophical

---

[1] *Le réalisme chrétien et l'idéalisme grec* is the title of Laberthonniére's second book, published in *1904*. Both it and the *Essais* were placed on the Index in *1906*.

[2] Except, that is, for an essay on St John of the Cross in the *Bulletin de la Société française de philosophie* in *1926*. A number of his works since have been published posthumously, thanks to the efforts of his friend, Louis Canet. Of particular interest among these is *La notion chrétienne de l'autorité* (*1956*).

position was in general pragmatist or activist.[1] The meaning of a truth, he explains, is chiefly to be gauged by the services it renders and the consequences with which it is pregnant—in short, "by the vivifying influence which it exercises over the whole body of knowledge". To understand dogmatic truth, as Catholic Christianity presents it, this principle has to be clearly understood. For the problem today is not that of the truth of particular dogmas but of the use and meaning of dogmas as such. To the modern mind the very concept of dogma is a stumbling-block. Truth, that is, is not a decision of authority, nor can it be established, in the way of the traditional apologetic, by arguments extrinsic to the truth itself. A further difficulty is that historically dogma can be shown to be an amalgam of scriptural imagery and ancient metaphysics. In any event, however, the very idea of dogma as a complete system of intellectual truths lacks credibility for the now obvious reason that it does not consist of knowledge which the modern mind is confident of possessing. Indeed, the basic objection to the traditional view is precisely that of a false intellectualism. Dogma is not a statement of truth in the speculative or theoretical order; it adds nothing to the sum of positive knowledge and is not comparable to a scientific hypothesis. Take, for example, the doctrine of the divine personality. To give it definition, says Le Roy, is inevitably to fall into anthropomorphism, yet not to affirm it is to admit agnosticism. Similarly with the doctrine of Christ's resurrection; this cannot be expressed as an intellectual concept since Jesus' post-resurrection life, on the evidence of the gospels themselves, is of a different kind from that which ended on the cross. Again, the doctrine of the real presence proves how difficult it is to present a mystery in rational terms, inasmuch as the dogma itself denies that the presence is in any way perceptible to sense. It exists for faith and cannot be made part of a general conceptual scheme.

But what dogma can do, so Le Roy contends—and this he holds to be its true function—is to provide rules of practical conduct, prescriptive guidance to the religious and moral life. Thus the doctrine that God is personal really means: Conduct yourselves in your relations with him as you would in your relations with a human person. So too with the resurrection; what the dogma effectually says is: Let your relation

---

[1] But see L. S. Stebbing, *Pragmatism and French Voluntarism* (*1914*), pp. *59* ff.

to the risen Christ be what it would have been before his death, or what it is to your own contemporaries. And likewise with the real presence, which bids us adopt before the consecrated host exactly the same attitude as one would were Jesus actually visible.[1] The intellectualist does not of course deny the practical import of dogma, but for him it is secondary and implied, depending on dogma's primary sense as a theoretical statement. Theology, in other words, is made to precede religion—a reversal of the true order. Consider it, though, in the light of man's practical needs and its propositions become meaningful and relevant, and its symbolism powerfully suggestive.[2] Moreover, this pragmatic view indicates the real connection between dogma and thought. For the test of religious teachings is in experience, the meeting-place of the diverse orders of knowledge being the life of man himself—the area, that is, in which the Church's authority is justly exercised. Indeed, one can go further even and allow that dogma has some speculative role by virtue of its *negative* use. For although it does not determine truth positively, it at least excludes certain notions as erroneous. Thus, in insisting that God is personal, it rejects the idea that he is "a mere law, a formal category, an ideal principle, an abstract entity".[3]

5. The Movement in Italy

If the immanentist apologetic originated in France it was in Italy that it found its most eager exponents. Pre-eminent amongst these was Ernesto Buonaiuti (*1881–1946*), of the Italian Modernists, the best known outside his own country. His autobiography, *Il Pellegrino di Roma* (*1945*), provides therefore an authoritative account of the movement from the standpoint of one who at the time had been a very active participant, even if he later so far changed his views as to

---

[1] *Dogme et Critique*, pp. *25* f.

[2] A somewhat similar account of Christian doctrine has in our day been given by R. B. Braithwaite, *An Empiricist's View of the Nature of Religious Belief* (*1956*).

[3] Le Roy denied that his "practical" interpretation of dogma meant that there is no correspondence at all between religious doctrine and that unknown reality which it nevertheless attempts to express, or that dogmas can finally be reduced to arbitrary symbols. "Qu'on parle d'analogies, je le veux bien: ces analogies sont en quelque sorte les *harmonies vitales* que la réalité transcendante éveille en nous" (*op. cit.*, p. *96*.)

be able to dismiss the entire episode as, for him, "a youthful mistake".[1] But Italian Modernism was not primarily a theological movement; its bias was political and in favour of the Lega Democratica Nazionale, the leader of which was a priest, Don Romolo Murri (*1870–1944*), who in theology was a decided conservative.[2] As a theological movement, however, it drew its inspiration chiefly from France, although Tyrrell's influence was considerable, and von Hügel too gave it his strong support.

Among biblical scholars the Barnabite, Giovanni Semeria (*1867–1931*), author of *Dogma, gerarchia e culto nella chiesa primitiva* (*1902*), and Salvatore Minocchi (*1869–1943*), editor of *Studi religiosi*, were the most prominent, the former being known also as an eloquent preacher and much liked as an engaging personality. In *1903*, the two men, who were close friends, paid a visit to Leo Tolstoy that aroused a good deal of comment. On its lay side the movement won the adherence of a group of energetic young men who, with the poet, novelist and senator, Antonio Fogazzaro (*1842–1911*), founded the review *Il Rinnovamento* in January *1907*. Fogazzaro himself was a fervent disciple of Rosmini, a keen advocate of church reform and a vigorous critic of the "immobilism" by which the Church seemed to him to be gripped.[3] His own principal contribution to Modernism took the form of a novel, *Il Santo*, published in *1905*.[4] In this he propounds the idea that what is needed for the reform of the existing Church is the emergence of a great saint, probably a layman and a man of both liberal

[1] Thus in *Una fede e una disciplina* (*1925*) he wrote: "The modernist crisis, it is true, caught me up completely and swept me into its explosive centre. But I was quickly disabused, and all that was paradoxical and untimely and eccentric in the—admittedly very noble—programme of the movement, which thought it would straight away make the Church irresistibly effective, thanks to a basic renewal of its attitudes and outlook, soon fell away like dross. No one around me believed this, and I was left to the risks of my solitary pilgrimage." Cf. M. Ranchetti, *The Catholic Modernists* (*1969*), pp. *9* f.

[2] On Murri's scholasticism see Loisy, *Mémoires*, ii, pp. *520* and *561*, and iii, p. *95*. The Lega was concerned about ecclesiastical reform, but according to Buonaiuti "it had no truly religious intention and implied no attitudes that were actually opposed to the spirit of orthodox Catholicism" (*Il Modernismo cattolico*, ed. *1943*, p. *133 n*).

[3] See T. Gallarati-Scotti. *La vita di Antonio Fogazzaro* (*1920*; new and corrected edition *1934*).

[4] An English translation appeared a year later, when the original was placed on the Index. Fogazzaro's last novel, *Leila* (*1911*), was something of a retractation.

vision and intense spirituality. The character so depicted in the novel declares:

> The Catholic Church, which proclaims herself a minister of life, today fetters and suffocates everything within her that lives with a young and vigorous life, and props up all that is falling to ruin and decay. . . . The Church is not the hierarchy only, but the universal assembly of the faithful, a *gens sancta*.[1]

Indeed the Church is prey to four "evil spirits"—those of falsehood, clerical domination, avarice and obstinate fixity in the ways of the past; to which charge the pope—himself a saintly figure—is made to reply that all this may well be so, but his own role is far less simple than that of the single-minded reformer, since he has to govern men as they are, steering his course among them not only according to charity but with prudence.

Two anonymous Modernist statements appeared in *1907*, the first an open letter, *Quello che vogliamo*, addressed to Pius X from a group of priests in answer to a discourse of his (April *1907*) in which he alluded to "rebels" who "spread abroad under artful forms" certain "monstrous errors" on the evolution of dogma and other matters;[2] the second, entitled *Il Programma dei modernisti*—it in fact was the work of Buonaiuti—an extended reply to *Pascendi*.[3] This latter objected that the encyclical had distorted the truth about Modernism by presuming to explain it in terms of a particular philosophy rather than recognize it for what fundamentally it was, an assertion of the rights of historical criticism even in the sphere of faith.

> So far from our philosophy dictating our critical method, it is the critical method that has, of its own accord, forced us to a very tentative and uncertain formulation of various philosophical conclusions, or better still, to a clearer exposition of certain ways of

---

[1] Quoted by A. L. Lilley, *Modernism: a Record and Review* (*1908*), p. *132*. The character which Fogazzaro here created was essentially a personification of his own ideals. Cf. Ranchetti, *op. cit.*, p. *109*.

[2] An English translation (*What We Want*), introduced by A. L. Lilley, came out in the same year.

[3] On the question of the authorship cf. Rivière, *op. cit.*, p. *405*. Cf. also R. Murri in *The Hibbert Journal*, *1926*, p. *664*. *Pilgrim of Rome*, edited by C. Nelson and N. Pittenger (*1969*), contains a selection of translated excerpts from Buonaiuti's writings, including *Il Pellegrino di Roma*.

thinking to which Catholic apologetic has never been wholly a stranger.[1]

The *Programma* then goes on to argue that the scholastic type of apology has no persuasive power for the contemporary mind and that a new apologetic, neither scholastic nor agnostic, must replace it; an apologetic, that is, which "not only coincides with that more generally assumed by the philosophy of today, but is also in continuity with the general results of the criticism of science". If, as the encyclical avers, Modernists are "immanentists" it is because they are conscious of "a living and acting spirit which, amid all the contingencies of its surface life, bears in itself a restless hunger for the Divine, and comes to live a more noble life only on condition of recognizing this hunger and satisfying it with the religious experience that its surroundings and historical setting naturally impose upon it".[2] Further, in distinguishing the "Christ of faith" from the "Jesus of history" Modernists do not suppose that from an ontological point of view the historical Christ did not include those ethical and religious insights and values which Christian experience has gradually become aware of by living the gospel life.

Religious facts include mysterious meanings which pure science misses. Faith, with its peculiar power, penetrates to these meanings and feeds on them. It does not create them; it feeds on them.[3]

As an answer to the misrepresentations of *Pascendi* the *Programma* was effective enough, but as a positive statement of Modernist aims its merits were those only of a fighting manifesto, compensating in boldness for what it lacked in depth. As soon as it appeared (October 29) a "blanket" excommunication fell upon all concerned in its publication. The struggle, however, was continued in the pages of the *Rinnovamento*, whose editors had earlier declared "without pride but without weakness" their intention to persist in claiming, for themselves and others, "the right to think and study with greater trust in the Catholic Church". But in December, Cardinal Ferrari, archbishop of Milan, in whose diocese the review was published, pronounced an excommunication on editors and publishers alike. In the following

---

[1] *The Programme of Modernism*, p. *16*.
[2] *Op. cit.*, p. *125*.   [3] *Ibid.*, pp. *138* f.

January, Buonaiuti launched his own journal *Nova et Vetera*, but this ran for less than a twelve-month, although his *Rivista storico-critica delle scienze teologiche*, started in *1905*, survived until September *1910*. Romolo Murri's *Rivista di cultura* made a brief re-appearance at the beginning of *1909*, but the game was up. In the ensuing June several of Murri's books were put on the Index and before the year was out *Il Rinnovamento* itself ceased publication. Modernism as a movement was finished.

6. Condemnation

The first of the two papal acts in condemnation of Modernism was the decree *Lamentabili sane exitu*, of July *3*, *1907*, listing as objectionable 65 propositions containing allegedly Modernist teaching. The main sources were the writings of Loisy, but Tyrrell too was drawn upon, and there were side-glances at Le Roy and even Archbishop Mignot. Presented in schematic form and in the Latin tongue they were calculated to give the impression of a deliberately constituted body of heretical doctrine *Pascendi dominici gregis*, which followed on September *8*, went further and purported to offer a systematic account of the whole Modernist programme. The new school of exegesis was denounced root and branch, but the encyclical's loudest thunder was reserved for the "agnostic" or "immanentist" philosophy on which the Modernist innovations were asserted to be based. The language is often intemperate; the course of speculative thought since the Middle Ages, for example, is dismissed as "the ravings of philosophers", and the Modernists themselves are repudiated as traitors to the Church, "thoroughly imbued with the poisonous doctrines taught by her enemies" and "lost to all sense of modesty". That the document was the work of Pius X personally—himself no theologian, even at the scholastic level with which alone he had any familiarity—is not to be credited.[1] Yet for all its extravagance of tone it was a cunningly devised utterance, and if its aim was to rally the forces of reaction by depicting Modernism as an insidious heresy—the essence indeed of all others—it so far succeeded.

[1] A certain Fr Billot is said to have been responsible for the greater part of it, although other hands have been detected, including perhaps Cardinal Steinhuber's. Dr Vidler maintains that the principal author was Fr Joseph Lemius, an able Vatican theologian who died in *1923*. See *A Variety of Catholic Modernists*, pp. *17* f.

The second part of the document indicated the measures to be taken against the movement. An elaborate machinery of control, including secret "Vigilance" committees in all dioceses, was to be set up. Reports were to be sent regularly to Rome. Private delation was encouraged. No teacher suspected of Modernism was to be allowed to retain his post in any Catholic university or seminary. Books and periodicals of a like tendency were to be prohibited, and censorship tightened up. Even this, in the event, was deemed insufficient and in *1910* the pope imposed upon the clergy a stringently anti-Modernist oath (*Sacrorum antistitum*).[1] The episcopate did not protest, although many bishops acquiesced only with an uneasy conscience. Of opposition, in fact, there was virtually *nil*. In any case the pope's entourage was filled with a zeal for orthodoxy which for a time knew no bounds, and heresy-hunting, directed with obsessional zest by Mgr Umberto Benigni and his *Sodalitium Pianum*, became the quickest road to official favour. Scholarship, needless to say, fell a ready victim to the campaign. A well-known moderate, Pierre Batiffol, was relieved of his rectorship at the Toulouse Institut Catholique.[2] M.-J. Lagrange, by far the best biblical scholar which the church then possessed and himself a critic of Modernism,[3] had for a while at least to relinquish his position as director of the École Biblique at Jerusalem. The first volume of Duchesne's *Histoire ancienne de l'Église* turned up in the Index. Only with the succession in *1914* of a new supreme pontiff was this obstinately repressive policy slackened.[4] Benedict XV was a man of a different stamp from his predecessor—he had been trained in the school of Leo XIII and Cardinal Rampolla—and the European war had brought new and more pressing concerns. But Modernism was to remain a "dangerous" subject for Catholics until the Second Vatican Council (*1962–1965*)[5] began, willy-nilly, a process of re-appraisal, in which

[1] Feeling against the oath was strong in Germany, where professors in the state universities were dispensed from taking it. Cf. A. Houtin, *Histoire du modernisme catholique (1913)*, p. *333*.

[2] Cf. J. Rivière, *Monseigneur Batiffol (1929)*, pp. *56* ff. His book on the eucharist was placed on the Index.

[3] See *M. Loisy et le modernisme (1932)*.

[4] Pius X was canonized in *1954*, the first pope of modern times to receive the honour.

[5] Cf. A. Dru, "Modernism and the Present Position of the Church", in *The Downside Review*, April *1964*, pp. *103–110*. The encyclical *Divino afflante Spiritu* of Pope Pius XII on the promotion of biblical studies (*1943*) greatly eased the

men like Tyrrell—if not Loisy, impenitent in mind and caustic of tongue to the last—are coming to be seen in a new and more sympathetic light.

7. The Significance of Modernism

Was the Modernist movement, then, a failure? By the end of Pius X's reign it certainly appeared to be. Its leaders either were dead or had been silenced or had left the Church. *Romanità*, integralist and triumphalist, had seemingly swept its opponents from the field or cowed them into submission. The alternative of a modernized, "critical" Catholicism, with eternal Rome at its centre but able also to make its appeal to the twentieth century as an effective rival to non-religious humanism, was evidently not a viable option. Rome herself, after all, should know, and the sovereign pontiff had declared it to be so. The face which she had consistently turned against "progress" during the last century was to continue averted in the present. *On est catholique ou on ne l'est pas*, so the saying goes, and an institution identified with wholly absolutist claims, it might be thought, cannot compromise; the road taken at the Counter-Reformation must be pursued to the end. The Modernists themselves, moreover, had in effect subscribed to this verdict. Loisy, long before his personal condemnation, had realized that the new apologetic was unacceptable to Rome and hence, as an apology for Rome, meaningless. Tyrrell always believed passionately in the Catholic "idea", but had he not come to doubt whether between the idea and the historical fact a gulf did not stretch? Von Hügel, as the years elapsed, felt increasingly that the strivings and hopes of the crisis days belonged only to the past. Buonaiuti for a time and Miss Petre to her dying day were loyal to the Modernist cause, but such isolated resistance as theirs could not disguise defeat.

That the movement had its limitations and shortnesses of view is not to be denied. Intellectually it was very much of its period, dominated as it was by historicism, immanentism and pragmatism. Paradoxically, indeed, its adherents, as so-called Modernists, were in some

situation of the critical exegete, cautious though its language is. For a brief account of the influence of Maurice Blondel on French Catholic thought see H. Bouillard, *op. cit.*, ch. i.

E

respects even behind their time, if one considers the direction contemporary Protestantism—as in Rudolf Eucken, for example—was
already beginning to take, along with the circumstance that the
non-Catholic scholarship which so won their admiration was really
that of the later nineteenth century; although one has in fairness to
remember the total failure of official Catholicism to come to terms
with the intellectual challenge of the new age and that to the more
radical minds within the Church the survival of religion itself was
ultimately at stake. Loisy's view of Christianity seems always to have
been socio-humanitarian, and the explicit "religion of humanity"
which he afterwards embraced had an oddly dated, Comtist look.
Tyrrell, on the other hand, in the final years of his all-too-short life,
set his gaze towards a wider horizon, and for this reason his ideas
would appear to have greater relevance to the present problems of
Roman Catholicism, as in truth of Christianity at large. Inconsistent
and mercurial as he showed himself to be, he realized more acutely
perhaps than any of his contemporaries in the movement that the
intellectual interpretation of religion is bound to involve tensions the
satisfactory resolution of which may be impossible. *Christianity at the
Cross-Roads* proved even to his sympathizers an enigmatic book. But
of all his writings its message is the most pertinent for us today.

However, though the Modernists, naturally enough, faced the
difficulties of belief as they themselves saw them, and though their
efforts to meet these were resoundingly denounced by ecclesiastical
authority, the particular questions to which they addressed themselves
remain to be answered, if answer can be found. For a generation or so
the confident assurances of neo-orthodoxy tended to obscure the fact.
The world, it was said, must be instructed by the gospel, not the gospel
by the world. But modernity cannot be so easily disowned and the
postures of faith without reason are too awkward to maintain for
long. Theology in this latter half of the twentieth century has felt
itself obliged to resume the tasks which the liberals of sixty or seventy
years ago, among Catholics as among Protestants, took to be unavoidable. In the Roman Church the current ferment of ideas could well be
seen as an open renewal of the debate which Pius X had prohibited
and suppressed. That it should once again be forbidden by a Vatican
diktat is not now feasible. Catholicism, thanks to the modern media of
communication, is exposed to world opinion as never before. Argument

and protest will not be silenced by imperious gestures and heresy is no longer a word to scare any but the most timid. Nor can the non-Catholic Christian stand aside from the anguished discussion, for the crisis of Catholicism is that also of Christianity itself. And what its outcome will be cannot be foretold. But "we may be sure"—to quote Tyrrell's words—"that religion, the deepest and most universal exigency of man's nature, will survive. We cannot be so sure that any particular expression of the religious idea will survive."

PART I

LOISY

WHAT *IS* THE ESSENCE OF CHRISTIANITY?

In seeking to determine historically the essence of the gospel, the rules of a healthy criticism forbid the resolution to regard as non-essential all that today must be judged uncertain or unacceptable. That which has been essential in the gospel of Jesus, is all that holds the first and most considerable place in his authentic teaching, the ideas for which he strove and for which he died, not only such part of them as is held to be vital today. In the same way, to define the essence of primitive Christianity, we must seek the dominant pre-occupation of the early Christians, and all that their religion lived by. After applying the same analytical procedure to all epochs successively, and comparing the results, we can determine if Christianity has remained faithful to the law of its origin; if the basis of Catholicism today is that which supported the Church of the Middle Ages, or the early centuries, and if that basis is substantially identical with the gospel of Jesus; or if, on the other hand, the clear light of the gospel was soon obscured, to be freed from the darkness in the sixteenth century, or only in our own time. If any common features have been preserved or developed in the Church from its origin till today, these features constitute the essence of Christianity. At least, the historian can take account of no others; he has no right to apply to Christianity a method that he would not apply to any other religion whatsoever. To decide the essence of Mahometanism, we should take from the teaching of Mahomet and the Mussulman tradition not what we judge to be true and fruitful, but all that seemed most important to the prophet and his followers in matters of faith, morality, and worship. Otherwise, with a little good will, the essence of the Koran could readily be discovered to be identical with the essence of the gospel—faith in a benign and merciful God.

Further, there would be little logic in taking for the whole essence of one religion the points that differentiate it from another. The monotheistic faith is common to Judaism, Christianity, and Mahometanism; but we are not therefore to conclude that the essential features of these three religions must be sought apart from the monotheistic conception. No Jew, no Christian, no Mussulman will admit that his faith in one God is other than the first and principal article of his belief. Each will criticize the particular form that the idea receives in the creed of his neighbour, but none will deny that monotheism is an element of his own religion on the ground that it belongs also to the religion of others. The essential distinction between religions lies in their differences, but it is not solely of their differences that they are constituted.

It is, therefore, in the highest degree arbitrary to decide that Christianity in its essence must be all that the gospel has not borrowed of Judaism, as if all that the gospel has retained of the Jewish tradition must be necessarily of secondary value. Herr Harnack[1] finds it quite natural to place the essence of Christianity in the faith in God the Father, because he supposes, somewhat hastily by the way, that this element of the gospel is foreign to the Old Testament. Even if the hypothesis were well founded the conclusion drawn from it would not be legitimate. It might present itself to the mind of a Protestant theologian, for whom the word "tradition" is synonymous with "Catholicism" and "error", and who rejoices to think that the gospel was the Protestantism of the law. But the historian can see in it only an assertion, whose proof is still to seek. Jesus has claimed not to destroy the law, but to fulfil. We should therefore expect to find in Judaism and in Christianity elements common to both, equally essential to both, the difference between the two religions lying in that "fulfilment" which is the special feature of the gospel, and should form with the common elements the whole essence of Christianity. The importance of these elements depends neither on their antiquity nor on their novelty, but on the place they fill in the teaching of Jesus, and on the value Jesus himself attached to them.

The essence of the gospel can only be determined by a critical discussion of the gospel texts, the most sure and most clearly expressed

---

[1] In *Das Wesen des Christentums*. See Introduction, pp. *27* f. (Ed.).

texts, and not those whose authenticity or whose meaning may be doubtful. To build a general theory of Christianity on a small number of texts of moderate authority, neglecting the mass of incontestable texts of clear significance, would be to sin against the most elementary principles of criticism. Following such a method, a more or less specious doctrinal synthesis might be offered to the public, but not the essence of Christianity according to the gospel. Herr Harnack has not avoided this danger, for his definition of the essence of Christianity is not based on the totality of authentic texts, but rests, when analyzed, on a very small number of texts, practically indeed on two passages:— "No man knoweth the Son, but the Father: neither knoweth any man the Father, save the Son",[1] and "The kingdom of God is within you",[2] both of them passages that might well have been influenced, if not produced, by the theology of the early times. This critical pre-possession might thus have exposed the author to the misfortune, supreme for a Protestant theologian, of having founded the essence of Christianity upon data supplied by Christian tradition.

No great harm would be done, from the point of view of history, if it were not that these texts are isolated by having preference given to them over the others. It must be admitted that it is often difficult to distinguish between the personal religion of Jesus and the way in which his disciples have understood it, between the thought of the Master and the interpretations of apostolic tradition. If Christ had himself drawn up a statement of his doctrine, and a summary of his prophecy, a detailed treatise on his work, his mission, his hopes, the historian would submit it to a most attentive examination, and would determine the essence of the gospel, according to irrefutable testimony. But no such treatise has ever existed, and nothing can take its place. In the gospels there remains but an echo, necessarily weakened and a little confused, of the words of Jesus, the general impression he produced upon hearers well disposed towards him, with some of the more striking of his sentences, as they were understood and inter-preted; and finally there remains the movement which he initiated.

Whatever we think, theologically, of tradition, whether we trust it or regard it with suspicion, we know Christ only by the tradition, across the tradition, and in the tradition of the primitive Christians.

---

[1] Matt. xi. 27.   [2] Luke xvii. 21.

This is as much as to say that Christ is inseparable from his work, and that the attempt to define the essence of Christianity according to the pure gospel of Jesus, apart from tradition, cannot succeed, for the mere idea of the gospel without tradition is in flagrant contradiction with the facts submitted to criticism. This state of affairs, being natural in the highest degree, has nothing in it disconcerting for the historian: for the essence of Christianity must be in the work of Jesus, or nowhere, and would be vainly sought in scattered fragments of his discourse. If a faith, a hope, a feeling, an impulse of will, dominates the gospel and is perpetuated in the Church of the earliest times, there will be the essence of Christianity, subject to such reservations as must be made on the literal authenticity of certain words, and on such more or less notable modifications that the thought of Jesus must of necessity have endured in transmission from generation to generation.

"The essences of things are unchangeable", said the ancient philosophy, when considering the eternal types of contingent realities. To determine such an essence in Christianity, it must be transformed into a metaphysical entity, into a logical quintessence, into something resembling the scholastic notion of species, that certain theologians still fear to corrupt by admitting the idea of evolution. Herr Harnack seems also to fear that his essence of Christianity might be spoiled if he introduced into it any idea of life, of movement and development. On the other hand, he distrusts abstract essences, and has taken care not to give any theoretical definition of religion, which should be at the same time a definition of Christianity, although he maintains the Hegelian proposition that Christianity is the one absolute religion. He finds the essence of Christianity in a sentiment—filial confidence in God, the merciful Father. Therein is to lie all religion and all Christianity. The identity of this sentiment in Jesus and in all Christians, is to constitute the continuity of the religion and the unchangeableness of its essence.

But is this essence, even in these reduced proportions, actually unchangeable, and why should it be? Has the Divine mercy been understood in absolutely the same way by the apostles and by Herr Harnack? The apostles had a conception of the world, and even of God the merciful, somewhat different from the idea that is suggested in the peroration of "The Essence of Christianity". Now, sentiment is not independent of thought; if the idea change, the form of the sentiment will also change, though the sentiment retains its first direction, because of the Spirit that sustains it; and if on this point (the Divine merciful Fatherhood) the attitude of Christianity is held to be unchanged, because it retains the direction and the impulse of Christ, why should not its attitude towards other points be held unchanged for the same reason? What, for instance, of the hope of an eternal kingdom, constantly preached by Christ, and never allowed to perish by the Christian Church? What of the mission of the apostles charged to propagate this hope? What of Christ himself, Whose place as Messiah belongs to the Primitive Church, and has never ceased to occupy the thought of the Church from the beginning? What of all the different themes of evangelical teaching, of which not one has been regarded during the Christian centuries as accessory? All these elements of Christianity, in all the forms in which they have been preserved, why should they not be the essence of Christianity? Why not find the essence of Christianity in the fullness and totality of its life, which shows movement and variety just because it is life, but inasmuch as it is life proceeding from an obviously powerful principle, has grown in accordance with a law which affirms at every step the initial force that may be called its physical essence revealed in all its manifestations? Why should the essence of a tree be held to be but a particle of the seed from which it has sprung, and why should it not be recognized as truly and fully in the complete tree as in the germ? Are the processes of assimilation by which it grows to be regarded as an alteration of the essence present potentially in the seed, and are they not rather the indispensable conditions of its being, its preservation, its progress in a life always the same and incessantly renewed?

The historian cannot but refuse to regard as the essence of living Christianity a germ that multiplies without growing. Rather he should return to the parable of the mustard seed, comparing the new-born Christianity to a little grain. The grain was small, for the new religion was without the prestige of antiquity enjoyed by the ancient religions, still surviving, of Egypt and Chaldea; it was less, in external power, than Graeco-Roman paganism: it was even less, apparently, than Judaism, of which it must have seemed a variety, with no future, since Judaism rejected it. This grain, nevertheless, enclosed the germ of the tree that we now see; charity was its sap: its life impulse was in the hope of its triumph; its expanding force was in its apostleship, its pledge of success in sacrifice: for its general form this budding religion had its faith in the unity and absolute Sovereignty of God, and for its particular and distinctive feature that faith in the Divine mission of Jesus, which earned it its name of Christianity. All this was in the little seed, and all this was the real essence of the Christian religion, needing only space to grow to reach its present point, still living after all its growth.

To understand the essence of Christianity we must look to those vital manifestations which contain its reality, its permanent quintessence, recognizable in them, as the principal features of primitive Christianity are recognizable throughout their development. The particular and varied forms of the development, in so far as they are varied, are not of the essence of Christianity, but they follow one another, as it were, in a framework whose general proportions, though not absolutely constant, never cease to be balanced, so that if the figure changes, its type does not vary, nor the law that governs its evolution. The essence of Christianity is constituted by the general features of this figure, the elements of this life and their characteristic properties; and this essence is unchangeable, like that of a living being, which remains the same while it lives, and to the extent to which it lives. The historian will find that the essence of Christianity has been more or less preserved in the different Christian communions: he will not believe it to be compromised by the development of institutions, of creeds, and of worship, so long as this development has been ruled by the principles verified in the first commencement. He will not expect this essence to have been absolutely and definitely realized at any point of past centuries; he will believe that it has been realized more or less perfectly from the beginning, and that it will continue to be realized thus more and more, so long as Christianity shall endure.

Herr Harnack does not conceive Christianity as a seed, at first a plant in potentiality, then a real plant, identical from the beginning of its evolution to the final limit and from the root to the summit of the stem, but as a fruit, ripe, or rather over-ripe, that must be peeled, to reach the incorruptible kernel; and Herr Harnack peels his fruit with such perseverance, that the question arises if anything will remain at the end. This method of dismembering a subject does not belong to history, which is a science of observation of the living, not of dissection of the dead. Historical analysis notices and distinguishes, it does not destroy what it touches, nor think all movement digression, and all growth deformity. It is not by stripping Christianity leaf by leaf that the law of its life will be found. Such a dissection leads of necessity to a special theory, of philosophical value doubtless, but of little account from the positive standpoint of history. It is not for the theologian (unless in quite a personal exercise of his intelligence), and still less is it for the critic, to seize religion on the wing, dismember it, extract a something and declare it unique, by saying, "This is the essence of Christianity". Let us regard the Christian religion in its life, observing by what means it has lived from the beginning and is still sustained; let us note the principal features of this venerable existence, convinced that they lose nothing in reality or importance, because today they are presented to us under colours that are not those of a former time.

To reduce Christianity to a single point, a solitary truth that the conscience of Jesus has perceived and revealed, is to protect religion against all attacks far less than might be expected, because it is thus almost put out of touch with reality, and deprived of historical support, and of every defence against the reasoning faculty. Christ is presented as a man who had but one true thought among many false ones, and those that are now held erroneous and valueless are not those that occupied his attention the least. If the sole truth that he revealed fails to make its appeal, there is nothing else to look for from him; and to feel this incomparable truth, to find it more true than the rest of his conceptions, the only truth in fact among them, to see in it absolute religion, it is not enough merely to contemplate it, but a kind of intellectual and moral enthusiasm is also demanded, prepared to see only this and be content.

L'Évangile et l'Église
(trans. by Christopher Home), pp. *8–21*

THE CHURCH

Thus to reproach the Catholic Church for the development of her constitution is to reproach her for having chosen to live, and that, moreover, when her life was indispensable for the preservation of the gospel itself. There is nowhere in her history any gap in continuity, or the absolute creation of a new system: every step is a deduction from the preceding, so that we can proceed from the actual constitution of the Papacy to the Evangelical Society around Jesus, different as they are from one another, without meeting any violent revolution to change the government of the Christian community. At the same time every advance is explained by a necessity of fact accompanied by logical necessities, so that the historian cannot say that the total extent of the movement is outside the gospel. The fact is, it proceeds from it and continues it.

Many objections, very grave from the point of view of a certain theology, have little or no significance for the historian. It is certain, for instance, that Jesus did not systematize beforehand the constitution of the Church as that of a government established on earth and destined to endure for a long series of centuries. But a conception far more foreign still to his thoughts and to his authentic teaching is that of an invisible society formed for ever of those who have in their hearts faith in the goodness of God. We have seen that the gospel of Jesus already contained a rudiment of social organization, and that the kingdom also was announced as a society. Jesus foretold the kingdom, and it was the Church that came; she came, enlarging the form of the gospel, which it was impossible to preserve as it was, as soon as the Passion closed the ministry of Jesus. There is no institution on the earth or in history whose status and value may not be questioned if the principle is established that nothing may exist except in its original form. Such a principle is contrary to the law of life, which is movement and a continual effort of adaptation to conditions always new and perpetually changing. Christianity has not escaped this law, and cannot be reproached for submission to it. It could not do otherwise than it has done.

The preservation of its primitive state was impossible, its restoration now is equally out of the question, because the conditions under which the gospel was produced have disappeared for ever. History shows the evolution of the elements that composed it. These elements have undergone, as they could not fail to undergo, many transformations; but they are always recognizable, and it is easy to see in the Catholic Church what stands today for the idea of the Heavenly kingdom, for the idea of the Messiah, the maker of the kingdom, and for the idea of the apostolate, or the preaching of the kingdom, that is to say, the three essential elements of the living gospel, which have become what they were forced to become in order to endure at all.

The theory of a purely inner kingdom suppresses them and makes an abstraction of the real gospel. The tradition of the Church keeps them, interpreting them and adapting them to the varying condition of humanity.

It would be absurd to desire that Christ should have determined beforehand the interpretations and adaptations that time would exact, since they had no reason to exist before the hour which rendered them necessary. It was neither possible nor useful for Jesus to reveal to his disciples the future of the Church. The thought that the Saviour left to them was that they must continue to wish, to prepare, to await and to realize the kingdom of God. The view of the kingdom has been enlarged and modified, the conception of its definite advent fills a smaller place, but the object of the gospel remains the object of the Church.

As a matter of fact, it is worthy of notice that the Church, for all her advanced age, for all her apparent want of anxiety as to the imminence of the final judgment, and for all the long future she anticipates still on the earth, regards herself nevertheless as a provisional institution, a transitional organization. The Church of the world, called the Church militant, is, as it were, the vestibule of the Church triumphant, which is the kingdom of Heaven realized in eternity, still held to be possible in the fullness of time. If the dimensions of the evangelical horizon have changed, the point of view remains the same. The Church has kept the fundamental idea of Christ's teaching: no terrestrial institution realizes the kingdom finally, and the gospel only prepares the way for the accomplishment. It is easy to divine why theologians, like Herr Harnack, abandon evangelical eschatology. But the question at issue is only to know if eschatology was not historically an essential element of the gospel, and if the Church, which has retained this essential element, is not the veritable continuation of Christ. What if the gospel eschatology were at bottom the expressive symbol of complex and indescribable realities; what if the eschatology of the Church be also a symbol, always striving for perfection, of the same expected benefits, the traditional theologian can still support it, and so continue to find the essence of the gospel where Jesus desired to set it. It means that Jesus and the Church have their eyes raised always in the same direction, towards the same symbol of hope, and that the Church maintains the attitude of Jesus, towards the kingdom of Heaven.

In their warfare against tradition, the most enlightened Protestant theologians, those who, like Herr Harnack, recognize a kind of relative necessity in the Catholic development, argue none the less eagerly about it, as though it were not evident that the desire to restore Christianity to its primitive form and organization is really a desire to condemn it to death, and as if change were not the natural condition of its preservation and the expression of its vitality. They are less exacting for themselves, when concerned to justify their own religious convictions, unlikely as they are to be confused with the gospel of Jesus. What else do they do but adapt the gospel to the needs of their special consciences? The Church also, from the beginning, adapts the gospel to the needs of the men she addresses.

It is not the personal adaptation that continues the ministry of Christ, the preaching of the "good news" and the preparation of the kingdom of Heaven. Even among Protestants, the directing tradition has a considerable influence on the way the Divine word is understood, and without this tradition the effects of the written gospel on the mass of believers would probably be very slight or not always salutary. In all Christian communities there is a service of the gospel which ensures the transmission and application of the Master's word. The Catholic Church is such a service formed by the centuries and continuous from the beginning. To be identical with the religion of Jesus, it has no more need to reproduce exactly the forms of the Galilean gospel than a man has need to preserve at fifty the proportions, features, and manner of life of the day of his birth, in order to be the same individual. The identity of a man is not ensured by making him return to his cradle.

The Church, today, resembles the community of the first disciples neither more nor less than a grown man resembles the child he was at first. The identity of the Church or of the man is not determined by permanent immobility of external forms, but by continuity of existence and consciousness of life through the perpetual transformations which are life's condition and manifestation. Setting aside all theological subtleties, the Catholic Church, as a society founded on the gospel, is identical with the first circle of the disciples of Jesus if she feels herself to be, and is, in the same relation with Jesus as the disciples were, if there is a general correspondence between her actual state and the primitive state, if the actual organism is only the primitive organism developed and decided, and if the elements of the Church today are the primitive elements, grown and fortified, adapted to the ever-increasing functions they have to fulfil.

It is the very duration of Christianity that has caused this evolution. If the end of the world had arrived in the years that followed the publication of the Apocalypse, the ecclesiastical development would not have taken place, and the Church even would hardly have existed. But the world did not perish: the Church retained a reason for existence and retains it still. Her history is that of the gospel in the world, and to find that the history is not that of the religion of Christ is only possible if the religion is placed outside history and the actual world.

If the Church were entirely a political institution, such as Herr Harnack conceives and represents her, it is certain that she would have nothing in common with the gospel, and would simply have to be regarded as the successor of the Roman Empire. We have already seen in what sense the Church really succeeded the Empire. The memories and the tradition of the Empire, conditioned, so to speak, the action of the Church, but did not change her essential character. Whatever can be said, it is a long step from Leo XIII to Trajan, from bishops to pro-consuls, from monks to legionaries, from Jesuits to the Pretorian Guard. The pope is not king, in so far as he is pope, and the question is still of the Universal Church, not of the Empire. The Catholics do not regard the pope as their sovereign, but as their spiritual guide. Although they receive their investiture from the pope, the bishops are not simple delegates either in law or in fact; if the pope is the successor of Peter, the bishops are the successors of the apostles, and their ministry is not of a political order nor purely administrative. It is only by way of metaphor that the faithful can be compared to an army. Secular priests and monks do not preach the policy of the pope, even when he has one; they preach first of all the gospel, with the traditional interpretation the Church gives, and the kingdom they endeavour to extend is that of the gospel, not that of the pope, so far as that is distinct from the kingdom of Christ. Even the Jesuits, founded to defend the Roman Church against Protestant and antipapal reform, are not political agents, but preachers of religion and religious educators, whatever may be thought of their methods and their special tendencies. The political side of the great institution, Catholicism, is naturally the one that first strikes those who are outside it, but it is wholly external, even accessory. Seen from within, the ecclesiastical organization is essentially of a religious order, and has no other reason for its existence than the preservation and propagation of religion in the world. Although the whole Catholic development, superficially observed, seems to tend solely to augment the authority of the hierarchy, or rather of the pope, the fundamental principle of Catholicism has never ceased to be the very principle of the gospel. The faithful do not exist for the sake of the hierarchy, but the hierarchy for the sake of the faithful. The Church does not exist for the sake of the pope, but the pope for the sake of the Church.

Of course, the Church has put on in many respects the form of a human government, and has become and still remains a political power. None the less, she has always desired, and still desires, quite a different end. The fact that she is of political importance, and that politics must reckon with her, is the inevitable consequence of her existence, and became certain as soon as Christianity had spread sufficiently through the Roman Empire. That she should set herself up as a political power, treating with governments as an equal or as a superior, negotiating religious affairs with them as international treaties are negotiated, is a special and transitory form of her relations with human powers. In this sense the Church has not always been a political power, and may cease to be one. The actual situation now is a legacy of the past, to be dealt with only with precaution. But it is possible to foresee in the future a general comity of civilized nations, wherein the Church, as a spiritual power, in no way political in the present sense, should lose none of her prestige, none of her independence, none of her moral influence. Are not politics falling more and more from the hands of managers of men, into the hands of managers of affairs, and will they not finally remain completely there? What would the Church gain by treating directly with such men in all that regards herself, and what interest would they have to occupy themselves with such matters?

We may even go further, and conjecture that the Church, when dealing with those who recognize her authority, will find a procedure more conformable to the fundamental equality and personal dignity of all Christians. In the universal levelling of ranks which is in prospect, the members of the ecclesiastical hierarchy may be less great personages in the eyes of the world, without in any way losing the rights of their ministry, which will assume again, more visibly, their essential form of duties.

In any case, it is not true that ecclesiastical authority is, or ever was, a species of external constraint repressing all personal activity of conscience. The Church is an educator, rather than a dominating mistress: she instructs rather than directs, and he who obeys her only does so according to his conscience, and in order to obey God. In principle, Catholicism aims, as much as Protestantism, at the formation of religious personalities, souls masters of themselves, pure and free consciences. It is true, the danger for Catholicism is that of desiring too much to govern men instead of simply elevating their souls. It cannot be denied, that its tendency, reacting against Protestantism has been towards the effacement of the individual, towards the careful guardianship of men, towards a control of human activity which by no means makes for the development of initiative. But it is only a tendency. It would be going almost too far to say that there is in the Church a "legion", whose religious and political ideal is that of a society regulated in all matters of thought and action by a kind of military discipline. Yet the main defect of such an ideal is not precisely that it is contrary to the gospel, but that it is dangerous, and impossible to realize.

The gospel of Jesus was neither wholly individualistic in the Protestant sense, nor wholly ecclesiastical in the Catholic sense. It addressed itself to the mass of mankind in order to establish the free society of the elect; is it possible to form an idea of the development of personality or of the form of government in the kingdom of Heaven? It is the Life and persistence of the gospel, which have made of it a permanent principle of religious and moral education, and a spiritual society where the principle is put in force. The principle has no hold without the society, nor the society without the principle. Protestantism and Herr Harnack wish to keep only the principle. It is a conception which lacks consistence and reality. Catholicism stands for both principle and society. Historical circumstances have made the social organization seem to compromise the principle more or less, even in some sort to appear to threaten it still. But it is the condition of all that lives in this world to be subject to imperfection. Whatever reservations the historian may make in details as to the way in which the action of the Church is or has been exercised, he cannot deny that Catholicism

F

has been, and is still, the service of the gospel, continued since the days of the apostles.

The power of adaptation recognized in the Roman Church is its best title to the admiration of the impartial observer. It does not follow that the Church alters either the gospel or tradition, but that she knows how to understand the needs of the time. It cannot be too often repeated that the gospel was not an absolute, abstract doctrine, directly applicable at all times and to all men by its essential virtue. It was a living faith, linked everywhere to the time and the circumstances that witnessed its birth. In order to preserve this faith in the world, a work of adaptation has been, and will be, perpetually necessary. Though the Catholic Church has adapted, and still adapts, the faith, though she adapt herself continually to the needs of new ages, that is no proof that she forgets the gospel or despises her own tradition, but that she wishes to display the value of both, and has confidence that they are flexible and capable of further perfection.

Ibid., pp. *165-178*.

CHRISTIAN DOGMA

It is only by starting from a scholastic conception, abstract and unreal, of revelation and of dogma that a conclusion is reached condemnatory of all the fruit of Christian reflection upon the object of Christianity. It is clear that if the unchangeable essence of the gospel had been only faith in God the Father, all Christian development of doctrine, as well as of ecclesiastical organization and ritual, would have been a vast aberration. But besides the fact that the gospel is not to be summed up in such a belief, it would be absurd to suppose that the statement of this faith could remain unchangeable, or become so if it were judged expedient for mankind to content themselves with it. If the attention of the first believers had not been directed towards the Son of God, it would have turned to the Father himself, and become occupied with his nature and relations with the world, thus leading speculation back to cosmology. Interest would have been roused in this goodness, which had its essential significance in relation to mankind, its historical manifestations would have been tentatively defined, or, at any rate, its secret action in each believing soul, a process leading thought again to

Christology and the economy of Divine Grace. Sooner or later attention would have been brought to bear on the normal conditions of evangelization, and the problem of ecclesiology would have arisen. Doctrinal Christian development was inevitable, therefore, and in principle, legitimate; on the whole, it has served the cause of the gospel which could not exist as a pure essence, but being constantly transformed into living doctrines has itself lived in these doctrines, whose development is therefore justified in fact.

It is easy to say that the Catholic Church does not even recognize the existence of this development, and condemns the very idea of it. Perhaps it would be nearer the truth to say that she has never had consciousness of it, and that she has no official theory concerning the philosophy of her own history. That which is taught by Vincent de Lérins, modern theologians (except Cardinal Newman) and the Council of the Vatican, touching the development of dogma, applies in reality to the definitely intellectual and theological phase of its development, not to the first budding and formation of beliefs, or at least includes in an abstract definition, much work for which this definition is no adequate expression. It is just the idea of development which is now needed, not to be created all at once, but established from a better knowledge of the past. The acquisition of this new dogma will have no different effect to that of the old ones. These latter were not contained in primitive tradition, like a conclusion in the premises of a syllogism, but as a germ in a seed, a real and living element, which must become transformed as it grows, and be determined by discussion before its crystallization into a solemn formula. They existed as more or less conscious facts or beliefs, before they were the subject of learned speculations or of official judgments. The Christological dogma was, before everything, the expression of what Jesus represented from the beginning to Christian consciousness; the dogma of grace was the expression of the Divine work accomplished in the souls that were regenerated through the gospel; the ecclesiological dogma was the expression of the permanent position of the Episcopate and the pope in the Church. If ever a dogmatic conclusion is formulated on the subject of Christian development it will almost certainly be an expression of the law of progress which has governed the history of Christianity from the beginning. Till now, Catholic theologians have been especially preoccupied with the absolute character that the dogma derives from its source, the Divine revelation, and critics have hardly noticed the relative character that its history makes manifest. The efforts of a healthy theology should be directed to a solution of the difficulty, presented by the unquestionable authority faith demands for dogma, and the variability, the relativity, the critic cannot fail to perceive in the history of dogmas and dogmatic formulas.

We have seen how the whole development of Christian doctrine is not outside the faith, but within the faith, which dominates it entirely. The traditional principle and the religious sense have always overcome the need of scientific adaptation, and have saved the originality of Christianity. The ancient dogmas have their root in the preaching and ministry of Christ, and in the experiences of the Church, and their development in the history of Christianity and in theological thought: nothing else was possible. Further, it is no less natural that the creeds and dogmatic definitions should be related to the state of general human knowledge in the time and under the circumstances when they were constituted. It follows that a considerable change in the state of knowledge might render necessary a new interpretation of old formulas, which, conceived in another intellectual atmosphere, no longer say what is necessary, or no longer say it suitably. In such a case, a distinction must be drawn between the material sense of the formula, the external image it presents, related to ideas received from antiquity, and its proper religious and Christian significance, its fundamental idea, which can be reconciled with new views of the constitution of the world and the nature of things in general. The Church still repeats every day in the creed of the apostles, "He descended into Hell, He has ascended to Heaven". These propositions have for many centuries been taken literally. Generations of Christians have followed one another believing Hell, the abode of the damned, to be beneath their feet, and Heaven, the abode of the elect, above their heads. Neither learned theology nor even popular preaching maintains this localization today: and no one any longer will hold that he can determine the place of the soul of Christ in the interval between his death and his resurrection, nor that of his glorified humanity since his ascension. The real dogmatic meaning of these sentences remains unaltered, because by them is always taught a transitory relation of the soul of Christ with the just under the ancient law, and the glorification of his risen humanity. May we not say, looking at the transformation that the apparent sense of the formulas has undergone, that the theology of the future will again construct a more spiritual idea of their content? It is quite true that the Church corrects its dogmatic formulas by means of distinctions, sometimes rather subtle. But, in so acting, she continues in the way she has walked from the beginning, she adapts the gospel to the constantly changing condition of human life and intelligence.

It is not indispensable to the authority of belief that it should be rigorously unchangeable in its intellectual form and its verbal expression. Such immutability is not compatible with the nature of human intelligence. Our most certain knowledge in the domains of nature and of science is always in movement, always relative, always perfectible. It is not with the elements of human thought that an everlasting edifice can be built. Truth alone is unchangeable, but not its image in our minds. Faith addresses itself to the unchangeable truth, through a formula, necessarily inadequate, capable of improvement, consequently of change. When Jesus said, in all solemnity, "Verily I say unto you, There be some of them that stand here, which shall in no wise taste of death, till they see the Son of man coming in His kingdom".[1] He put forward a dogmatic proposition much less absolute in reality than in appearance; He demanded faith in the approaching kingdom, but the idea of the kingdom and of its proximity were two very simple symbols of very complex matters, and even those who were the first to believe must have attached their minds more to the spirit than to the letter of this statement, to find it always true. The dogmatic formulas stand in the same position as the words of the Saviour, and it is no demonstration that they are objectless, to discover at any given moment that the reality has passed them by.

The singularly defective logic which seems to preside over the formation and growth of dogmas is in no way difficult to understand, and may even be called normal, by the historian who considers the proofs of faith as expressions of its vitality rather than the real reasons of its origin.

Nothing is more precarious, from the point of view of the ordinary rules of human reasoning and textual criticism, than certain arguments

---

[1] Matt. xvi, 28.

by which the gospel is founded on the Old Testament, and Catholic Christianity on the whole Bible. The work of traditional exegesis, from whence dogma may be said to proceed by a slow and continuous elaboration, seems in permanent contradiction with the principles of a purely rational and historical interpretation. It is always taken for granted that the old Biblical texts and the witness of tradition must contain the truth of the present time, and the truth is found there because it is put there. Catholic theologians had a right appreciation of this state of affairs when they laid down the rule that the infallibility of the Church applies to dogmatic definitions, not to the preambles that stated the reasons for them, even when the preambles were expressed in the official declarations of councils and popes. A distinction of this kind would be useful for the New Testament, wherein the resurrection of the dead is proved by the text, "I am the God of Abraham, and the God of Isaac, and the God of Jacob",[1] the independence of the Christian from the Mosaic law by the history of Hagar and Sarah,[2] and quotations from the ancient Scripture applied generally in a sense that did not originally belong to them. As for tradition, it suffices to recall how the Fathers and theologians prove the Trinity of Divine Persons by the words of Genesis, "Let us make man in our image, after our likeness",[3] and by the three angels that visited Abraham;[4] how the two swords that Peter is said to have carried at Gethsemane[5] demonstrated according-ing to Boniface VIII and the medieval doctors the double power, spiritual and temporal, of the popes. It is well known, also, how texts, in themselves perfectly clear, like the lamentations of Job and the psalmists over the annihilation of man by death, the assertions of the Saviour and the apostles upon the approaching end of the world, the saying of Christ as reported by John, "The Father is greater than I",[6] are not held to mean that which they obviously signify.

May it not be said that, in the order of things moral and religious, human logic has no care for itself, that the effort towards improve-ment runs ahead of the reasoning that justifies it, and that it bears within itself a truth superior to all the arguments that seek to establish it? Thus the best apology for all that lives lies in the life itself. All the scaffolding of theological and apologetic argument is only an attempt, and a necessary one, to figure the relation of the past to the present

---

[1] Mark xii, *26*.　　[2] Gal. iv, *21–31*.　　[3] Gen, i, *26*.
[4] Gen, xviii, *2*.　　[5] Luke xxii, *38*; John xviii, *10*.　　[6] John xiv, *28*.

as well as the continuity of religion and religious progress from the beginning. The artifices of interpretation serve ceaselessly to enlarge and spiritualize the meaning of the symbols, to promote the development and intelligence of religion by the ever renewed perception of analogies, higher and more worthy of their mysterious object. External imperfections, which are above all imperfections relative to us, to the critical knowledge of the sources of history and to the modern education of intelligence, do not render this great work vain nor prejudice the importance of its results. If the gospel had been a philosophical thesis, the thesis would have been very badly constructed and developed, but as the gospel was a living religion, the theological work of Christian centuries testifies that this religion has really lived, as an infinitely powerful movement, of which those who supported it and whom it supported had only a partial consciousness, the whole of whose depth, those who today attempt to analyse it are incapable of sounding. How vain it is to proclaim the end of dogma because the doctrinal flower of this great life appears withered, and to imagine that the fruitfulness of Christian thought is definitely exhausted, and that the old tree can never again renew its adornment for a new epoch, a new springtime!

From the moment the gospel is believed, it is impossible not to think of the belief, not to work at the thought, and so produce a theology of faith. It is equally impossible to keep the faith without transmitting it, for it demands to be communicated, being universal hope and charity; and it cannot be communicated without a certain teaching, a dogma regularly put forward for belief. There is a mastership of the faith. Reasoning in the abstract, it is possible to say that faith springs up in the soul at the contact of the gospel as expressed in its text. But in fact, faith is born of Christian instruction, and the gospel is explained to those who are taught to believe. The distinction of masters and pupils is therefore inevitable. It is impossible that no science of religion should exist, or that it should be indifferent to the preservation of faith in cultivated society. Equally is it impossible that this science should be accessible to all, that all should be doctors of religion. From the beginning all the faithful could not be apostles. Under the conditions which are prescribed for the gospel in this world, masters are needed to propagate it, and doctrines to express it. A durable society, a Church, can alone maintain equilibrium between tradition, which preserves the heritage of acquired truth, and the incessant toil of human reason to adapt ancient truth to the new needs of thought and knowledge. It is inconceivable that each individual should recommence the interrogation of the past on his own account, and reconstruct, for his own use, an entire religion. Here, as elsewhere, each is aided by all, and all by each one.

It is no longer a matter for astonishment that the Church presents herself as an infallible mistress to those believers who venture forth without her. Her attitude is as easy to understand as that of the Protestant theologians who, seeing the powerlessness of the individual to formulate a creed for others besides himself, and knowing no other religious principle than individualism, take refuge in one solitary idea, which they wish to believe is alone evangelical and accessible of itself to all souls. But their hypothesis has the inconvenience of being unfounded and impracticable, whilst the Catholic hypothesis is a real institution that continues the real gospel. It was not without reason that Luther retained a dogma, and that organized Protestantism tends to orthodoxy in spite of itself.

Is this the same thing as to say that Christian dogma thus becomes a ready-made belief, before which it is wise to bow, without too close investigation, lest contradiction be called for? Even as the constant flexibility of ecclesiastical teaching brings it about that no conflict of dogma with knowledge can be considered as irreducible, so the very character of this teaching causes the authority of the Church and its formulas to be not incompatible with individuality of faith, and does not necessarily bring with it that perpetual subserviency which seems, to Protestant theologians, the normal condition of the Catholic believer. The Church does not exact belief in its formulas as the adequate expression of absolute truth, but presents them as the least imperfect expression that is morally possible; she demands that men respect them for their quality, seek the faith in them, and use them to transmit it. The ecclesiastical formula is the auxiliary of faith, the guiding line of religious thought: it cannot be the integral object of that thought, seeing that object is God himself, Christ and his work; each man lays hold of the object as he can, with the aid of the formula. As all souls and all intelligences differ one from the other, the gradations of belief are also of infinite variety, under the sole direction of the Church, and in the unity of her creed. The incessant evolution of doctrine is made by the work of individuals, as their activity reacts on the general activity, and these individuals are they who think for the Church while thinking with her.

Ibid., pp. *212–225*

CATHOLIC WORSHIP

The conception that Protestant theologians readily form of the worship in spirit is no more rational than evangelical. It is impossible to unite men in a worship that is purely an affair of the soul, and it would be vain to impose such worship on human beings, who are bound by their physical conditions, and can only think through their being able to hear and to speak. Their religious life cannot be independent of every sensible element, which aids them to become conscious of it, to define and affirm it. Jesus was the first to give his disciples a formula of prayer; he observed the practices of Jewish worship; he never recommended to his followers a worship without external forms, and never intended to establish such a worship. The saying of Christ in the Gospel of John, as to the worship "in spirit and in truth", does not oppose a purely inner worship to an external one; but the worship that may be called inspired, spiritualized, the Christian worship known to the evangelist, and animated by the spirit given to the faithful, is substituted for a worship localized at Jerusalem or on Mount Gerizim.

The same evangelist who gives the formula of worship in spirit, gives also the formula of the Incarnation; the two correspond to one another; God is a Spirit, as is also his Word; the true worship is spiritual, since it is founded on the communication of the Divine Spirit. But just as God the Spirit is made manifest in the Incarnate Word, so the life of the Spirit is communicated and maintained by spiritual sacraments, the water of baptism, the bread and wine of the Eucharist. The system of John is a perfect whole; neither the discourse to Nicodemus nor the instruction concerning the bread of life contradict the statement made to the woman of Samaria, and the whole agrees with the conception of the Incarnation, the Divine manifesting itself in the human, the spiritual acting in the sensible, the eternal reality figured in the terrestrial symbol and communicated by it. Catholic worship does nothing but apply the theory of John, and this theory was the description of the evangelical fact.

From the point of view of pure reason, the efficacy of the sacraments is not so very difficult a thing to conceive. It is with the sacraments as with ordinary language, the virtue of ideas passes into the words, acts through the words, is communicated really, physically, by the words, and only produces its effect on the mind by the aid of the words. Therefore it is fair to speak of the virtue of words, for they contribute to the existence and fortune of ideas. In so far as an idea has found no formula capable of striking the mind by a clearness, at least in appearance, by its simplicity and its vigour, it has no power of action. It is true that the action of the formula depends on the historical circumstances of its production, but this fact by no means lessens the analogy between words, the natural expression and indispensable means of communication of ideas, and the sacraments, the expression of inner religion and means of communication with God. The significance of the sacramental symbols has also been determined by the historical circumstances connected with their establishment and use. Thence comes their efficacy; they are signs appropriate to their end, as words can be appropriate to the expression of thought; they are Divine signs because they are religious; they are Christian, because they proceed from Christ. On all these grounds they are efficacious, and their power comes not from him on whom they are conferred, but is exercised in him and upon him; it is bound up with the tie that links them to Jesus, which makes them, as it were, actions of Christ living in the Church, and it is conditioned at once by the special application of the symbol to him who receives it and by the disposition it finds in him.

These considerations help to make clear the doctrine of the Catholic Church regarding the sacraments, and the essential harmony of this doctrine with the gospel. This is not the place to set forth the theory of the efficacy of the sacrament in itself, as a definite institution of Christ, in its substance and its form, that cannot be modified without destroying its effect. The formulas of sacramental theology, like the greater number of dogmatic definitions, were conceived in opposition to assertions rejected by the Church as erroneous, namely, that sacraments have no real efficacy, that they do not come from Christ, that the choice of them is arbitrary and without relation to the effect. Positive doctrine, as a counterblast to condemned opinion, is always capable of explanation and of progress. It matters little that sacraments are held to be composed of form and of substance; there would be nothing unsuitable in abandoning these notions of ancient philosophy artificially applied to the sacraments, and considering them in themselves, taking them for what they are, namely, religious acts, endowed with supernatural efficacy. This efficacy does not belong to them merely as religious acts, but in so far as they are the acts of religious Christians, related to Christ through the Church, men in whom Christ lives and acts, as he lives and acts in the Church and the Church's teaching.

The life of a religion consists not in its ideas, its formulas and its rites as such, but in the secret principle which first gave an attractive power, a supernatural efficacy, to the ideas and formulas and rites. The sacraments have no meaning for the Christian except through Jesus or his Spirit acting in the material symbol; they figure and realize the constant action of Christ in the Church. Jesus established them so far as they are a permanent institution proceeding from him, powerful through him. The incontestable and important changes undergone in the management and arrangement of several of them do not deprive them either of their character or their value as sacraments of Christ. The Church has always believed that she possesses in herself the Spirit of Jesus to direct her in all things. The action of the Spirit is linked to the forms of her government, her teaching and her worship. The sacramental institution is not an inert instrument, but a principle, a mode of action transmitted from Christ to the Church, susceptible of varied application, changeless only in itself, its general direction and essential form. The Church regulates its progress and action, regarding herself as the authorized interpreter of the intentions of its founder, and of the suitable way to execute it. The sacramental system is the historically established form taken by the Christian institution, the Church, inasmuch as it is a sanctifying organization through which the immortal Christ continues to act.

It is, perhaps, true that God is the only Grace, as he is the supreme good of man and his final end. But human life cannot be resolved into a simple act of union with God, to contain the whole of religion. It is written that the "Grace of God" is "manifold",[1] and truly it must adapt itself to very varied conditions of existence, bringing God to

[1] 1 Pet. iv, 10.

them, whose inexhaustible nature can no longer be summed up for man in a single aspect. The activity of the Father is not exhausted by the single movement of pardon. Why should not his permanent assistance be recalled and guaranteed by material symbols? These symbols take nothing from the Divine majesty, if it is well understood that their efficacy is in no way magical, and if, instead of interposing between God and man, they only remind human beings of the constantly beneficent presence of their Creator. Nor does the administration of the sacraments come between man and his Supreme Master, to take the place of God. The social character of Christianity exacts a regulation of external worship and a division of duty in the acts which constitute it; but none the less is there a direct relation between God and all those who, under different titles, participate in the symbolic actions of Christian ritual? God is no farther from the simple believer than from the bishop or the priest. Clerics and laity come together to God, pray together, are sanctified together. There is between them not only a "diversity of gifts and of ministrations", as St Paul says, but "the same Spirit"[1] is in all. The gospel is not the enemy of order, and it is difficult to see how the regular economy of Divine service can impede the operation of the grace of God.

Every religion is sacramental; every religion is also more or less *deifying*, offering man a means of raising himself to Divinity, conceived first by analogy in the image of man. Perhaps it would not be very difficult to prove that the worship of man is, in all known religions, associated in some way with that of God. But in pagan worship this association is made definitely, to the detriment of divinity, whose essential feature, that of remaining infinitely above humanity, is not recognized. Christianity avoided this confusion, while satisfying, by the worship of Jesus and the sacraments co-ordinated therewith, that need of deification which seems inseparable from human nature. It renders to Christ the worship the Jews rendered to the hidden God, Whom no human being could look on and live. It has been able to do so without falling into Polytheism or man-worship, because it distinguishes, in the object of its adoration, the Eternal God and the human nature in which this God was manifested on earth. Christ is none the less seated on the right hand of the Father, and humanity is

[1] 1 Cor. xii, 4, 5.

raised in him up to Divinity. It may be said that humanity adores itself in Jesus, but it must be added that, so doing, it forgets neither its own condition nor that of God.

Herr Harnack does not expressly condemn the worship accorded to Christ, but he regards it all the same as a kind of idolatry, born of ancient polytheism. For him, the worship of Jesus is no more legitimate than the dogma of his divinity. Did the apostles adore Christ even when they had acquired belief in his resurrection? Was Jesus for the first Christian generation any other than a Divine mediator, with whom, and through whom, men could pray to and worship the Father, instead of one to be worshipped? But these circumstances only serve to make more evident the need of a worship deifying humanity, since from a rigorous monotheism, whose formula has been strengthened rather than weakened, was derived the worship of a human being, whose human character has never been denied, though his divinity has been proclaimed; while, after this, Christian piety has made for itself a whole hierarchy of intercessors from heavenly spirits and spiritual ancestors, as though to aid Christ in his position of intercessor, and at the head of them has set the Virgin Mary.

Neither the worship of Christ nor the worship of the saints could be part of the gospel of Jesus nor does either belong to it: they arose spontaneously, and have increased one after the other, and then together, in Christianity as it became established. All the same, the worship, both of Jesus and of the saints, proceeds from what may be called, in all truthfulness, the primitive revelation, the revelation that has never been specified in a formal doctrine, that mankind bears in the depths of its religious consciousness written in indistinct characters. The sole article that constitutes this unexplained revelation, that Jesus manifested in himself and in his life as much as in his teaching, and was the first to show in a clear and intelligible manner because he realized it in himself, is that God reveals himself to man in man, and that humanity enters with God into a Divine association. Man had always believed it, and only understood it vaguely; Jesus made it intelligible, and from that moment, as it were, the direction of prayer was changed, and the mythological cloud dissipated, while at the same time the barrier of law and verbal revelation was overthrown. The most Divine thing in the world is not the crash of the thunder, nor the light of the sun, nor the unfolding of life; it is beauty of soul, purity of heart, perfection of love in sacrifice, because this is the sovereign gift of God to man, the grandest work and supreme manifestation of God in the universe. In this way Jesus revealed to men the secret of God and religion, because God was in him revealing himself; in this way men felt that in Jesus they possessed God revealed to them. The impression was deeper among the Gentiles, who knew not God, than among the Jews, who knew him better, but were accustomed to adore him in his redoubtable majesty. It is certain that the eternal principle of the passage of the Divine through the human then received a new application, very clear and very fruitful, that this application was the Christian religion and the worship of Jesus, and that it could be nothing else.

This application of the principle itself refused to be limited to the worship of Christ. All those who bore witness to the revelation of God in Jesus, who had not feared to die rather than disavow their certainty, who had demonstrated its power by the practice of Christian virtues, and had died in the peace of the Lord, all these equally received on their foreheads a ray of Divinity. It was not the full light, the unmeasured communication of the Spirit and of the glory of God, but it was a part of this gift, to be saluted with reverence.

In fact, it is as an extension of the worship of Jesus that, from the Catholic point of view, the worship of the Virgin and the saints is justified. The saints live, not only in the memory of the Church, but in her present work, by the lasting influence of their personal activity, and of the ideal signified by their name. Worship of them, like that of the Virgin and of Christ himself, has become what it might and ought to have become under the circumstances and in the times where it has developed. The Christian spirit gave life, and still gives it, to practices apparently trivial, and easily becoming superstitious; but the point at issue is whether those who follow them do not find Christ therein, and whether they would be capable of finding him more easily elsewhere. From the actual point of view, the Virgin and saints are religious types inferior to Christ, but united to him, leading to him, acting though him and for him. From the point of view of theological symbolism and popular conception, Christ alone is the mediator, all-powerful by reason of his Divinity; the Virgin is a subordinate intercessor all-powerful through Christ; and the power of the saints is equally subordinated to that of Jesus.

It may be said that the government of this world, even of moral things, should not be divided into provinces according to specialities which recall a little too vividly the lesser gods of paganism. Yet all that ever was has an eternal life and action in God, wherein all things abide. He who suppresses intercession is on the way to suppress prayer. Is it not true in the strictest sense for the Catholic, that he goes to God through Jesus, to Jesus through the saints? Is it not true that Christianity endures by the force of all its past, from Jesus to the Christians of our own day, worthy of the name? Is it not true that all the fruits of the gospel in Christianity are still the gospel? Is it not true that to have recourse to the saints is to have recourse to Jesus—to Jesus, then to God; and that to turn to God with a simple faith is to rise above one's self, to enter into religion and make it a personal reality? Is it not true that by all these means the Protestant finds so vulgar and so ridiculous—by wearing a scapulary, by telling beads, by gaining indulgences on the merits of saints for this life or for souls in Purgatory—the Catholic places himself effectively in the communion of the saints, which is the communion of Jesus, which is the communion of God?

Assuredly it would be wise to moderate this worship in some of its manifestations, and above all to make clear its real significance. The general considerations which allow, from the Christian point of view, prayers of intercession, as a means of attaching the soul to God by the intermediary of those in whom God was especially made manifest, demand also that these prayers should be different in spirit from pagan superstitions, and should not be sustained by wild imaginations. After all, it will be said, if St Antony of Padua has not really the power to cause the recovery of things that are lost, the winning of the great prize in the lottery, the gaining of diplomas by devout but lazy students, it is possible that a naïve credulity may provide the hope of supernatural intervention that is solicited in these cases, so that the religious and moral value of such prayers is not superior to that of the requests commonly addressed to pagan deities: far better recommend students to deserve success by their work, advise all to look to their affairs and count at once on Providence and on themselves for the success of their enterprises.

Nevertheless the apparent puerilities of devotion are less removed from religion than they seem. The face of the world is twofold. Man is placed between nature, where all seems inevitable, and consciousness, where all appears free. The universe for him is a gigantic mechanism, which encompasses him on all sides, and will overwhelm him without mercy if the opportunity arises; and, at the same time, it is the revelation that a Being, good and omnipotent, gives of himself. The contradiction evident in the conduct of man demanding to be freed from inevitability, exists also in the world, where necessity and liberty meet in opposition. No prayer is insignificant or ridiculous for the man of faith, so long as it does not misrepresent God in his goodness and respects his sovereignty. No prayer is justified as an act of pure reason and of perfect piety, save by the uprightness of its intentions, its application to duty, and submission to the Divine will. Taken solely in its natural and primitive significance, the Lord's Prayer in some respects would be as open to critical objection as a prayer to St Antony of Padua to recover an object that has been lost. Would not the demand, "Give us this day our daily bread", considered in its strictly historical meaning, be subversive of social economy? Practically, as a general rule, the adult healthy man can and should earn his bread with his own powers. Today, the Christian requests that this activity be blessed by Heaven, but the original sense of the words he uses was very different. In the same way the meaning of the request, "Thy Kingdom come", is very different for the modern Christian from the sense the first converts attached to it. Thus the prayer derives its value from the feeling that prompts it and determines its moral efficacy, not from the occasion that provokes it, not even from the good to which it seems directed. This efficacy of prayer is independent of its formal fulfilment, and is no more a matter of question for the Christian than the personal existence of God.

It must not be imagined that sentence of condemnation has been passed on the worship of saints, of relics, of the Virgin, and of the Saviour himself because such worship appears to the historian as a concession to the tendencies of popular religion. It is essential that every religion that lives should be a concession of this kind, though Christianity may be asked to raise the character of the concession by the spirit that informs its worship and its practices. The tendencies in question are a fundamental law of religion, and a condition of religious development. All is well so long as the forms of worship are not esteemed beyond and at the expense of the spirit that should animate them. The Church is unable to suppress the religious instinct, and is little disposed to leave it to itself: she sets out to regulate it, and devotions are to her a means of maintaining religion. The piety of any Catholic nation does not, perhaps, represent the ideal of Catholicism, but it is all that Catholicism can obtain from that nation. What can be asked of the Church beyond a constant effort to obtain more than has as yet been given? This effort exists. Herr Harnack recognizes that devotions paid to the Sacred Heart, the Holy Virgin, and others, have become in the Catholic Church a source of blessing and a means of reaching the good God. This is because the Christian spirit has penetrated to the depth of the devotion, and set the gospel there. These devotions, far from being a hindrance to religion, are a support to it, just as the sacraments do not take Christ from the believer, but give him to him.

Protestant critics, when they express surprise that the Christian spirit is still found in Catholicism in spite of the Church, faith in spite of dogma, true piety in spite of the multiplication of external rites, take for obstacles the real guarantees and normal conditions of the good that the gospel, now become a religion, has given to the world, good that their own speculations on the pure essence of Christianity are unable to procure. Does not Protestantism itself exist as a religion through that amount of ecclesiastical organization, official doctrine, and confessional worship that it has retained?

It is true that as a result of the evolution, political, intellectual, economic, of the modern world, as a result of all that may be called the modern spirit, a great religious crisis, affecting Churches, orthodoxies, and forms of worship, has arisen to a greater or less extent everywhere. The best means of meeting it does not appear to be the suppression of all ecclesiastical organization, all orthodoxy, and all traditional worship—a process that would thrust Christianity outside of life and humanity—but to take advantage of what is, in view of what should be, to repudiate nothing of the heritage left to our age by former Christian centuries, to recognize how necessary and useful is the immense development accomplished in the Church, to gather the fruits of it and continue it, since the adaptation of the gospel to the changing conditions of humanity is as pressing a need today as it ever was and ever will be. It is no part of the present book to say what difficulties—more apparent, perhaps, than real—this work may encounter in the Catholic Church, nor what incomparable resources exist for it, nor in what way the agreement of dogma and science, reason and faith, the Church and society, can be conceived

G

today. This little volume is full enough if it, has shown how Christianity has lived in the Church and by the Church, and how futile is the desire to save it by a search after its quintessence.

Ibid., pp. *259–277*

"AUTOUR D'UN PETIT LIVRE"

"There is a time", says Ecclesiastes, "to keep silence, and a time to speak". The author of a little book bearing the title *The Gospel and the Church* believes that he has observed the precept of silence long enough. Now he will speak.

What he is going to say is not an apology, for he judges that neither he nor his work has need of self-justification. But a few remarks seem fitting in regard to what has taken place concerning the book, and the book itself can be amplified on certain points which therein were treated only lightly.

The archbishops of Paris and Cambrai, the bishops of Autun, Angers, Bayeux, Nancy and Perpignan have prohibited the reading of *The Gospel and the Church* in their dioceses. As a priest the author respects these judgments. . . .

The archiepiscopal order, dated January *17, 1903,* was motivated by the fact that the work had been "published without the *imprimatur* required by the Church's laws", and was "of its nature such as seriously to disturb the belief of the faithful on the fundamental dogmas of Catholic teaching—notably the authority of the scriptures and tradition, the divinity of Jesus Christ, his infallible knowledge, the redemption wrought by his death, his resurrection, the eucharist and the divine institution of the sovereign pontificate and the episcopate". Since it would have been superfluous to insist that the book's object was to defend all these beliefs on the terrain of history as against Protestant criticism, the author wrote to the cardinal archbishop in a letter of February *2, 1903:* "It goes without saying that I condemn and repudiate all the errors which are capable of being deduced from my book were one to place oneself, in order to interpret it, at a standpoint wholly different from that which I have had to adopt in the writing of it."

Some have considered this "retractation" insufficient. But there has not been nor could there be any such retractation. The author freely condemns all the misinterpretations that have been put on his text through taking for a system of theological doctrine what was only a modest attempt at historical construction. He used the gospels as historical documents, according to the warrants presented by the diverse elements which have entered into them. He did not touch on the dogma of biblical inspiration, nor on the Church's inherent authority as to the dogmatic interpretation of Scripture. He set out to depict the historical physiognomy of the Saviour; he formulated no sort of definition regarding Christ's transcendent relationship with God. He analysed the teaching of Jesus concerning the kingdom of heaven and its imminent coming; he did not draw from it any conclusion on the theological question of Christ's human knowledge. He attributed to St Paul the theory of redemption; he carefully refrained from contesting that Jesus was the Saviour of humanity. He remarked that the resurrection was not properly a fact of the historical order and that it cannot strictly be demonstrated under this aspect; he did not deny that Christ was raised. He tried to indicate the historic relation between the sacraments—the eucharist notably—the ecclesiastical hierarchy, the Roman pontificate and the episcopate and the reality of the gospel and the circumstances in which Christianity was born and grew up; he threw no doubt on the legitimacy of Catholic doctrine regarding the divine institution of the Church and sacraments. He confined himself to presenting the state and significance of the witnesses, dwelling on matters of history and avoiding those of faith.

His letter to Cardinal Richard[1] was not a disavowal of his views as a historian but an act of respectful deference in conformity with ecclesiastical discipline. It discreetly removed the error into which those had fallen who had taken an historical account of the gospel for a series of objections to Catholic dogma, and it upheld all the book's conclusions as to its true object. As a mere historical sketch, the little volume was submitted to the appreciation of all competent persons free to criticize it according to their capability and put it to such use as suited them. If the archbishop of Paris and other prelates judged the reading of the book to be especially hazardous for the members of their dioceses this in itself did not alter the state of the question at issue, and as it conveyed nothing to the author he could base any qualification of his work only on the further progress of his researches.

[1] The archbishop of Paris (Ed.).

The primary condition of all scientific work is liberty. The primary obligation of a scholar, Catholic or otherwise, is sincerity. The author of *The Gospel and the Church* dealt with Christian origins after the fashion proper to an historian and in accord with his personal responsibility. He confesses to being, in the meagre catalogue of his accomplishments, without the idea of science as approved by his superiors. He did not put before the public a Sacred History for the use of catechists, nor a manual of theology for the seminaries—works of a kind from direct control of which the Church cannot relieve itself. He addressed himself simply as an individual, long given to the historical study of the Bible, to the task of replying as critically or as scientifically as possible, to a learned Protestant and a man very well known who had sought to define the essence of Christianity in terms of history alone. That is why he had not seen and still does not see, what importance could be attached to the appearance in the forefront of his work either of the *nihil obstat* of a theological censor or the *imprimatur* of a bishop.

In order to satisfy those who have blamed him he would have had to destroy the historical character of his work—in other words, to render it useless for the end he proposed. Still more seriously, he would have had to substitute for opinions which he believes to be historically true, others which he believes to be and perhaps are false. In November *1893*, when a professor at the Catholic Institute of Paris, he was deprived of his chair, without further explanation, by the governing body of bishops for having published in *Biblical Teaching*,[1] a review which numbers some two hundred subscribers, the following sentences:

> The Pentateuch, in the condition in which it has come down to us, cannot be the work of Moses.
>
> The first chapters of Genesis do not present an authentic history of the origins of mankind.
>
> The books of the Old Testament as wholes, and the different parts within each, do not have the same historical character. All the historical books of Scripture, even those of the New Testament, have been subject to an editorial procedure much freer than that of modern historiography, and a certain liberty of interpretation is the legitimate consequence of the freedom which obtained in their composition.

[1] *L'Enseignement biblique* (Ed.).

The history of the religious doctrine contained in the Bible betrays
a genuine development of that doctrine in all the elements that
constitute it: viz., the ideas of God, of human destiny, and of the
moral laws.

It is hardly necessary to add that for an independent exegesis the
sacred books, in all that pertains to the science, do not rise above the
views common to antiquity, and that these have left their traces in
the biblical writings and even upon the beliefs they contain.

Since then these scandalous propositions have come to be looked
on as elementary truths. They have been taken up again—Heaven
preserve me from saying that anyone has actually borrowed them!—
under one form or another, over the past ten years, by the most
reputable Catholic exegetes—indeed by a considerable number of
those whose recent appointment to the pontifical commission on
biblical studies rested on the confidence of Pope Leo XIII.

In October *1900* the ex-professor began a series of articles in the
French Clergy Review[1] on the religion of Israel. The cardinal archbishop
of Paris forbade their continued publication, declaring that the first
of them ran contrary to the Constitution *Dei Filius*, of the Vatican
Council, and the Encyclical *Providentissimus Deus* of Pope Leo XIII, on
the study of Holy Scripture.

In what exactly this contradiction consisted, the author has never
discovered. The historicity of the first chapters of Genesis was still in
question, and doubtless the authority of Scripture and the foundations
of revelation were believed to be in danger inasmuch as, speaking as an
historian, he had confessed himself lacking in information regarding
the primal age of mankind, to have found in the Bible only very
uncertain and incomplete data concerning the history of Israel before
the monarchy, and to be able to reconstruct the milieu in which
Hebrew monotheism was born only conjecturally and in accordance
with historical probabilities. No serious scholar, however, even a
Catholic one, would seek to assign a date to the creation of the world,
as does the catechism used in the diocese of Paris, nor maintain that the
Bible really does contain the annals of the human race from its
beginnings down to Abraham and Moses, nor pride himself on knowing the historical circumstances of the Hebrew exodus, nor contest

---

[1] *La Revue du clergé français* (Ed.).

that the practices of the Israelitish cult, analogous to those of Israel's still older neighbours, more or less depend upon them for their origin.

He who permits himself to recall these facts does not complain of the episcopal action, which he respects and understands in precisely the same way as he understands the condemnation of *The Gospel and the Church*; but he believes it possible to derive from the past some light and consolation under present difficulties. He cannot regret not having been able to dissemble in order to comply with an authority which appeared to be concerned only with its own rights and to have but slight idea of the situation created for Catholic exegesis, apologetics and theology by the advances of biblical criticism and the general movement of modern science.

For it was a terrible fate—and this has to be said once and for all—for a priest called, fifteen or twenty years ago now, to study and practise Biblical exegesis scientifically, that he should have had an open mind and a sincere tongue. What disclosed itself to him was an immense field of investigation the existence of which the received teaching had scarcely allowed him even to surmise. The work already accomplished by Protestant and rationalist exegesis, though incomplete, was nevertheless enormous. What it amounted to was the recovery, confused still but tending to become ever clearer, of a vast historical scene—that of the origins of Christianity. It was a history which, as history, past centuries neither knew nor comprehended, any more than they did the remote antiquity of the East or of Greece or Rome. Finally, he saw the necessity for Catholics themselves to contribute to this recovery, as to every other development of human knowledge, on pain of cutting themselves off from the society of the educated and preparing for themselves in the near future a much graver crisis than any which the Christian faith had undergone since it came into existence.

The most enlightened of the men of the preceding generation who had glimpsed this difficult task confined themselves to timid ventures. It even seems that some of them despaired of the future of Catholicism in our land and that they had made up their minds to die, honourably and peacefully, in defence of positions they knew to be indefensible. A single difficulty paralysed them. The venerable name of tradition, almost a synonym for the Catholic faith, appeared to them to cover, like an impenetrable shield, the entire heritage of the past, nor were they unaware that the leaders of ecclesiastical opinion—I do not say the heads of Church—were not disposed to contemplate the requirements of an intellectual development which in no wise touched themselves. What had been the fate of the representatives of political liberalism? What welcome had been accorded the efforts of intellectual liberalism? It was no longer a question of liberalism in theory; it was one of liberty to practise, of getting to know the truth. But is it not, all of it, a matter of "liberalism" and concession to error to those who are not able or do not wish to learn anything outside their supposed tradition, or to understand anything which does not feed the insatiable appetite for domination?

In spite of everything and everybody, however, a movement began from different sides simultaneously, and since the circumstances imperiously demanded it, it persisted and grew in face of all opposition. Question after question cropped up: first that of Biblical inspiration; then those concerning the origin of the Pentateuch, the nature of the historical books of the Old Testament, the origin and nature of the gospels—St John's Gospel in particular; and lastly the question of dogma, its origin and development, the relation of the Church to the gospel, and the general philosophy of religion. This struggle for the truth was not a pitched battle but a sort of guerilla warfare in which each stood by himself and answered only for himself. Only, what these guerilla-fighters had in view were no more than unscientific and self-destructive ideas, whereas their adversaries attacked the men themselves and, to refute them the more easily, besought authority to act against them.

The spectacle of disinterested scholars seemingly hunted like dangerous animals is hardly one to add to the glory of the Church of France! For the past ten years, with no help from the outside world, which nevertheless had some reason to succour them, they have raised their eyes to the thrones whereon sat the bishops whom the Holy Spirit has appointed to rule the Church of God. Beneath the pectoral cross is there not the heart of a father, and beneath the golden mitre the understanding of a teacher? They ask themselves whether these princes of the holy city do not feel for them in their anguish, whether they do not encourage them in their efforts, whether they do not comprehend the aspirations of the century which is marching on and leaving the Church far behind it. With one or two rare and honourable exceptions, those who sit on these thrones remain unmoved and cold, as if the priest who also is a man of science had become alien and suspect to them. It does not even occur to them to question him. "A bishop does not discuss, nor refute; he condemns", was the remark of one of the prelates who censured *The Gospel and the Church*. Indeed from time to time one sees the bishop extend his cross not to guide the exegete in his painful and exhausting efforts to make good the neglect of past years, but to give him a solemn knock.

The fact is that the object of these assaults is a phantom exegete who has behind him an idea. Each time he bites the dust up springs the idea again a moment later, smiling and strong, and the exegete's shade resumes his dangerous pursuits. You do not kill ideas with a blow from a crozier.

Pope Pius XIII at last came round to thinking it advisable for the exegete to be consulted on matters of exegesis, just as one consults doctors about illnesses and lawyers about litigation. He likewise realized that it is prudent nowadays to study the subject in depth before delivering judgments. This wise course will sooner or later be copied in France. The day perhaps will come when it will not be from having yielded to the seductions of a false science, or from possessing a restless and ill-balanced mind, or from lack of docility towards papal instructions, or from want of respect for the bishops and loyalty to the Church, that Catholic authors dare to treat scientifically the problems which non-Catholic learning has raised concerning religion. It is no less than high time to provide for the needs of intelligent people, and if the efforts so far made have still yielded only imperfect results such is the condition of any human undertaking. One's duty is to try. And when one considers the nature of what has to be achieved there can be no crime in success that is only partial.

The situation is such that silence or reserve on the part of Catholic scholars on certain particularly delicate questions cannot contribute to the peace of consciences. The points at issue, of themselves, challenge the minds of our contemporaries. It is this condition of things, above all else, which "seriously disturbs the belief of the faithful on the fundamental dogmas of Catholic teaching". Were we not to explain, for those capable of reflection, the true state of the facts they would inform themselves from the writings of Protestants and non-believers, and the attitude itself of some ecclesiastical authorities could lead them to think that the official creed of the Church contradicts history and that the Catholic faith is incompatible with knowledge of the truth as to the origins of Christianity. What really disturbs the faithful in regard to Scripture is the impossibility, for a man judging according to common-sense, of reconciling what the Bible plainly is as a book with what the theologians seem to affirm as to its absolute and universal truth. What really disturbs the faithful in regard to tradition is the impossibility of reconciling the historical evolution of Christian doctrine with what the theologians seem to affirm as to its immutability. What really disturbs the faithful in regard to the divinity of Christ and his infallible knowledge is the impossibility of reconciling the natural meaning of the most authentic gospel texts with what the theologians seem to teach about the consciousness and the knowledge of Jesus. What really disturbs the faithful in regard to the redemption wrought by the death of Christ is the impossibility of considering as adequate to the economy of salvation a theory conceived in ignorance both of men's actual history in this world and of the history of religion within humanity. What really disturbs the faithful in regard to Christ's resurrection is a simple reading of the gospels as compared with the assurance with which our apologists proclaim the absolute agreement of the witnesses and the historical character and reliability of the facts. What really disturbs the faithful in regard to the eucharist and to the institution of the pontificate and the episcopate is the immense effort they have to put themselves to, and have to go on putting themselves to, in order to find in the gospel texts a full and complete determination of these matters, relative to the existing state of ecclesiastical doctrine.

This disquiet has been growing for near on a century, in proportion to the advance within our civilization of the knowledge alike of the universe and of antiquity. The progress of science raises the problem of God in new terms, the progress of history those of Christ and the Church. It is this threefold problem which forces itself on the attention of Catholic thinkers. In no way does it depend on the unfortunate little work about which so much fuss has been made. The author of *The Gospel and the Church* dealt with it only in part, and of this part he has sketched but one aspect: the historic relation of the Church and the gospel. Granting that we know what the gospel of Jesus was, how are we, from the standpoint of history, to understand the process of Christian and Catholic development? It would be wholly absurd to say that this book actually gave rise to this question, which has existed since the days of Luther and has only assumed a new form in recent times because of critical work on the gospels. The issue now, in fact, is one of seeing how the gospel, which proclaimed the imminence of God's kingdom, produced the Christian religion and the Catholic Church. The problem is a complex one, incapable of a simple solution.

A ready-made answer does exist: that Jesus in the course of his earthly life deliberately founded the Church as we know it, with its pope and its bishops, the symbol of its doctrine and the sacraments of its worship. If this answer has no place in *The Gospel and the Church* it is because there was no intention of putting it there; and there was no intention because there was no possibility of doing so. For the historian, the Church followed the gospel of Jesus; it is not formally part of that gospel. It came into being by a necessary process of evolution whereof one has only to establish the conditions. Any disquiet of faith, on this particular point, is but the consequence of the incompatibility between the ready-made answer just alluded to and the facts of history.

One had tried, then, to show that the Church truly was founded by Christ since in a very real sense it has only been a continuation of the gospel and an actualization of the kingdom of Heaven. The entire ecclesiastical institution—hierarchy, dogma and cult—is justified, in respect of historical continuity, as a development serving the gospel and as a fulfilment of the heavenly kingdom. Thus the Church was not merely the inevitable but also the legitimate outcome of the gospel. As for the divine truth of gospel and Church, it was not the book's object to demonstrate it. History, of itself, supplies no proof of such truth, which is not to be found, in its wholeness, on the surface of things, in what presents itself to critical experience, but mainly in their inner life and in the action of the gospel on the souls of men.

What, therefore, is proposed is an explanation, in itself incomplete yet to be judged sufficient as an historical insight, of the Christian movement from its beginnings in the Gospel. If this explanation is defective it nevertheless is by works of the same essential nature— though better—that its imperfections will be corrected. . . . *The Gospel and the Church* was written in order to explain how the Catholic principle, from its inexhaustible fecundity, can adapt itself to all forms of human progress. But in the past this adaptation was not accomplished without effort. So will it also be in the future.

Autour d'un petit livre, pp. v-xxviii, xxxvi

L'ÉVANGILE ET L'ÉGLISE IN RETROSPECT

The Gospel and the Church was not exactly what it appeared to be. It was not merely a defence of Catholicism against the criticisms of liberal Protestantism. There exists an official Catholicism, intransigent, registered in the formularies of the most recent councils and papal encyclicals and embodied in the Roman Curia—a huge political machine wherewith the papacy manages the affairs of religion. Of this latter type of Catholicism the author in no wise sought to establish the legitimacy. Rather, his intention was discreetly to point out its defects and its dangers. Or better, the twofold object that he had in view was—without fuss—to instruct the Catholic clergy as to the real state of the problem of Christian origins, whilst at the same time demonstrating, as against Protestant criticism, that this in no way rendered an apology for Catholicism impossible; that, on the contrary the Church would appear as a necessary and proper development of the gospel, and that what *was* rationally untenable was the liberal Protestant position itself, with its supposed "essence" of Christianity rediscovered only in our own day after having been lost for more than eighteen centuries.

This critical exposition undoubtedly spelt ruin for the "absolute" doctrines of official Catholicism. Orthodox theologians also took care—hardly necessary—to prove that the book contradicted their ideas in regard to revelation, the historical authority of the gospels, and the divinity of Jesus Christ and the divine institution of the Church and sacraments. Quite without vanity the author could have prided himself on defining much better than they wherein his opinions derogated from the official teachings of Catholicism. If he abstained from refuting this teaching it was because his intention was not to combat it but to suggest its reform, which he saw to be indispensable for the good of the Catholic Church. The achievement of such a reform belonged only to the Church itself, and he endeavoured, with all possible accommodations and precautions, to awaken it to the necessity of such a reform. An idle endeavour, were it to have no chance of success, but whatever one may say, a morally honest and loyal one. For the Church has always known how, when the need arises, to set aside or disregard old formulas that have become somewhat too embarrassing, and one asks of it nothing more than to ascertain whether a certain number of such formulas may not be found in its present repertory.

That an absolute agnosticism underlay *The Gospel and the Church* the head of the Roman Church evidently meant to be understood from his encyclical *Pascendi* on the doctrines of the Modernists. But not only is this objection an exaggeration, it cannot in any way be justified. What affords some pretext for it is the historical critical way of posing questions, as also perhaps the absence of a basic philosophy to be set in opposition to the theories of liberal Protestantism. But the impression of scepticism which the perusal of an historical critical study leaves upon the minds of dogmatists is attributable only to themselves—to the excessive rigidity of their understanding and to what is "absolutist" and false in their viewpoint. And if *The Gospel and the Church* contained no general philosophy of religion it is because there was no occasion to produce a systematic account of the subject. The author still believed himself able to maintain the substantial value of the Christian teaching, and he left it to the Church itself— that is, to those of its representatives best authorized by their situation and enlightenment—to undertake the task of orientating its teaching in the direction which circumstances seemed to demand. This attitude contained nothing of political opportunism. In some respects it has more in it of what nowadays is called pragmatism. . . . The author's intention was to stay as close as possible to traditional Catholicism so as to sacrifice only that which appeared to be irremediably condemned.

There is no question, moreover, that it would not be easy to gather from *The Gospel and the Church*—especially with the help of a commentary supplied by *Concerning a Little Book*[1]—a general philosophy capable of explaining whatever, from the standpoint of the official theology, seemed inexplicable or incoherent or heterodox in that enigmatic little volume. In it there was discernible the idea of an immense force at work in the world and manifesting itself within humanity in a

---

[1] *Autour d'un petit livre* (Ed.).

flowering of the reflective consciousness, a forward-thrust of intellect, a broad aspiration towards moral good and justice, and a growing sense of what is comely in the order whether of visible forms or of the emotions or of action. Of this great human movement Christianity was one of the aspects most fully realized. And of Christianity the Roman Catholic Church remains the most authentic representative. Her future was in her own hands. She could if she wished, and if she could so far forget her past and sufficiently modify her excessive claims, make sure of her future by working effectively for the advancement of mankind. The final article in this philosophy was a hope which the Church herself is now bent on destroying. In the remainder she has seen only a negation of her dogma—which is why she raises the cry of agnosticism. But, on this showing, there are today many agnostics in the civilized world, and even, one may fear, among those who still profess to be Roman Catholics.

L'Évangile et l'Église,
Preface (*1914*) to the fifth edition (*1929*), pp. *1–6*

PART II

TYRRELL

REVELATION

When theologians take the dogmas or articles of the creed and use them as principles or premisses of argumentation, when they combine them with one another, or with truths outside the domain of faith, so as to deduce further conclusions to be imposed on the mind under pain of at least "constructive" heresy, the resulting doctrinal system is what is here meant by theologism. We have called it a pseudo-science, not because it takes its principles blindly on faith—given the testimony of an omniscient and infallible witness, what could be more reasonable? —but because it treats prophetic enigmas and mysteries, which of their very nature are ambiguous and incapable of exact determination, as principles of exactly determinable intellectual value, and argues from them accordingly. We propose to call this *the dogmatic fallacy*, and may now proceed to make good our contention.

It may here be assumed that the Divine which is immanent in man's spirit does naturally and inevitably, at a certain stage of his mental and moral progress, reveal itself to him, however dimly, as a *vita nuova*, a new sort of life, the life of religion, with its needs and its cravings for self-adjustment to realities lying beyond the bourne of time and place; that, reflecting on this need, man seeks to explain it to himself by various religious conceptions and beliefs; and that, with regard to such explanations, it serves the purpose of an instinctive criterion or selective principle, as the appetite of an animal does in regard to its fitting dietary. It is chiefly and more immediately as a determinant of conduct, as consciousness of right and wrong, that this manifestation of the Divine will is experienced. Man lives long before he possesses a scientific theory of life, even before he reaches those ruder practical explanations of its nature and functions that are forced on him at the very dawn of reflection. Yet the science is there from the first, implicit in life itself. So too the practices and observances of religion precede the explicit formulation of those truths by which, nevertheless, the said practices are determined. They form the skeleton which grows in and with the living body; it is not first constructed apart and then clothed with flesh, and nerves, and sinews.

What revelation (considered actively as the self-manifestation of the Divine in our inward life) first defines for us is therefore a certain mode or way of life, action, and conduct. It is only later, and in the second place that our intelligence begins to reflect on this process and tries to picture it and understand it, to invent a philosophy or a history to explain it, and still more for the practical purpose of registering or fixing our experiences, of communicating them and comparing them with those of others. If we consider the generic characteristic of these explanations, to wit, the affirmed existence of superhuman transcendent beings beyond the range of ordinary experience, with whom, nevertheless, man stands in close practical relations of subjection and dependence, it is plain that the way of life or mode of action whereof these imaginings are explanatory must have reference to a world or order of existence beyond, above, yet closely related with, the world of daily experience. In this sense the teaching of religion is a popular substitute for metaphysics, so far as this latter stands for that part of philosophy which deals with the ultra-phenomenal; but it differs radically in that metaphysics, in obedience to a merely intellectual need, is deduced from a scientific reflection on the totality of phenomena, whereas religious beliefs are, in obedience to a practical need, explanatory only of the facts and phenomena of religious life, and are therefore only indirectly representative of the world to which those phenomena have reference. They are determined by life, sentiment, and conduct, whereas the rational "theology" of the metaphysician precedes and determines his practical life so far as it affects it at all.

In the main, then, religious belief is directly explanatory and justificatory of religious life and sentiment. These latter are, in the first instance, determined by the nature and action upon us of that order of things to which they have reference, and not by our knowledge of that order. Certain suggestions or occasions first awaken the religious need into consciousness; and then, by experiment, co-operation, tradition, we determine a complete code of *fas* and *nefas*, of piety and impiety. Lastly, reflection sets the imaginative intelligence to work to construct some picture, idea, and history of the world to which this code strives to adjust our conduct.

So far, then, revelation (considered objectively) is a knowledge derived from, as well as concerning, the "other world", the supernatural. But its derivation is decidedly indirect. What alone is directly given from above, or from beyond, is the spiritual craving or impulse with its specific determination, with its sympathetic and antipathetic responses to the suggestions, practical or explanatory, that are presented to it, whether casually or by the industry of the reflective religious intelligence. Here is the true "Urim and Thummim", laconic as the voice of conscience, deigning no information beyond "yea" and "nay", according to our questionings. To find the object which shall explain this religious need and bring it to full self-consciousness is the end and purpose of the whole religious process.

Every man has the power of shaping some rudimentary language for himself—a power which tradition and education render unnecessary, except so far as the language he has been taught may on occasion prove too narrow for his needs. So too revelation, in the above sense, is accorded to most men; but religious tradition and education are usually beforehand to wake up the religious need and to overwhelm it with the treasures of the collective spiritual experience and reflection of the past. They are few who ever master this tradition in its entirety; fewer still who rise above it or revolutionize it. It is these last, however —the great founders and reformers—who alone are credited with being the recipients of revelation from on high, whereas in truth they often but reap what has been sown by multitudes of forgotten labourers. There is, however, little doubt that an intense feeling, passion, or emotion will in some instances incorporate itself in congenial imaginations and conceptions; that from the storehouse of the memory it will, as it rushes outwards, snatch to itself by a sort of magnetism such garments as may best set it forth on the stage of thought. In respect to such conceptions and visions the recipient is almost as passive and determined as he is in regard to the spiritual emotion so embodied. Hence these presentments of the supernatural world seem to be quite specially inspired, to possess a higher authority and to come less indirectly from God than those that are deliberately sought out in explanation of the life of religion. Yet in fact their only superiority is that they may indicate a stronger, purer, deeper impulse of the Divine

H

Spirit; not that they are any more directly representative of those invisible realities known to us merely by the blind gropings of love. All revelation truly such is in some measure or other an expression of the Divine mind in man, of the Spirit of God; but it is not necessarily a Divine expression of that spirit; for the expression is but the reaction, spontaneous or reflex, of the human mind to God's touch felt within the heart, and this reaction is characterized wholly by the ideas, forms, and images wherewith the mind is stocked in each particular case.

But in thus allowing that the rudest religious beliefs are inspired so far as they originate purely in a spontaneous effort to interpret the workings of grace in the heart, we do not for a moment equalize them otherwise than generically; nor do we forget that there is here, as in other spheres of human life—in art, in science, in politics, in ethics—a true progressive tendency and a firm criterion of such progress, the criterion of life amplified and invigorated, or life contracted and impoverished. If the whole field of experience, if that world from which the philosopher draws his metaphysical theology, may in some sense be called a revelation of God, yet we shall be keeping closer to the original and historical sense of the term "revelation" if we refer it to those presentations of the other world which are shaped and determined by man's inward religious experience, individual and collective. Here it is that man seems to be guided and taught, not through the ordinary ways of knowledge, but more or less supernaturally, by a Divine Spirit in direct communication with his own; and this in the interests of conscience and duty and worship, not in those of speculative curiosity. Hence the peculiarly sacred character attached to revelation as distinct from theology. For the former, God is felt to stand guaranty, whereas the latter is fallible with the fallibility of the human mind. And yet it is to their eventual confusion as truths in the same order, to the ascription of Divine authority to theology and of scientific or philosophic exactitude to revelation, that the mischievous results of theologism must be traced.

But in what sense are religious revelations divinely authorized? What sort of truth is guaranteed to them by the "seal of the spirit"? In accordance with what has been already said we must answer—a truth which is directly practical, preferential, approximative, and only indirectly speculative. What is immediately approved, as it were experimentally, is a way of living, feeling, and acting with reference to the other world. The explanatory and justificatory conceptions subsequently sought out by the mind, as postulated by the "way of life", have no direct Divine approval. Again, the Divine approval of the way and the life (and therefore indirectly of the explanatory truth) is mostly preferential, it is a favouring of one alternative, not as ideal and finally perfect, but as an approximation to the ideal, as a "move in the right direction".

To take the inspired imagery of revelation as representing the Divine mind in the same way as a philosophy or science represents the human mind; to view it as a miraculously communicated science, superseding and correcting the natural results of theological speculation, is the fundamental mistake of theologism. Yet like all widespread and persistent errors it is a very natural one, as natural as the belief in geocentricism. It needs no slight degree of critical development to distinguish *momenta* in a phenomenon that seems to be given all at once and is therefore taken in the lump, *i.e.* to discern the soul of the act from its body, its essence from its accidents, the action of grace from the reaction of nature, the warmth of the heart from the light which it kindles in the mind, the infusion of Divine love from the inspired image in which it clothes itself or from the theological concepts in which it is afterwards clothed by our reflection.

The story of the birth of our dogmatic theology is now fairly well made out. Dr Paul Wernle, in his *Die Anfänge unserer Religion*, with perhaps a somewhat too indiscriminate antitheological bias, shows the process by which a religion, that in its origin and spirit was so largely a protest against that theologism which builds a theology on the letter-value of spiritual and prophetic utterances, and makes the Word of God of none effect through the vain traditions of men, came itself to lapse into that very same fallacy. While admitting that religion without some sort of dogmas, some sort of beliefs and symbols of the other world is as impracticable as ordinary life would be without some rude practical knowledge of ourselves and our surroundings; while even allowing that theology, though not essential, may be as helpful to religion as science is to daily life; yet it is all but impossible to imagine the Christ of the synoptics, the advocate of the poor and simple against the intellectual tyranny of lawyers, scribes, and theologians, attaching the slightest religious value to the theologically correct formulation of the inscrutable mysteries prophetically symbolized by the Heavenly Father, the Son of Man, the kingdom of God, etc., or making salvation to depend on any point of mere intellectual exactitude.

In its first form the Christian revelation was altogether apocalyptic, prophetic, visionary in character. The ethical teaching of the gospel was not considered as part of it, or as in any wise new. The kingdom of Heaven, its nature, the circumstances of its advent—this was the "good news"; but the repentance, the preparation for the day of the Lord, lay simply in walking in the paths of holiness, already trodden and marked out by the saints and prophets. But of these apocalyptic teachings the prophetic spirit was the criterion, even as it was the author; they were at first avowedly the setting forth of the future ideal order in figurative and imperfect language, borrowed from a lower order of reality; and, while thus understood, the only opposition with natural experience which they had to fear, and did encounter, was with the history of the future, which they seemed to predict more or less ambiguously. Very early, however, arose the apologetic desire to show that, as the Spirit gave to children and weaklings a virtue and self-control exceeding that of the philosophers, so it gifted them with a miraculous wisdom or philosophy which turned pagan light into darkness. Hence the endeavour to argue deductively from prophetic visions to scientific conclusions; to discover the highest philosophical systems embedded in the Christian revelation, and then to find gropings after Christianity, thus interpreted, in all the best philosophies. Forthwith the resulting system, compounded of prophetic revelations and philosophical theories and conceptions, is proposed for general belief as a divinely revealed *Weltanschauung* or general philosophy, as having all the oracular authority of a prophecy with all the exactitude of a scientific theology. Here we have theologism full-blown in all its hybrid enormity, *i.e.* a would-be science governed, not by a scientific, but by a prophetic criterion.

Concurrently with this transformation of revelation into a revealed theology there arises a parallel and dependent perversion of the notion of faith into that of theological orthodoxy. Faith is now an intellectual assent to this revealed theology as deriving directly from the Divine intellect; it is no longer the adhesion of the whole man, heart, mind, and soul, to the Divine Spirit within—primarily a spirit of life and love, and only thereby a guide or beacon leading the mind gradually to a fuller instinctive apprehension of the religious truth implicit in the inspirations of grace.

So long as the Christian revelation was felt to be an utterance of prophetic enthusiasm, a communication of visions whose correspondence to the felt realities of eternity was more or less enigmatic and inexact, variations of form were not considered prejudicial to its truth. Prophets, like poets, may deal quite differently, yet quite truthfully, with the same theme. But, as soon as it pretended to be a revealed philosophy and to possess a more or less literal and exact correspondence to fact, substantial variations of form were felt to be inconsistent with the oneness and unchangeableness of truth. As mysteries of faith, the threefold personality of God, or the godhead of Christ, could not come in conflict with theological monotheism or the metaphysics of nature and personality, but as theological statements they had to be squared with the requirements of intellectual unity.

One inevitable result of this intellectualising of revelation was the sterilizing (due to other causes as well) of the sources of prophetic inspiration. Under the tyranny of a dominant classicism, art and poetry dry up; yet this at most is the tyranny of a fashion, not that of a divinely-revealed immutable standard. To force prophetic or poetic vision to take certain theological shapes and forms under pain of anathema is to silence and quench that spirit, the breath of whose life is freedom. Tried by such standard orthodoxy, the prophets who could not prophesy to order and rule were discarded as charlatans and impostors, and gradually their whole caste fell into discredit; nor was their function as agitators and reformers compatible with a conservative ecclesiastical institution, such as that into which the primitive communities were being fast welded. Such additions and modifications as the canonized doctrinal system subsequently received were chiefly the work of theological reflection, deduction, explanation, controversy, definition.

The current theological, philosophical, and historical beliefs and conceptions, in which the original Christian afflatus or enthusiasm embodied itself, being thus canonized as part and parcel of a revealed theology, and as being therefore God's own philosophy of existence and of human history, the whole force of the Christian religion, with all its highest sanctions and motives, was thrown into the scale against the progress of knowledge and, thereby, of civilization. All those categories, philosophical, scientific, and historic, all those readings of the world and of history, that were involved and presupposed in the canonical traditions and scriptures, were imposed by conscience upon the understanding as the Word of God, as matter of Divine faith, to be questioned only at the peril of one's immortal soul. So closely interwoven are all the parts of the kingdom of knowledge that this meant its entire subjection (at least in the event of conflict) to the ultimate control of revelation now identified with dogmatic theology. The superiority of this so-called revelation over reason was no longer that of a higher kind of truth over a lower, excluding the possibility of conflict in the same plane, of prophetic mysteries veiled from the impertinent scrutiny of reason, but only that of a higher truth in the same plane or order.

Quite apart from the juridical and physical coercion so freely resorted to by ecclesiastical authority, the very conception of a divinely revealed doctrinal system, ramifying out into every corner of the field of knowledge, held the Christian intelligence for centuries captive to the Christian conscience. No philosophical speculation, no scientific or historical discovery, could merit consideration or toleration which seemed to come into conflict with a divinely revealed theology. Reluctantly, as time went on, and as the hopes of a near Parousia yielded place to a prospect of possible centuries of delay and of an intervening ecclesiastical era, the idea of development or growth had to be admitted to justify undeniable additions and alterations forced on the Church by the necessity of adapting her teaching to new times and regions and circumstances, to new forms of thought and speech. Yet in theory, at least, this theological development allows of no transformation of those scriptural and primitive conceptions, with all their now largely obsolete historical and philosophical presuppositions, in which the Spirit of Christ first uttered itself. These are to be developed, like the immutable first principles of geometry, by combination with one another, or with truths of natural reason and experience outside their own order. Revelation having ceased with the apostles, it is only in and through these primitive conceptions that we retain any sort of distant and mediate contact with the facts and realities which dogmatic theology defines, and by which its truth may be experimentally verified and criticized. In sight of these facts and realities, were they still present to us, we might venture to re-adjust these their earliest expression to our own mode of thought and speech; but now such a criticism is impossible. It is therefore a necessary supposition of dogmatic theology that the scriptural and apostolic utterances were faultlessly and divinely perfect, not merely as symbols, but as theology, history, and science; that it is itself practically like an abstract science in being delivered from these revolutions and changes of governing categories which befall sciences ever confronted and controlled by the experiences which constitute their subject-matter. Such, then, is the theoretical immutability of dogmatic theology. Needless to say, it is an impossible and unattainable ideal.

Through Scylla and Charybdis; or, The Old Theology and the New,
pp. *204–216*

BELIEF AND TRUTH

1. The Truth of Beliefs

In its external expression a religion consists of a body of theological and ethical propositions, as well as of sundry rites, ceremonies, institutions, and disciplinary observances. As the rite or sacrament has its visible and spiritual side, its value as a fact in the will-world; so . . . each ethical or theological statement is sacramental and belongs at once to the world of the natural understanding, and to the world of faith and spiritual reality. It is as to *faith* and *morals* (*i.e.*, as to spiritual and religious valuations) that the scriptures and traditions of the Christian Church claim to be divinely guided into all truth, as it were, by an unerring Spirit or sentiment, which selects or casts aside such materials as are offered by the thought and language of each age and people for its embodiment—a Spirit which, itself unchanged, changes the fashion of its outer garb to suit every variety of custom and tradition. That texture of philosophical, scientific, and historical beliefs, which the religious sentiment of Christianity has inspired and in which it has embodied itself, claims to be in harmony with the rest of human knowledge, of which it is but a part, and so far, to be true with the truth of the understanding; but its religious truth lies in "the Spirit that quickeneth", in its fidelity to the facts of the will-world compared with which "the flesh", the merely mental value, "profiteth nothing". From every new ingathering of knowledge the same Spirit can weave itself a living garment of flesh, not less, but more pliant to its purpose of self-manifestation than all previous garments.

The world of appearance, as we have said, is simply subordinate and instrumental to the real world of our will and affections in which we live the life of love and hate, and pass from one will-attitude to another in relation to other wills than our own. This will-life becomes religious as soon as we rise to a distinct knowledge of a Divine Will as the head and centre of the will-world. In this region truth has a practical and teleological sense—it is the trueness of a means to its end, of an instrument to its purpose; and like these truths it is to some extent conditioned by what we know and believe about its object. But this will-adjustment is the end of all such knowledge and belief, and constitutes its religious value. Hence the *religiously* important criticism to be applied to points of Christian belief, whether historical, philosophic, or scientific, is not that which interests the historian, philosopher, or scientist; but that which is supplied by the Spirit of Christ, the *spiritus qui vivificat:* Is the belief in accord with, is it a development of, the Spirit of the gospel? What is its religious value? Does it make for the love of God and man? Does it show us the Father and reveal to us our sonship?

Such religiously true beliefs have been either created or shaped or selected under the influence of religious inspiration, that is, of the sacred enthusiasm kindled by some piercing intuition, some vivid perception of the realities of the will-world to which they correspond.

We may usefully distinguish a threefold truth or correspondence to reality in that organic body of beliefs known as the Christian creed. First, they may be viewed externally as woven into the tissue of our natural understanding, and as forming elements of our whole history and philosophy of the world—of our attempt to put things together coherently and to connect religion with the rest of our knowledge. Thus the existence and the nature of God, the immortality of the soul, the freedom of the will, may be viewed as constitutive elements of our philosophy; the birth, death and resurrection of Christ, as links in the chain of history.

Secondly, as a man's spirit and character may be revealed and known by his reading of history and by his view of the world and life, by the colour they derive from the glass through which he sees them, by the shape to which his receptivity moulds them, so the spirit of Christianity is revealed and known in the creed. This truth of the creed's correspondence to the Spirit of Christianity is only another aspect of its practical or "regulative" truth. It is by living in the light of these beliefs, by regulating our conduct according to them that we can reproduce and foster the Spirit of Christ within ourselves. They furnish us with an effectual guide to eternal life.

Thirdly, a mere fiction may be practically serviceable in art or industry; and even the natural life of soul and body may be aided for a time and in particular cases by useful illusions. But no mere fiction, no pure illusion, no lie can be practically serviceable to life on an universal scale. For life depends on agreement with Nature; that is, on truth. Rogues and liars prosper just so long as there is a majority of honest men to lie to; but a community of rogues could not hold together; their theory of conduct is untrue to the nature of human society. Beliefs that have been found by continuous and invariable experience to foster and promote the spiritual life of the soul must so far be in accord with the nature and the laws of that will-world with which it is the aim of religion to bring us into harmony; their practical value results from, and is founded in, their representative value. Not indeed that the spirit world can be properly represented in terms of the natural world. But as we can speak of thought in terms of extension, or of will in terms of mass and motion, on account of certain analogies between the two; so we can be sure that between the Christian understanding, or formulation of religion as embodied in the creed, and the eternal realities of the spirit world there exists a certain analogy whose precise nature is hidden just because we cannot compare its terms as we can those of thought and extension. And the reason of this assurance is found in the universally proved value of the creed as a practical guide to the eternal life of the soul—a proof which is based on the experience not of this man or that, however wise or holy, but of the whole Christian people and of the Church of the Saints in all ages and nations, on the consensus of the ethical and religious *orbis terrarum*.

Lex Orandi; or, Prayer and Creed, pp. *53–58*.

2. Belief in God

As we here use the term, religion is the will-attitude of the soul towards God considered as a person, as that Sovereign Will which is the head, bond, and centre of the will-world. It is precisely under the aspect of goodness, or rather, since the will's ultimate object is never an abstraction, under the aspect of a Being in the act of loving, and willing, and causing, every possible kind of goodness and truth and beauty, that God is our principal will-object, the term of our unqualified love and worship and reverence. All else that we believe about him is but an amplification of his aspect. So far as he belongs to that world of our understanding which systematizes our experience with a view to converse and outward action, he is viewed as the First Cause, as Self-existent, Infinite, Eternal; or perhaps he is misconceived in some way or another, and some of his attributes distorted or denied. As the object of theological science we may *know* him more or less; but we do not *believe* in him. To believe in him is to reckon with him as a reality, and by free-choice to shape and adapt our inward and outward life with reference to that reality—yielding to it or resisting it.

The simplest can believe in him, however incorrectly they may understand him or apprehend all the philosophical implications of Necessary Being. To reckon with God as a reality, to enter into social relations with him, does not necessarily mean leading a good life. The rebel who wilfully resists and defies authority confesses its reality by his defiance as much as he would by his submission. We do not beat the air or resist the void. Hostility is as real as friendship. Hence the distinction between belief and love is well founded and is consistent with the assertion that belief involves a practical attitude of the will, and does not stop short with a barren assent of the mind. "The devils believe and tremble"; their trembling is the very embodiment of their belief; for them God is not merely accepted by the mind, but is felt as an obstacle to the will.

The reasons and proofs that are commonly given for the existence of God are not always those that have historically given birth to the belief in his existence. Rather they are after-justifications of a belief that has risen independently of them, and represent an attempt to harmonize it with the rest of our understanding. Historically the belief has been fashioned by the religious needs of man's nature, and so far as it is true to that nature it must be justifiable by any philosophy that is true to the same. Truth is the same whether approached from the practical or the speculative side; what is really good, is true; what is true, is really the best.

In the measure that men have obeyed their inborn attraction towards the ideal, feeling their way from one conception of the spiritual world to another according as this or that has proved its greater efficacy as a practical guide to inward life and growth, the notion of one supreme personal Spirit, almighty, all-wise, all-holy as Source, Centre and End of the will-world has gained acceptance universally—*semper, ubique, ab omnibus;* and has thereby proved its accord with the ultimate realities on which the laws of man's higher life are founded. The practical advantages and life-values of the great unifications of physical science are not more immediately apparent or indisputable than the moral and spiritual advantages resulting from the conception of the Infinite as being a personal Spirit or Will, giving unity of origin, centre, and aim to the otherwise aimless and chaotic multitude of finite wills; from the conception of this God as super-corporeal; as one rather than many; as just and holy rather than merely wise or powerful; as all-seeing, all-judging, rather than limited. Growing better, men have formed and approved these beliefs rather than their contraries; and approving them have grown still better, and have thus verified them experimentally.

It is plain that these beliefs are at first expressed simply and directly in the terms of things familiar to us, just as if they had been given us through our sense like the facts of history or science; and belonged to the world of appearances. But our mind, with its need of unity and coherence, cannot tolerate the confusion that would result from taking them in their simple literality, and at once sets about explaining them as analogously true in some way that will harmonize with the rest of our systematized knowledge.

It tells us that these beliefs will bring chaos into our understanding unless we are quite clear that, between the being and nature of God and that of all the creatures he has made there is no common measure, no relation of more and less, but an absolute difference *in kind;* that nothing can be said in just the same sense of him and of any creature. This is what we mean by his infinity—not that he is indefinitely, endlessly, greater in measure and degree than anything we know in the way of being unity, personality, spirit, knowledge, power, cause, will, goodness; but that he includes these in one simple absolute perfection in some way more different from them all than thought is from matter or than desire is from force. In him, what we call will is exactly the same thing as what we call knowledge, or being, or unity, or goodness; in us all these things are as distinct as possible and have nothing in common. He cannot strictly be grouped with anything so as to be one of a class: but only by way of analogy. We call him *a* spirit, *a* person, as if he were one of a number of such; yet he is not one, or individual in the way that we are. He is a spirit only so far as this means that he is not corporeal; he is a person because most certainly he is not impersonal. What he *is* includes all that by which spirit excels body, and by which personality excels impersonality, and by which individuality excels indefiniteness and confusion. We do not even believe in *a* God, for this would imply a possible or conceivable multiplication of Gods; but only in God, for could we conceive him adequately we should see that the idea of his replication was incoherent and absurd.[1]

That it is not so to us now, only shows that we cannot now think of him, cannot make him *an* object of our thought, cannot oppose him to ourselves as another self, without at once putting him into a class with other objects of our thought and so making him finite in the image and likeness of creatures. This transformation is however necessary if we are to enter into social relations with him—if we are to think of him, love him, pray to him. As head and centre of the will-world he must be *represented* by us as *part* of that finite spiritual organism; as the First of Creatures; as making himself man for our minds; as *a* power, *an* intelligence, *a* will indefinitely greater than, but of the same kind as, our own. Man cannot deal practically with what the heart of man has never conceived, with what is neither the self nor the not-self; with what is as distinct from him as the latter, yet quite differently distinct; as close to him as the former, yet quite differently closer with a relation that is necessarily *sui generis* and unknown to finite experience, he cannot deal with the Absolute in its absoluteness.

[1] That it does not now strike us at once as inconceivable that the self-existent should be multiplied or extended is because the only "self" and the only "existence" that our understanding (as distinct from our intuition) knows is finite and limited and therefore can be conceived as multiplied. Again it is because we are forced to conceive God's existence in terms of our own and as of the same sort, that we do not at once see the *necessity* of his existence, the impossibility of his non-existence—our own sort of existence being merely contingent. It is only by roundabout reasoning that we are brought to see that there must be a higher kind of being than our own to account for our own; one whose existence is necessary and which cannot be measured by any finite measure.

The fiction of God's finitude and relativity is therefore a necessity of man's religious life. But the interests both of intellectual truth and of religion require us to recognize this fiction as such, under pain of mental incoherence on one side, and of superstition and idolatry on the other. For, to make God finite is to bring him inside creation as its principal part or factor, just as a monarch is part of the society he governs; but to mistake this imaginary importation for a reality, to view God's immanence as that of a veritable *anima mundi*, part and parcel of the whole, revealed in Nature just as the soul is revealed in the body, would falsify all the calculations of our mind. Again, worship is not less idolatrous because the idol is greater than all other creatures put together. The reverence due to even the most marvellously gifted of our fellow-creatures differs altogether in kind from that due to the Giver on whose bounty we both alike are beggars; just as fraternal differs essentially from filial affection. This sentiment of adoring (latreutic) reverence owes its unique quality to the sense, however vague, of the absoluteness and infinitude which characterize its object, as being that which alone can satisfy the spiritual hunger which no idealization of the finite, however great, could possibly satisfy. To lavish this sentiment on anything short of God is the very essence of idolatry. Yet if they cannot find bread, men will eat earth in their vain efforts to stay the imperative cravings of their nature; for the appetite is there, as a vague uneasiness, from the very first, long before it arrives by way of experiment and failure at a distinct expression and understanding of itself and of its object.

The finite image, therefore, under which God is presented to us for the practical purposes of religion could not be universally useful to that spiritual life by whose exigencies it has been fabricated were it not grounded in the ultimate nature of things; were it not representative of the infinite at least by way of analogy. There is a representative correspondence between a musical score and the music itself through which one stone-deaf from birth might be taught to produce effects, to exercise control, in that sound-world which has no direct place in his consciousness. Yet we cannot say that he knows nothing of the sound-world, that he has no evidence of its existence; we can only say that he does not know it in its own terms, but in terms of sight or touch. Though we know God's kind of being only in terms of our own, the infinite only in terms of the finite, yet he is not therefore unknowable or unknown; nor is our action void of all effect in the order of Eternity.

Confusion as to this fundamental point is at the root of nearly all the difficulties we experience in endeavouring to reconcile the chief mysteries of faith with our natural understanding. Hence we have tried to put the matter clearly at the outset.

We have seen then how this popular notion of God as a personal spirit in our own image and likeness is true to the needs of our religious and moral life; and how it is true for the mind only so far as it is taken to represent the Divine order of being analogously in terms of the finite.

Ibid., pp. 71–80

3. The Incarnation

(i)

Apotheosis, the deification of heroes, is a frequent manifestation of the natural idolatry of the human mind. A low conception of the meaning of divinity, the fanatical exaggerations of hero-worship, the fertility of the myth-making faculty, the craving for a god in our own image and likeness, combine with other causes to make the error easy and almost inevitable. Nor are incarnation-beliefs less easy of explanation where gods, conceived more or less in the form and fashion of men, may well be imagined as mixing with mortals and even marrying into the race. In such superstitions or diseases of the religious sense, we must not let the perversion blind us to the value of that which is perverted, or overlook the natural exigency or appetite that gropes blindly for satisfaction in these husks of truth. Rather we must recognize in them bizarre "dreamings of things to come", troubling "the prophetic soul of the wide world"; uncouth embryo shapes of the fuller faith that is ours, vain essays of inexperienced humanity to interpret its own nature and needs. We must moreover distinguish the principle of variation from the principle of selection; the various fallacies, truths, half-truths, and errors, the good, the evil and the mixed motives, that have first almost accidentally suggested and shaped these beliefs, from that practically proven religious value that has determined their survival. The desire to bring the human and divine, this world and the other, into closer relation; to rend the dividing veil of the heavens; to lift man up to the throne of the immortal gods: to draw the gods down to the sorrows and weaknesses of man's mortal lot has rarely dictated and originated, but it has mostly sustained and won credit for beliefs of this kind—beliefs which, so far, may have served, in default of better, as a rude language or channel of communication between men and that Unknown God whose goodness they ignorantly worshipped under the image and likeness of some creature of their brain.

Yet, as in other instances, it was needful that the little seed of truth should perish in order to live again in a higher form; that a purer and better conception of the Divine Nature should first put such a gulf between Creator and creature as to make apotheoses and incarnations unthinkable and blasphemous, and that a clearer apprehension of the infinitude of God's greatness should prepare the way for a belief in the infinitude of his mercy and condescension, and in the mystery of the Son of God made man to make men sons of God.

Thus while Christianity with its Trinity of Divine persons, its God-made-man, its pantheon of divinized men and women, is open to the superficial charge of being a falling-away from the purer monotheism of Jew or Mahometan, and a reversion to the old pagan polytheistic type, it is rather to be regarded as taking up into a higher synthesis those advantages of polytheism which had to be sacrificed for the greater advantages of a too abstract and soul-starving mono-theism. For as has already been said, the unsocial conception of the divinity as a solitary infinite spirit, out of all fatherly and friendly relationship with the finite, is as untrue for deeper philosophical reflection as it is for the best instincts of the spiritual life. Nor has Judaism been really content with it; God as the God of Israel, as the God of the individual soul, as the Father of the human race is already limited and incarnate for the mind that so regards him; he is virtually a "God with us".

The belief in the Godhead of Christ is the capital and central creation of the Spirit of Christ. A mystery for metaphysics, its meaning as a practical rule of speech, sentiment and conduct is within the appre-hension of the simplest follower of the Galilean fisherman who first accepted it. For to believe a truth is to reckon with it as with a reality, whether welcome or unwelcome; it is to adapt our will to it as to a new factor of the world with which we have to deal. Here it means to speak of Christ, to feel and to act towards him as towards a person who, being one and the same, possesses distinctly all the attributes of divinity and of humanity; it means for us that the life and death of Christ are the life and death, not of the divinest of men or of the greatest of prophets, but of God. What saint or prophet could dare to say, "Take and eat; this is my body"? Who but God is the bread of the soul's life?

Christocentricism, the direct adoration of Christ as personally identical with God, is the essential characteristic of Christian as distinct from any purely theistic religious sentiment. The Catholic doctrine is far less a creation of theological reflection than of the selective power of the Christian spirit rejecting the variations of heretical curiosity—Arian, Nestorian, Monophysite—as inadequate to its needs, as untrue to the laws of its life. It is a synthesis of all their religious values and a correction of all their deficiencies. No incarnate aeon, no created Wisdom or Logos could bridge the gulf between the finite creature and the infinite Creator; no alliance with a servant could win us the adoption of sons. The chiefest of his angels are but ministering spirits; and those nearest his throne are not, as measured by Infinity, appreciably nearer than we are. It is himself we need to see and handle and no angel from his face. Nor yet are the higher exigencies of religion satisfied by any sort of Nestorian Christology. Between person and person the separateness is irreducible; no relation of closeness that leaves this opposition unconquered or that falls short of that of personal identity between the God-Christ and the Man-Christ can lend the same emotional and practical value to the life at Nazareth and the death on Calvary. Saint of Saints, Prince of Prophets and Martyrs, First-born of every creature, the Man-Christ were at best a divinely-given ideal of perfect humanity—God's shadow but not his substance and very self.

If in revolt against this merely moral or juridical union of the human and Divine in Christ, the Monophysite secures unity of person at the cost of blending or confusion of the two natures into something that is neither one nor the other, he seems to relapse from pure mono-theism into an essentially pagan mode of thought inconsistent with a right estimate of the unchangeableness and infinitude of the Godhead. Still more, he robs the Incarnation of its principal religious value; for it is as being both perfect God and perfect man, as leading two different lives at once, that Christ fulfils the ideal of a mediator. For this reason the instinct of the Christian spirit has ever been hostile to any sort of Docetism that would deliver Christ from any of the blameless and natural limitations of our human nature, and so make him less of a mediator touched with a feeling for our infirmities, tempted in all points as we, yet never yielding to sin. It is the faith that God not only knows this sad life of ours but that he has actually lived it and consecrated it, which has transformed the bitter water of our affliction into the wine of joy and gladness. It is therefore Christian devotion rather than Christian metaphysics, the need of the soul rather than the need of the intellect, that has selected the orthodox faith in preference to heterodox error.

(ii)

That God, in his own simple and mysterious perfection, realizes, while he infinitely transcends, the highest idealization of human excellence; that so far he is man, and that in striving after the ideal completion of our nature we are likening ourselves to God, making ourselves his sons; that since our spiritual life requires we should conceive him in our own finite likeness (as another, though indefinitely greater, personal spirit in relation with our own, endowed with like faculties working under like conditions), this conception must have some equivalent representative value—all this seems more than probable to that deeper theistic philosophy which reckons with the whole man, and not merely with the rational understanding.

By its doctrine of the Incarnation the Christian spirit expresses this truth in the language of fact, and brings it home effectually to the imagination and emotion of the flesh-clad spirit of man. The aforesaid ideal of the Perfect Man which is swallowed up and transcended in the infinitude and simplicity of the Divine Perfection is, as it were, hewn out of that eternal rock and set in all the beauty and definiteness of its outline before us for our eyes to see and our hands to handle, being yet bound to God by the tie of personal unity and not severed after the manner of other creatures. In Christ, that aspect of the Godhead which is the highest our human standards can measure, and under which God is the postulate of our moral and religious life, is thrown into bright relief against what to us is the inscrutable darkness, but is

I

really the blinding brilliance, of that absolute perfection which embraces but infinitely transcends it:

> So the All-Great were the All-Loving too,
> So through the thunder comes a human voice
> Saying: O heart I made, a heart beats here,
> Face, my hands fashioned, see it in myself.

"He that hath seen Me hath seen the Father; how sayest thou then: 'Show us the Father'?" Christ is the most perfect translation of the Divine Nature and Character into terms of human nature and character; whatever there is in him of truth and grace, of wisdom and mercy, of strength and love, all that and infinitely more is contained in the simplicity of the Divine Perfection which it is his mission to unfold to us. The Catholic and Christian spirit has refused to regard him as mediating between an angered Master and his rebel servants, as commissioned by these latter to overcome the reluctance of the former. God so loved the world that he gave his only-begotten Son, that he "sent him into the world" as ambassador to plead the Father's cause with his erring children; to win them to a belief in his loving-kindness—a belief which was hard for them so long as, being themselves merciless and unforgiving, they were bound to conceive him in their own image and likeness. Nothing could be more unlike the various pagan and superstitious notions of mediation and atonement.

Christ is thus the incarnation of the eternal humanity, *i.e.* of humanity as it is involved and merged in the simplicity of the Divine Perfection and identified with God. But humanity stands here for the manhood of an unit, not for the whole race of Adam as bound together physically, spiritually, and morally into one living social organism. Through Christ whose human nature is knit and woven into the continuity of its substance this collective humanity is indirectly linked to the Godhead and thereby to its own eternal ideal. Through Christ in whose manhood the ideal manhood is realized, grace is spread abroad among men in order slowly to realize the ideal race, people, or kingdom of God. Through him who is a Son of God by Nature in virtue of his personality, all men can receive power to become sons of God by adoption fashioned to the pattern of Christ's human spirit and character. For the infinite riches and potentiality of the Spirit of Christ could not find adequate expression within the compass of any single mortal life however full and varied, but needs to be manifested in every variety of time and place, character and circumstances; in its social no less than in its individual effects; in combination with strength and weakness, wisdom, and simplicity, culture and barbarism, riches and poverty, age and youth, antiquity and modernity.

Brought to the test of life, how does this doctrine compare with pagan beliefs in apotheoses and incarnations springing from and fostering unworthy views of the dignity of God and man? Surely the truth of Christ's humanity, taken in connection with that of his divinity, is one that has, more than all others, renewed the face of the earth. It has turned a feeble and ineffectual speculation of philosophy into a living effectual truth of religion; it has brought home to the heart of mankind the infinite value of the individual soul, the ineffaceable dignity of personality; it is a belief to which we owe that slow movement of liberation, which is lifting our race from conditions of brute competition to that of free children in the same household; a belief through which the old scholastic speculation about the angels, affirming that each was a species in itself and could not, without contradiction, be repeated or multiplied, has come to be verified of man viewed on his spiritual side. Jesus, the Son of God by nature, and every man the brother of Christ by nature and adoption—is a belief which gives us an insight into the world of wills and explains a thousand mysterious instincts of unity and sameness, which else we should never have been able to formulate. The oneness of all men with one another in Christ; and their oneness with God through Christ, is the foundation of all practical and affective religion as summed up in the duty of Charity; and this is the religious value of our belief in "Jesus Christ— His only Son—our Lord". All that is added in the Nicene and Athanasian creeds as to the precise nature of the hypostatic union—"Begotten of the Father before all worlds: not made; consubstantial with the Father; by whom all things were made", and so forth; all this is but protective of the simple truth that Christ is God; and that God is in Christ, reconciling the world to himself.

Again, the doctrine of the Incarnation which is given us by the spirit of Christianity and which is the intellectual expression of the implications of the Christian sentiment of Divine love, is also the supreme consecration of that sacramental principle which is so potent a factor in the development of spiritual life. The precise relation of reality to appearance, of inward to outward, of the spirit to the flesh, of active freedom to passive necessity, of the determining to the determined, is one of the persistent problems of the soul the solution of which seems to evade that rational understanding whose forms are derived from, and whose language is adapted to, the lower member only of each antithesis; and which can figure the relation of its own sphere to the higher only in terms of those relations that obtain between the contents of the lower. Only by giving the soul certain attributes of the body can it figure to itself some analogy of the tie between body and soul.

The sacramental principle, as demanded by the exigencies of Christian sanctity, gives us at least a practical answer whose proven fidelity to the laws of life warrants our faith in its fundamental truthfulness. A neo-platonic or puritanical abhorrence of the sense-world as radically and irredeemably evil and hostile to the spiritual life marks the first crude revolt against mere pagan Naturalism or against the abuse and corruption of the sacramental principle. A partial correction of this extreme is found in the "sacramentarian" view of Nature as a symbolic expression or sign of the spiritual order, as of something separate and distinct, with which it has no causal connection except so far as by enlightening man's intelligence it may occasion some movement of his will and affections. And this is analogous to Nestorianism in Christology; and receives a sort of Monophysite correction in the view that conceives the relationship between Nature and Spirit, Outward and Inward, after the fashion of a material mixture or confusion of substance. All these errors have been excluded by the *Lex Orandi*, by the instinct of the Christian spirit, which teaches us that Nature is the instrument of our healing as of our hurt: "Peccat caro; mundat caro". Unconquered and blindly obeyed, Nature stands as an impenetrable barrier between man and God; conquered and brought under the will it becomes the organ of the divinity, the channel of communication between spirit and spirit—not merely symbolizing but effecting what it symbolizes. Thus the sacred humanity of Christ is the sacrament of sacraments; for there the subjugation of the natural to the spiritual is absolute as in no other; his manhood is no mere finite symbol of the divinity, but is Divine; not mingled nor confounded with divinity, but united to it personally: Christ is for us effectually that which he reveals and signifies. In him the redemption of

Nature, the conversion of evil into good, of poison into medicine, reaches its unique culmination; through him and in union with him the visible order becomes the sacrament, the effective symbol, of the invisible.

But while this relationship between the Godhead and manhood of Christ is intelligible in terms of its practical consequences for us, in itself it cannot be represented to our mind except by halting analogies. If we are so vague as to the precise meaning of human personality; as to the relation of body and soul; and still more as to the relation of creature to Creator; we are not likely to form any very coherent representation of the "Hypostatic Union". At best it is a name for that hidden mystery in which the practical truth of our conceptions of Christ is founded.

We may illustrate it from psychology which gives us cases of so-called divided personality, but which are rather cases of double nature in the same personality—cases where two complete and separate systems of knitted memories, ideas, feelings, habits, passions, are developed in the same person who may be, but often is not aware of this doubleness of nature, mind and will. Or, with the Athanasian Creed, we may illustrate it from the normal union of soul and body— of two substances in one person. Or we may illustrate it from the ethical side of personality as an absolute and unique subjection of the created will to the Divine, destroying every vestige of "otherness" and passing beyond all other finite sanctity, *in aliud genus*, making the sacred humanity not merely a separable instrument but a living inseparable organ of the Divine will. Taken as defective metaphors these comparisons are helpful; taken as more than this, they are false and misleading. What they point to lies beyond the range of our mental vision for ever, since it demands a comprehension of the Infinite.

Ibid., pp. *147–163*

4. Belief and Historical Fact

Christianity is an historical religion; that is to say, it proposes certain historical facts, no less than theoretical statements, for our belief; and as these latter have to be reconciled with the philosophy of our understanding—with our world-theory, so the former have to be reconciled with our reading of history. Jesus Christ is not a purely ideal creation like King Arthur, but an historical personage; he has a place, not only in the world of thought, but also in the world of fact. Our construction of either world must find room for him. In and through him the ideal has been realized, the Word has been made flesh and has dwelt among us.

As a mere dream of the religious sense the gospel might have been a divinely inspired work of great spiritual fruitfulness, like the *Divina Commedia* or the *Pilgrim's Progress;* it might have conveyed a true God-given revelation of the absolute order in the clothing of analogy; it might have possessed a regulative and practical truth as a guide to life, as a way of taking things. Many who hold it to be no more than a dream, freely admit that it has been thus beneficent; but they must also allow that it has been beneficent to a great extent just because it was held to be solid fact and not simple dream-stuff.

Between the inward and the outward, between the world of reality and the world of appearances, the relation is not merely one of symbolic correspondence. The distinction that is demanded by the dualism of our mind does not exclude, but implies and presupposes, a causal and dynamic unity of the two. Our view of the value of the outward world should be "sacramental" rather than "sacramentarian", that is, we should look upon it as being an effectual symbol of the inward, in consequence of its natural and causal connection therewith; and not merely as signifying truths to our intelligence, which can become effectual only through the subsequent action of our will.

If certain beliefs are universally fruitful of spiritual progress it is, as we have said, because they are rooted in fact, and possess at least an analogous representative value; it is because through them we are put into relation with reality. And this relation is one of action and reaction; of giving and taking, taking and giving. The beliefs are not arbitrary, like algebraic symbols, but are, like our sense-perceptions, the natural response of our mind to the influence of its surroundings. We are passive before we are active; we receive impressions before we attempt to imagine their causes and laws; or to govern our action in the light of such imaginings. Thus by experience we feel our way to more and more adequate conceptions of the world we live in. It is because God's influence in us or upon us is from the first that of a father, that we at last come to believe in his fatherhood; but the belief makes him more effectually a father than ever; just as every truer hypothesis about Nature multiplies our communication with Nature and leads to fuller knowledge and power.

Hence the belief is sacramental; it not merely signifies the relation of which it is the natural issue or evidence, but it also effects and deepens that relation. There can therefore be no ultimate conflict between what is true for the religious life and what is true for the understanding —philosophical or historical. In the measure that a creed has regulative and practical truth, it is also representative, however mysteriously, of the same world which our understanding strives to reconstruct from the data and in terms of outward experience. That the two reconstructions, using different and partial data and proceeding by such diverse methods, should often disagree both negatively and positively, is only natural. The criterion of faith (taken widely) is simply the practical one of proved universal religious value, "Quod semper", etc. The believer is justified in showing that philosophical and historical reasoning tallies with, or does not contradict his belief, but in this he plays the role not of believer but of philosopher or historian. Further, in case of conflict, he is justified in preferring to hold on to an otherwise rationally indefensible belief until its religious value is accounted for and saved in some higher truth.

Thus a Unitarian might deny the Trinity until he were persuaded that the Unity of God was saved and transcended in that doctrine; or the Incarnation, until he were convinced that it was compatible with the Divine immutability. Faith will never allow him to deny a belief of proved religious value.

As our philosophy is a putting-together of all experience, past as well as present, with a view to understanding this world as it is, and dealing with it rightly, so too our creed is based largely on the data of history, on what has happened to us personally, and to our race from the beginning, in regard to our spiritual life and our dealings with God. There, more especially, though also in every other section of experience, the Ideal has been slowly realizing itself, the Word has been embodying itself. Religion is not a dream, but an enacted, self-expression of the spiritual world—a parable uttered, however haltingly, in the language of fact. It is not an arbitrary working hypothesis shaped at one stroke by some comprehensive genius, but a construction that has been forced upon us and verified by our experience, step by step, and part by part. Hence it is, that certain concrete historical facts enter into our creed as matters of faith. Precisely as historical facts they concern the historian and must be criticized by his methods. But as matters of faith they must be determined by the criterion of faith, *i.e.* by their proved religious values as universally effectual of spiritual progress; as implications of the spirit of Christian charity and sanctity; as selected by the exigencies of the development of the inner life of the soul. The unity of all experience forbids any ultimate contradiction between the results of these separate criteria; but it does not exclude the possibility of superficial and temporary contradictions. The believer will desire and endeavour to play the part of historian and to harmonize every seeming discord, often with more zeal than discretion or ingenuousness. But he will always be justified in holding to the faith-taught facts until he is convinced that their religious value is in no way imperilled by the results of historical criticism.

Our reading of history is in some sort a "perception"; that is to say, from certain points, hints and suggestions which are all that is really given us, we construct what we call an "object", but what is more truly "pro-ject", inasmuch as nine-tenths of what we imagine ourselves to see is thrown out into the object by our own fancies, memories, expectations, inferences, associations—just as in a dim light we shape every shadow according to our fears. Taken as a whole, the Christian reading of history, the religious interpretation of the aforesaid points, hints and suggestions will frequently differ from the readings inspired by other and counter interests. In many matters it has had to yield to historical criticism and may yet have to yield; but of its substantial justness, faith can have no doubt; nor can it have any doubt even as to details which are essentially bound up with any indispensable religious value. Such facts, however, faith holds by their religious, not by their historical, side. To believe that Christ was crucified under Pontius Pilate, or even that he rose from the dead and ascended into Heaven, may need as little faith as to believe that Wellington won the battle of Waterloo. Faith holds to these facts as fruitful of eternal life, and on purely conscientious and religious grounds; *Lex orandi, lex credendi*—the rule of prayer is the rule of belief.

Ibid., pp. *164–171*

THE NATURE OF CHRISTIAN DOCTRINE

Doctrines and dogmas belong to the understanding. The understanding is before all else an instrument of life and action. In its lowest form life consists in response, by way of selective self-adaptation, to the impression of the moment. Next, memory and association make it possible in various degrees, by a *semblance* of inference, to pass from the near and present to the distant and future. The present impression now calls up to mind those past sequences and groupings with which it is associated; and, just so far as Nature is uniform, such memories, clustering round the immediate impression, give a wider outlook, by means of which action can be adapted to a wider world than what is given us in that immediate impression. The thieving cat perceives not only the milk, but the chastisement which followed the theft on some previous occasion, and acts now on a wider view of the world than formerly.

But the aid which mere memory thus affords to our limited outlook is very fallible, and is itself limited by the range of our past experiences. Aided by the reflex notions of uniformity and law, the understanding enables us to go by inference beyond the range of actual experience, *ad infinitum* so far as uniformity is assumed to be universal; and thus to adapt our action to conditions infinitely distant in time and space. The building up of our understanding is the work of reason, reflecting on observation, and aided by language through which we appropriate the collective understanding of the society into which we are born. This understanding strives to reconstruct mentally that mechanism of Nature with which we have to deal, and which we can use and master just so far as we understand it. So far as Nature is irregular our understanding is of no use to us as a guide; where law fails, inference fails. Though the understanding assumes universal law and regularity of grouping and sequence as the very object of its quest, it can never possibly attain to more than a bare outline of the infinite complexity of the concrete; it will always be to Nature what a pocket-map is to the city of London—a sufficient guide in certain matters for certain practical purposes. The pocket-map will not tell one where the traffic is blocked at any given moment. That men find interest and pleasure in the mere exercise of the understanding for its own sake, does not show that its true natural purpose is other than life and action; any more than the acrobatic art proves that legs and arms were made for contortion. Every faculty in health is exercised with pleasure, and has a sort of life and action apart; but this is wholly subordinate to the total life and action of the entire organism, constituted by the harmonious and orderly functioning of all its members conspiring to a common end. The violent divorce of the understanding from the hierarchy of our spiritual faculties, and its deification as an end in itself, invariably leads to an idle, hair-splitting, cobweb-spinning intellectualism. As an instrument of life, its truth means its trueness to its purpose; its efficiency as a guide to the absent and the future. It can never hope to comprehend the entire mechanism of Nature, short of which its comprehension of any part of the system must be imperfect. But, from the observation of such parts it can make hypotheses of ever-ascending values, according as they unify more and more of the previous irregularities; but as being necessarily an attempt to describe the whole in terms of some part such hypotheses are always inadequate. Yet they have an approximate, a regulative, an equivalent truth; as, for example, when we speak of Nature as a mechanism or an organism or a kingdom.

The proper matter of the understanding, so conceived, is that world of the outer senses common to us all; in which our animal life is lived; which is our medium of intercommunication, the basis of our language and symbolism. So far as spiritual realities need to be discussed and spoken about, so far as they are to regulate our outward action, they must first be understood, *i.e.* they must be represented by some non-spiritual symbol and placed somewhere in the map of our understanding as factors of the space-and-time world; they must enter into that "schematization" of experience by which we guide our speech and conduct. Moreover, so far as the sequences and groupings of our inward religious experiences are regulated by law, and can be brought under control, some construction of the spiritual world in terms of the natural understanding is a necessity of spiritual life—some figurative presentment of (*e.g.*) a kingdom of Heaven which, however speculatively inadequate, will be practically true as a means of guiding our feet into the way of peace. All that ascetical and mystical teaching which is directed to the government of the very inmost movements of the Spirit is of necessity couched in metaphorical language, and offers at best a sort of guidance from analogy. "The kingdom of Heaven is like unto" something which it is not; nay, it is not even strictly a kingdom; what it *is* we cannot understand or say, though we can feel and know.

The doctrinal and dogmatic system of Christianity is the understanding of the mental construction of that spiritual world to which we are related by the life of charity. It is fabricated by the public Christian understanding inspired by the Spirit of Christ; and has the same authority for the individual Christian as the natural life-theory or world-theory, as the history and science, which he inherits together with the language of the society into which he is born. Alone, he might construct some very crude and elementary doctrinal system from the data of his personal religious experiences; but if he is to be more than a wolf-man, he must appropriate the gathered fruits of past generations. Avowedly this construction of the Church's understanding is built on lines laid down by Christ in his doctrine of the Father, the Kingdom, the Messiah. But it has been notoriously expanded step by step with the expansion, explication and development of the Christian spirit. The function of religious doctrine is first of all to fix and embody the inward sentiment begotten of contact with the Divine; to describe it as accurately as it can be described in the language of another world. Sentiments can only be described indirectly by their occasions, causes and effects. Thus the story of the Prodigal Son describes the inward phenomenon of conversion only indirectly, and that by way of analogy—it is a spiritual state somewhat akin to that which would be produced by such circumstances.

To speak of charity or love as a simple homogeneous sentiment, varying only in quantity, is an obvious mistake. Love is exactly specified by its motive and object and is never twice the same; always immeasurably complex.

The Charity of the Christian Spirit, which in Christ was raised to its maximum of enthusiasm, is a love of God and of mankind in God; it is characterized at once by a particular apprehension of the nature of God and of the nature of man, and of their relations to one another both in this life and in the beyond; by the apprehension of a certain supernatural and spiritual system of wills, centred round the Divine will, and destined to a continual expansion and development in comformity therewith. This specifying or characterizing object, from its very nature, is not one that admits of being properly, or otherwise than metaphorically, expressed in terms of the natural understanding. At most, we can say: The sentiment is analogous to that which would be yielded were such and such things true.

The Christian creed even in its most elaborate form is mainly a closer, though indirect and analogous, definition of the Christian spirit. It is, however, more than this. It is also a guide to life as expressed in speech and action. We are to live with reference to a world conceived in these terms, and by so living we shall deepen and develop the spirit of Christian charity. We are not only to speak, but to act, as though the Absolute were a spirit of threefold personality—Father, Son and Spirit; Creator, Redeemer, Sanctifier of mankind. Christ is to be to us, for purposes of life and action, the Son Incarnate, very God of very God; the Host is to be, not the symbol, but the verity of his Body offered in sacrifice on Calvary; Mary, the immaculately conceived and ever-virgin mother; and so of the rest.

But what sort of truth or trueness is this? How does it differ to say: "The host shall be to us *as* the Body of Christ"; and to say: "I shall but symbolize that Body"?

This objection would hold good did we contend that the truths of the creed were *purely* regulative, were mere arbitrary fictions with no relation to ontological reality or to the necessary nature of things. Such pure fictions may suffice to guide the hand of art, but not the hand of Nature. No conception whatsoever of the order of Nature or of the order of Grace can conduce, widely and regularly, to the development of the natural or spiritual life, except in virtue of a certain approximative agreement with ontological reality. Life is the very test and measure of its truth; or, in other words, its practical truth is grounded in its speculative truth. But then, in the case of religious truth, this ontological ground is not to be sought in the empirical and physical order of reality, but in the spiritual and "metempirical", in the realm of the Absolute, beyond Time and Space. There alone it is that the ontological values of these doctrines are to be sought, which err, not as overstatements, but as immeasurably defective understatements of the truth. If the Host is not materially and literally Christ's Body, it is so really and super-really and not merely symbolically; and the practical, regulative and relative truth of this dogma is rooted in its ontological truth—"Eye hath not seen; nor ear heard; nor the heart of man conceived" those inwardly felt truths which the understanding, inspired by the Spirit, presents to our eye and ear and conception.

The Church (*i.e.* institutionized Christianity), as we have said, presents this creed, this body of symbolized eternal realities, to the mind and understanding of her children as a means of waking, forming, and educating in them that same Spirit which gave birth to these conceptions. But we must not suppose that the revelation was given to her from heaven in the same way as she gives it to us—as it were, from an external teacher. If man could not begin to live till he was presented with a map of Nature, he could not live at all. It is by living that he is enabled to construct such a map for himself. So too the Christian creed is the fruit of the Christian life as lived first by Christ, subsequently by the Church; it was he who gave it its first mental expression and embodiment in the doctrine of the kingdom of God; and upon that basis the rest has been slowly built up by the Church under the dumb guidance of the Spirit. "Dumb", because it is analogous to the guidance by which the fire leads a blind man towards itself through his experience of greater or lesser warmth; or to the manner in which the roots of a tree are guided to the water. No modification of doctrine that is not life-giving, that does not foster and develop charity, can survive; it lacks the truth or trueness of correspondence to the Spirit of Christ.

"There is a double truth in religious doctrine as in poetry, which in this respect resembles religion in that it uses certain truths of history or science, in order through them to communicate certain affections and will-movements. What is historically false may be poetically true; though, in certain cases the truth of the fact is a condition of the poetical truth; nor will fiction always serve as well as fact. In the case of religion, which regulates our relations with the will-world, and does not rest in solitary unrelated feelings and emotions, indifference to fact is not tolerable, except in the sense that religious value can never be so tied to any accidental error as to perish by the discovery of the truth, which must always be eventually a gain to religion, whereas it may often be a loss to poetry. That texture of philosophical, scientific and historical beliefs, in which the religious sentiment of Christianity has embodied itself by a process of inspiration, claims to be in harmony with the rest of human knowledge, of which it is but a part, and, so far, to be true with the truth of the understanding; but its religious truth lies in 'the Spirit that quickeneth', in its fidelity to the facts of the will-world, compared with which 'the flesh', the merely mental value, 'profiteth nothing'. From every new ingathering of knowledge the same Spirit can weave itself a living garment of flesh, not less but more pliant to its purpose of self-manifestation than all previous garments. Hence, the religiously important criticism to be applied to disputed points of Catholic belief, whether historical, philosophic, or scientific, is not that which interests the historian, philosopher, or scientist; but that which is supplied by the Spirit of Christ, the *Spiritus qui vivificat*. Is the belief in accord with, and a development of, the Spirit of the gospel? What is its religious value? Does it make for the love of God and man? Does it show us the Father and reveal to us our sonship?

In saying that the great end of religious dogma and doctrine is the revelation and communication of the Spirit; or the figuring-forth of ontological realities that belong to the eternal order of being, and are but shadowed in the world of time and space, we do not mean that these doctrines are of such stuff as dreams are made of.

True, even men's dreams and purely poetic creations are shaped by the Spirit that is within them. Christ, in common with all religious teachers, embodied much of his Spirit in what was avowedly parable and fiction. The Church deals extensively in symbolism as an instrument of spiritual formation and instruction. To a large extent it is indifferent whether a principle be illustrated by a fact or a fancy. Who cares or need care whether the story of the rich Man and Lazarus, or the story of Job be history or fiction? The religious truth which the Spirit utters in both cases has to do solely with the nature of God, the nature of man, and their relations to one another. Apply this criterion steadily to much in the way of doctrine that is supposed to be vital simply as history, or as science, or as physical fact, and it will be clear that we should have as little right to resent the denial of the empirical side of those doctrines, as we should have to feel that we had been basely deceived on discovering that the story of the Samaritan was a mere fabrication.

But a man's spirit not only determines his dreams and voluntary fictions and is revealed in them; it also largely controls the building up of his mind and understanding, whence its character may as surely be inferred. Fallible as man is in his quest of truth, he has no wish to fail when he endeavours to put history together, or to construct some system of science, philosophy, ethics or theology. The inevitable minglings of false with true in his results are involuntary, and he labours incessantly to purge out the dross and to approximate towards the unattainable goal of perfect truth. In this labour he is largely guided by some ruling idea, principle or spirit which exercises a stimulating, selective influence in his use of the material from which he builds. For, as has been said, the understanding is an instrument of life and is fashioned to those ends to which life is directed. Men do not care to know, nay, they do not and cannot even see, what *in no way* affects them or can affect them.

There is then a double truth to be noticed in all this work of a man's understanding, so far as it is determined and inspired by his spirit—(1) its correspondence to the facts and laws of the world to which it professes to be a practical guide; (2) its correspondence to the character of his own spirit. Under the first aspect it may be more or less false, and yet perfectly true under the second. Thus a man's ethical system, his code of right and wrong, may be most faithfully determined by his hedonism, or his altruism, or his idealism, or his patriotism. But his judgment as to the sort of conduct which subserves these ends will be faulty in a thousand matters. His system is true to his spirit, but not altogether true to facts; true as a revelation of himself, not as a revelation of the world.

Christianity as a doctrinal system, as a construction of the understanding, is a selection not of poetical, but of theological, philosophical, ethical, scientific and historical beliefs and conceptions, shaped and inspired by the Spirit of Christ. As such it has a double truth—its truth to the world of man's outer experience; its truth to the Spirit of Christ and to the order of eternal realities of which that Spirit is the product. Under the former aspect, it is a necessarily fallible approximation to natural truth; under the latter, it is an infallible approximation to supernatural and eternal truth. We must therefore distinguish the form from the matter, the principle of selection from the material selected. The Spirit of Christ seizes from the chaos of current beliefs— theological, ethical, historical—those that are most appropriate for its own embodiment and progressive expression, and weaves them into a garment adapted to the present stage of its own growth. If the choice and the weaving is its own, the matter chosen is the work of fallible man in his quest for truth. It is in the former, in the choice and the weaving, that the product of inspiration is to be sought; and not in the "beggarly elements" of man's devising; in the heavenly treasure, and not in the earthen vessel—*Spiritus est qui vivificat, caro non prodest quidquam*. If, therefore, in any point of philosophy, history or science, the traditional Christian belief should prove, as it so often has proved, mistaken, it matters as little as the discovery that Dives and Lazarus never existed; it is not *ad rem*. It only means that the revelation has been recorded in blue ink rather than in red or black. We can know God only as he reveals himself, not as he *is;* he was not much more disguised in the anthropomorphic theophanies of the Old Testament, when he walked and talked with Adam in the cool of the evening, than he is in every theological conception of our understanding, even the most spiritual and expurgated. That he should present himself to us as three persons in one nature is not more strange than that he should present himself as a person at all; and can only scandalize those who fancy that their conception of him as a personal Spirit has an adequate ontological, and not merely an equivalent practical truth. And the like is to be said of all particular beliefs of the creed wherein the Christian dogma of the Trinity is expanded, and which serve to fix, characterize and develop more fully the Spirit of Divine charity by which they have been inspired and shaped. In the measure that we live in the light of these doctrines of the Trinity, the Incarnation, the Atonement, the Virgin Birth, the Resurrection and Ascension, Heaven and Hell, Angels and Devils, the Church, the Sacraments, the Communion of Saints—we shall be brought into closer spiritual harmony with the "Absolute" which reveals itself to us in these forms through and in the mind of the Christian Church, stimulated and guided in its selection of beliefs by the Spirit of Christ. In no fuller way can God reveal himself than in man's thoughts about God, in man's reflections on the nature and meaning of the Spirit that strives with his own. No voice from the clouds 'mid the thunders of Sinai could win credence till submitted to that inward tribunal of the secret conscience.

The Church and the Future, pp. 80–91

DOGMA AND DEVELOPMENT

(i)

It may be urged against the whole theory of *Lex Orandi* (the theory, namely, of devotion as the determinant of dogma, of spiritual need as the guide of religious truth) that, as a fact, the greater part of Catholic dogma has been shaped by the results of theological curiosity, by the controversies of the philosophers and schoolmen; by anything rather than by the pure interests of inward religion. A partial answer is found in the contention that much of this intellectual construction is apologetic and defensive, a reply to the attacks or philosophical and historical criticism upon beliefs shaped originally by the exigencies of spiritual life. We may question the wisdom of meeting intellectual curiosity on its own ground, instead of taking refuge on the higher plane of the distinction between religious values and their historical and philosophical embodiment, still it is right to hold as much of the said embodiment as will bear the test of criticism, and not to yield to every wind of doctrine. Though primarily interested in religious truth, yet religion is also interested in all truths; more especially in those most intimately connected with her own, as being their contingent and actual, if not absolutely necessary, embodiment.

But a fuller answer is found in the fact that a sentiment or instinct is not directly creative or "revelatory" of the truth by which it is explained or justified, but is only selective of materials that are offered to it, choosing this or that somewhat blindly, according as it is felt to be more congenial, more approximate to the required truth, more satisfying to the soul's desire of what the world should prove to be. For every sentiment seeks and gropes after a certain environment, and (so far as it is a normal and universal sentiment) is warrant for the existence of such an environment. Though not itself inventive, yet the religious sentiment puts our inventive imagination and reason into play, with a success conditioned by the purity and intensity of the sentiment, on the one side, and, on the other, by the native vigour and the cultivation of the said faculties of invention and hypothesis. Such invention, though *a priori*, is not, like the romancing of the love-sick, merely poetical, but rather consists in a re-arrangement of the world

K

in accordance with desire; and yet in such a way as not to conflict with established and accepted truth, but simply to interpret doubts and uncertainties in a manner favourable to our hopes and longings. This power of inventive re-arrangement we observe in all great religious geniuses, whether affecting their reading of history or their interpretation of life and nature. Unchecked by a sense of the rights of criticism it often works havoc in the mind, and produces fruit of little or no permanent value to religion. Duly controlled by the critical conscience it is the chief instrument of theological progress, of those epoch-making, harmonizing hypotheses, which are hardly distinguishable from revelations except as the laboured products of talent are from the sudden inspirations of genius.

That the leading ideas of Catholic dogma, the ground-plan of its construction of the supernatural world, have been more or less consciously divined by the inventive faculty, inspired by the Spirit of Christian Love, must be allowed.

But there are other contributions in regard to which the functions of the Spirit have been purely selective, and which have been supplied by non-religious interests, good, bad and indifferent. Not to speak of that purely intellectual, theological curiosity and inquiry, which is often most active in the least reverent, which kindles a controversial ardour that is so falsely confounded with zeal for the truth, and which we may call the scholastic spirit, there are the religious notions and traditions already to hand when Christianity first comes on the scene; and there are the historical, scientific and philosophical convictions of each age and locality, with which Christianity must come to terms as far as possible, weaving such material into the texture of its teaching; and there are, alas! beliefs that have been suggested and fostered by unworthy motives, by the desire of temporal gain, or of spiritual ascendancy, or by superstitious fear, or selfishness—beliefs that represent the spiritual weakness or deadness of the numerical majority. Over all these the Holy Spirit exercises a selective criticism; for there is no inherent connection between the religious interest and those by which they have been dictated. Their origin has nothing to do with their truth. He who digs for lead may turn up gold, and truth often drops from lying lips. Of such beliefs it may be said: "Every plant that my Father hath not planted shall be uprooted"; it will wither away because it has not much root; or, in other words, because it will not endure the test of the collective experience of succeeding generations of the faithful, by which alone its religious serviceableness (and, by consequence, its fundamental truth) can be demonstrated.

(ii)

The public mind, sentiment, custom, morality, of a people or society, is an educational instrument and standard for the individual mind, which must be formed upon it and characterized by it in order to be capable of any critical reflection by which the said public standard may be improved and developed. Though fixed, relatively to the individual, the public mind is slowly progressive from generation to generation, through those accumulated criticisms and amendments of individuals, which have succeeded in approving themselves to the general sense. We may distinguish in the public mind a *formed* part which constitutes its bulk and mass, and a part in process of formation; a margin of uppermost surface of soft sensitive pliant matter, which will be the hard dead matter of the next generation, and whose formation is the task of the present generation. And in this task they have a responsibility to the past and to the future, which must limit and guide their work if they are not to break loose from the process which constitutes the life of humanity, and to apply the fallacy of crude individualism to one generation in relation to the multitude of its predecessors and successors. For as each man receives freely from his fellows, and must freely give, so too each generation, as it lives *from* the past, must live *for* the future; none is primarily *for* itself, but each one is part of a wider universal self, which lives in and through it.

To acknowledge an organic continuity between the succeeding generations, to recognize the whole process as the gradual unfolding and self-embodiment of one and the same Spirit, will save us from the fanaticism of that pseudo-revolution which would wipe out the past as wholly worthless, and bid us begin afresh at the very beginning—a behest that we simply could not obey if we would, since our whole mind and sentiment, however revolutionary, is shaped by our past. So far as there is some blind implicit justice at the root of the revolutionary sentiment, and so far as the revolution is proved to be healthy, fruitful, and enduring, it is simply because some deeper law of the process of social growth, long neglected or perverted to the hurt of orderly development, at last makes itself painfully felt in the general subconsciousness; it is because the community is sick and disordered in consequence of past irregularities, and must now go back upon that past, critically, till it finds the point of deviation; must destroy and reconstruct just so much and no more as is needful for its perfect recuperation.

It is no "propriety" of the past that it should be a complex tangle of false and true, evil and good, weakness and strength; the present and the future are subject to the same necessity. Of all men and movements Reformers and Reformations are the most one-sided, over-emphasis and under-emphasis being essential to their corrective influence, and being, moreover, the secret of their uncritical self-complacency, of their conviction that the present is all right and the past all wrong and the future all radiant. *Sicut erat in principio et nunc et semper*—man's nature, like God's, is unchanging; for ever, though in lessening proportion, false will mingle with its true, evil with its good, not merely intermixed as tares with wheat, but permeating and combined in a third nature or substance, that is neither one nor the other wholly.

I cannot, then, repudiate wholly, or wholly in any element, that life of the past—physical, mental, moral, social, religious—out of which I have grown; through and in which I have lived. I cannot, because in some particular I have carried on the process further or corrected its deviations here and there, forget that I, who judge it, and the principles by which I judge it, are its product and outcome, through which, rather, it judges, reforms and heals itself. In the measure, however, that the process becomes more deeply and fundamentally self-conscious in me or in my contemporaries; in the measure, that is, that we apprehend better the idea and law of human progress, we shall necessarily *appear* more radical in our criticism, *being* all the while more conservative, more strongly assertive of the oldest laws and constitutions of our general life.

Thus the only solid reformation of our religious conceptions and belief is to be sought, not in some brand-new "thinking-out" of the questions of God and the soul, without any respect whatsoever to the confessedly false and inadequate conceptions of the past, as though such attempts did not, even by their very crudities, testify to the existence and nature of the experience they strove to formulate.

Rather, we must recognize religion as one of the great constituents of this self-evolving life of humanity; as a sort of life that unfolds itself, like an organism, from age to age, that exhibits an immense variety of species and genera in different times and places, in all of which, collectively, its potentiality is progressively disclosed. It is only from such a study that we can hope to go on approximating, though never attaining, to an adequate conception of the nature of religion and of its implications about God and the soul; and, by means of such conceptions, to classify, to criticize fruitfully, to distinguish the higher from the lower, the normal from the abnormal and the morbid. It is in this general life, stretching like a spiritual vegetation over the whole earth, and from the dark past into the light of today, that we are to look for that wider revelation of God, in which the Christian revelation is included as central and supreme.

To bring all this scattered experience to one focus, to determine its meaning, to organize and control it in the light of a better understanding of its nature, is the result of social development viewed on its religious side. The religious, like every other element of human life —the physical, intellectual, moral, and political—gains indefinitely by that co-operation and division of labour whereby the experience of millions is heaped together, sorted and unified to the profit of each, and becomes a capital at the disposal of every one who chooses to appropriate it. In claiming to be Catholic and universal, the Christian Church has only claimed an ideal for religion which belongs to every element of man's life. The ideal science and morality and polity must be in some sense as catholic and universal as human nature itself—one with the unity-in-variety of an organism, not with the uniformity of a regiment.

(iii)

It is important to remember Kierkegaard's insistence on the great difference between spiritual and physiological development, which Newman and his school are too little conscious of. The former is self-wrought, the latter passively undergone; the former creative, the latter merely explicative. The organism is potentially at the beginning what it is actually at the end; its "idea" is present from the first, and shapes it to a vehicle of self-expression. Not so the character of a man or a nation. No two minds or moralities are alike. Each is absolutely original; self-built, according to a series of self-chosen plans. I gather wild flowers as I go along, and arrange them each moment, according to what I have got in hand, in some sort of harmonious unity. I gather more, and forthwith I break up the unity in favour of another more inclusive arrangement, which takes in all the old materials in new relations. The final arrangement is not implied in or exacted by the first. It is not a process of passive unfolding, but of active reconstruction. So it is with our gathering experience, of which the later additions are no way involved in the earlier. Every moment we unmake our world and build it anew. And this holds of the collective as of the individual spirit life; of the Church as well as of the Nation. What we have to look to is that in our hasty reconstruction we do not simplify by casting out and forgetting those elements of our past that will not fit in easily with our new synthesis; but rather gather up the fragments that remain, so that nothing be lost. We are all disposed to forget the disagreeable.

The "law" of spiritual development is a freely chosen path to good —one of many; that of organic development is a fixed path to a fixed form or determination of good; my bodily future is predictable, not my spiritual future. Who knows how a child will "turn out"?

Essays on Faith and Immortality
(ed. M. D. Petre), pp. *119–127*

CATHOLICISM

(i)

One of the results of the comparative study of religions has been to convince us that religion is just as necessary and universal a factor of general culture and civilization as language is; that it is "natural" to man in just the same sense. Like language or the arts of life, in all its infinite varieties and degrees of development, it is governed by one and the same end, and by certain generally uniform characteristics and methods. Gradually the genealogical tree, in which the parentage of religions each and all may be traced, is advancing towards completion, and shows us that the religious process is but an integral part of the great historical process of human civilization and development.

This conception confirms rather than denies the Catholic tenet of the Logos, which gives light to every man coming into this world, not one of whom is left without sufficient means of salvation. And since that light, at once transcendent and immanent, at once above and within Nature, guides all men to one and the same supernatural end, it is plain that the process is at once, and without contradiction, natural and supernatural.

As little as one civilization is as good as another, though all civilizations aim at the utmost plenitude of life; so little is one religion as good as another, though all religions aim at the same plenitude of truth and righteousness and of communion with the Divine. They differ infinitely in their methods and in the degree of their actual attainment. Nor is it the difference between the babe, the boy, the youth, and the man; for spiritual development is not like organic development—as has been already explained. The need they would satisfy, the end they would serve is the same; but it is understood with different degrees of truth and explicitness; and the means are determined partly by chance conditions, partly by free choice.

Yet in spite of this the religious process is one; and the unity of the need and of the end on one hand, and the unity of the human spirit on the other, secure a certain uniformity characterizing all religions; rendering the definition of "a religion" possible, however difficult, and making it practically easy to recognize a religion as such when we see it.

Now Catholicism with its priesthood, its sacraments, its ritual, its dogmas, its tradition, and all their uses and abuses is plainly a "natural" religion in the same sense as Judaism, Christ's own religion, was. It as plainly takes its place as a member in the universal family of religions, and presents the unmistakable family features. It is as evidently a product of the same general process by which God is bringing man into conscious relationship with himself.

Now one of the reasons for trusting Catholicism is because it is in this sense "natural"; because it is a growth, a part of a larger growth— *Nascitur non fit*. Its conformity to the psychological laws that govern the growth of religion everywhere proves it to be a product of those laws, which after all are God's laws. So far it is from God, and not, like thought-out systems, from man. There is a huge presumption in favour of what is "natural". Its adaptation to human nature in its entirety, to every factor of man's being, to every level of his culture, proves the Church's divinity—not as their proximity to rivers proves God's miraculous care for the needs of great cities, but as what is natural, in the adequate sense, is thereby proved to be Divine. A true religion is a growth and not a manufacture. The so-called founders of new religions have one and all sprung from old religions, which they have but modified and stamped with their individuality. They have been reformers, not creators. What seems the most original and independent religious experience of the solitary mystic has invariably some historical religion behind it, of which it is the unconscious product. Our seemingly simplest ideas and words have been elaborated by generations of organized human life. Revolutions have their own place, not in organic, but in spiritual developments, and do not break continuity. As little could one man create a new religion as a new language. A Chaucer, a Shakespeare, a Dante may at most inaugurate a new philological epoch.

But the true revolution must be wholly constructive; destructive only of what is destructive. It must take up in a higher synthesis all the truth and experience of the old system. It must obey, and not defy, the natural law of its development. Else continuity is broken. For reasons that may presently appear it seems to us Catholics that the Protestant synthesis is too crude and hasty a simplification in many ways, too artificial and reflex, that it has so far broken itself off in several respects from the natural religious process and suffered grave impoverishment.

On the other hand, what is so often used as a reproach against Catholicism—its various affinities with non-Christian religions, with Judaism, and Graeco-Roman, and Egyptian paganism, and all their tributaries—seems to us one of its principal glories and commendations. We like to feel the sap of this great tree of life in our veins welling up from the hidden roots of humanity. To feel so, to possess this sense of solidarity with all the religions of the world; to acknowledge that they are all lit, however dimly, by the same Logos-light which struggles, unconquered, with even their thickest darkness—this is to be a Catholic; this is to rise above exclusiveness and sectarianism, without in any wise falling into indifferentism; this is to be his disciple who, believing salvation to be of the Jews, found such faith in the Samaritan and the Gentile as he found not in Israel.

To have thus recognized the "natural" character of religion and of Christianity and of Catholicism is no novelty, but only an "explicitation" of the thought of the greater prophets, of Christ, of St Paul, of Tertullian, of Origen, of Clement of Alexandria—a thought which had to struggle long with opposing tendencies, traditional opinions and sentiments that have only gradually yielded and made way for its full manifestation in these latter days.

I am not concerned to defend this conception of Catholicism as a natural and therefore a Divine religion against those friends or foes of the Church who, using the term "natural" in a now unintelligible and obsolete sense, choose to stigmatize the view as rationalistic, naturalistic. I am only stating a consideration which, rightly or wrongly, weighs with certain minds in favour of Catholicism as distinguished from more artificial and reasoned-out syntheses—the products of man's freedom, rather than of God working, through the universal laws of man's nature.

(ii)

Allied with and dependent on this consideration there are others. Catholicism is characterized by a certain irrationality, incoherence, and irregularity—a certain irreducibleness to exact and systematic expression—which, far from being scandalous, is another presumption in its favour. As an illustration we might point to its Breviary or its Ritual—manifestly composite works—wrought at different times by hands guided in no two cases by quite the same ideas and principles, or by an adequate grasp of the exact meaning of preceding efforts. To criticize the result as guided by one steadfast aim and rule, to ask why this and why that, is to seek for a consistency that does not and could not exist in a product of spiritual development, whose regularity must be continually broken up by the accumulation of fresh experience, to be reconstituted by a new constructive effort. Catholicism as a religion of the people must in its growth betray the same sort of irregularities as the other co-factors of civilization, as language or social custom or traditional political institutions. It requires two principles for its development; one, a principle of wild luxuriance, of spontaneous expansion and variation in every direction; the other, a principle of order, restraint, and unification, in conflict with the former, often overwhelmed by its task, always more or less in arrears. The tangle and undergrowth of the forest is always more than the woodmen can cope with. The growth and fertility is not from them, but from God through Nature. They by taking thought can but secure the conditions of Nature's free play and fullest fruitfulness. By understanding and obeying her laws, art and cultivation can win her richer favours. Were they to fail wholly or in part, the forest would not forthwith disappear, but would at worst return to its primitive wildness. Thus its very wildnesses and barbarisms point to the natural character of Catholicism, and distinguish it from all planned-out philosophical religions, whose over-trimness is an indication of their poverty and exhaustion; for nothing that lives and grows can keep its shape long. Its durableness is therefore not dependent merely on the wisdom of its theologians, or the prudence of its officers, or this or that theory of its essence, or this or that form of its organization. As long as a fibre of its roots remains anywhere, it is capable of renewing itself and spreading abroad over the face of the earth. It has the durability and indestructibleness of the natural as against the transitoriness of the artificial. Because it is a natural religion Catholicism is full of compromises. In all the opposing elements of its syncretism there is a part-truth to which the religious spirit clings in spite of logic, and wisely. For a *syncretism*, a more or less violent forcing together of incompatibles, is the preliminary stage of an harmonious *synthesis* which can never be finally and fully realized just because new elements are ever coming in. Ground one against the other the fragments lose their angles in time, and approximate to coherence and continuity. Art can compel a premature and poorer unification by throwing out this or that recalcitrant member of the various antitheses; but God in Nature works slowly and surely through the unimpeded struggle of opposites.

Now it would be paradoxical to say that the greater incoherence of Catholicism were without more ado an argument in its favour; or that the mere completeness and tidiness of other systems were fatal to their claims. Nature is orderly; chaos is incoherent and not Divine. But when the order is suggested by experience and waits on experience it can never be finished and logically satisfactory; when it is complete and logical it means that irreducible tracts of experience have been artificially excluded from the synthesis.

True, the Anglican reproaches Roman Catholicism precisely because of its logical and artificial unity, and uses the above argument in his own favour. But first of all, minor controversies apart, Anglicanism is far more of the Catholic than of the Protestant type, and belongs to the same tradition more or less. Secondly, the objection identifies Roman Catholicism with its present dominant theological system, or its present ecclesiastical polity. These are but examples of the incoherence in question; parts of the whole, factors in the syncretism, elements at war with other elements; not to be thrown out but reduced and penetrated by the vital principle of Catholicism. Their persistence must be explained, their essential values must be saved, before their husks are discarded.

(iii)

Again; viewing religion as a natural process, as a factor in the general process of man's rational and spiritual development, it seems to us that in Catholic Christianity that process attains, not indeed to an impossible finality, but to a crisis that begins a new epoch. For in it the mystical process and the "moral" process (understanding "moral" widely, as including the "ought" of intellect, feeling, and will) run into one and recognize their former separateness as merely the result of imperfect enlightenment. The mystical need of conscious communion and self-adjustment with the super-sensible and superhuman world, to which the sensible and human world is felt to be subordinate, seems distinct from the "moral" need until the character of the superhuman order is realized as "moral", and till the voice of conscience —moral, intellectual, and aesthetic—is accepted as the Voice of God. Nor till then is it felt that obedience to every sort of conscience puts man in harmony with the universe of being, and is the very essence and inwardness of religious worship and sacrifice. Of the two, the religious interpretation of "morality" is a greater gain for mankind than the "moral" interpretation of religion. It is more important that the "moral" life should gain a mystical height and supernatural sanction as a life of union with the eternal and universal principle of all being than that the religious life should be, at once, levelled up and flattened down to the plane of "moral" symbolism. In Catholicism, conscience—moral, intellectual, and aesthetic—is raised to the throne of God, and worshipped with all that religion has ever offered in honour of its divinities. The whole system, centred round the crucifix, invests such "morality" with the awe and reverence due to the mysterious all-pervading, all-sustaining Will of the Eternal.

Here, then, it seems to us that the rationalizing anti-mystical tendencies of many other Christian bodies are impoverishing, both in their narrowed conception of morality as merely ethical, and in their reduction of religion to morality; and that they overshoot the mark in their revolt against the residues of non-ethical pagan religiousness not yet subdued in the Catholic synthesis. As for systems of independent conduct-morality they have yet to prove their ability to do what the Church has so often done on so large a scale for the masses. The ethical code she enforced was often more barbaric than Christian; yet she did enforce it, and precisely by *giving a mystical and religious depth to ethical requirements*, however crudely understood.

(iv)

Again; it seems to us that Catholicism is, more than other systems, a religion of the whole man, body, soul, and spirit, a religion for every stage of his culture, and not for one only; for every mood of his variability, and not only for the highest; for every sort of man, and not merely for a religious, ethical, intellectual, or social aristocracy; that it enters as an organic part into the whole process of civilization with its multitudinous interests; that it makes us sensible of our solidarity with, and dependence on, the whole of humanity, past, present, and to come; all this, of course, in virtue of principles and ideals to which it has never been wholly faithful or unfaithful, and in spite of discordant elements in the Graeco-Roman paganism over which the Christian leaven can never be fully victorious.

It is a religion of the whole man. A made and thought-out religion is governed by some theoretic and abstract view of man and of the hierarchic order of his faculties and exigencies. Not so, one that is slowly being shaped by the play of man's conflicting requirements over a world-wide area. In Catholicism we find the competing claims of his intellect, his feelings, his heart, his senses asserting themselves more or less discordantly and, as it were, fighting their way towards an unattainable ideal of harmonious agreement. We find mysticism and intellectualism at war; practical and contemplative religion looking askance at one another; externality and inwardness contending for the mastery; the asceticism of John despising the humaneness of Jesus. No interest of man's complex nature has been disregarded or unrepresented in deference to a forced and premature unification.

The modern psychologist, with his deepened knowledge of the subconscious self, of the nature and play of habit, suggestion and automatism, must confess that instinctively and experimentally Catholicism has always acknowledged and utilized these psychological laws and principles, which thought-out syntheses were bound to ignore as long as they were unrecognized by contemporary science. Perhaps nothing is more characteristic of the difference between Catholicism and that sort of scholastic Protestantism which ripened into the cold eighteenth-century deism than the attitude of the two systems towards the subconscious, towards that deep and wide-spreading basis of the visible emergent peak of our clear consciousness. Both accepted the crude definition of man as "a reasoning animal", but while Protestantism applied it to the condemnation of all that was not reason, Catholic experience ignored and belied it.

Thus Catholicism has always known, not theoretically but experimentally, the use and value of suggestion and auto-suggestion in the formation of habits good or evil, religious or otherwise. It has known the need of continually building-up and perfecting a complex mechanism of habit as the condition of a fuller and more fruitful exercise of free conscious action. It has learnt the utility of certain deliberately induced narrowings and concentrations of the field of vision, and of the range of interests, without which nothing great has ever been accomplished, and to which we owe the effectiveness not only of saints and prophets, but of scholars, discoverers, heroes, and conquerors. A psychologically false spirituality, in despising these almost mechanical bases and conditions of free origination, has fallen to the ground through striving to fly without wings. Suggestion, auto-suggestion, and fixed ideas are spiritually indifferent. They guarantee nothing for the truth or falsehood, goodness or badness, of what they impose upon us. But the true and the good must be so imposed on us by ourselves or by our educators; must be worked into the mechanical and automatic basis of our rational life, if they are to fructify and not to be as seed sown by the wayside.

And in the same way, Catholicism has learnt to recognize, allow and provide for the non-religious temperament, and for the religious temperament in its non-religious moods, in its states of mere potentiality, in its rudimentary stages of development. It has learnt that though men ought to, men cannot, pray without ceasing; that in the best of us the Spirit slumbers and sleeps through many of our waking hours; that in most of us its moments of full self-consciousness are few and far between; and that in the dull intervals we are left to the guidance of habits, formed or deepened in those better moments. Catholicism recognizes a certain lower goodness in these semi-conscious, automatic or merely mechanical species of activity, partly as disposing towards, partly as resulting from, intelligent self-chosen acts of goodness. When the mind is barren and feeling is dead, mechanical prayers and religious practices are not so merely and utterly mechanical but that they are also exercises and acts of conscience and freewill—earnests of "the better" we fain would offer if we could, in "the day of small things", when the flax smoulders without flame, and the bruised reed cannot lift itself upright. Catholicism refuses to despise the half because it is not the whole, or to confound little with nothing. In the bare-walled conventicles of pure reason, if the soul cannot do her best she can do nothing. In a Catholic temple she can do her second best or her third. There are altars to visit and candles to light, and beads to finger, and litanies to mutter, and the crucifix to gaze on, and a hundred little occupations not less good because others are so much better, or because abuses are easy and frequent. In short, man is psychological as well as spiritual—mostly the former; and in Catholicism he finds a lower psychological religion ministerial to the higher and spiritual; and this, not designed, or planned, or even quite acknowledged, but shaped by the necessities of humanity in the mass and on the average.

(v)

Similarly, Catholicism stands out as a religion of the whole man against the pedantry of a purely reasonable religion that would abolish the luxuriant—doubtless at times too luxuriant—wealth of symbolism in favour of a "ministry of the word" alone, taking "word" in its baldest literal sense; and that would limit the converse between God and man to what can be uttered in spoken or written language.

Yet all language is poetical in its origin. It tries to express the whole inner state—not merely the truth, but the emotions and feelings in which the truth is embedded; for the so-called "faculties"—mind, will, feeling—have not yet been marked off from one another by abstract thought. It is only later that the utility of exact ideas and corresponding verbal signs leads to prosaic precision, and turns what once were living metaphors into sober measurements. But outside this region of strict usefulness, and wherever man would utter his whole Spirit or receive the whole utterance of another Spirit, the language of poetry becomes indispensable; for inward feelings are not directly communicable, but only suggestible through their outward and natural signs. We know them in ourselves alone; in others we can see but their symptoms. Because religion is of the whole soul and of no single faculty, because it springs immediately from the deep root of our nature, and not from any one of the branches, therefore the converse of man with God, of the finite Spirit with the infinite, must of necessity be in the symbolic language of poetry; for it is the indistinct utterance of all that man knows, feels, and wills about God, and of all that God knows, feels, and wills about man. But not only is all exact lingual expression, but all possible lingual expression, inadequate to such fullness of utterance. In religion as in Nature, God speaks to every sense with a thousand voices, and bids us answer him again, as far as we can, in his own tongue. There is, then, no small pedantry of intellectualism in the notion that worship in Spirit and in truth must necessarily be conducted in circumstances of sought-out plainness, and divested of all appeal to the senses, the imagination, and the emotions; of all sacraments and symbols—a worship which would suffer no more of God's message to enter the soul than can find its way through the narrow slit of common sense, and clothe itself in the stiff primness of colourless prose. Of such worship Christ and his apostles—Jews as they were and lovers of the temple with its soul-stirring symbolism—knew nothing, nor has any religion ever thriven long on such a fallacy of puritanism strictly adhered to. If it has exercised a soul-compelling power over the masses, it is only because it has, in fact, appealed to more than the mere understanding through psalms and hymns, and through a preaching that was impassioned as well as argumentative; that addressed the eye as well as the ear; that spoke by glances, gestures, intonation, and all the symbolism of will and emotion. A strict "rationalizing" of worship would, therefore, mean an infinite impoverishment of the language of religion. One need not deny the advantages of a vernacular liturgy. Yet it may be that the mere "dumb-show" of a high mass, with all its suggestions of mystery, faith, and reverence, speaks more fully and directly to the Spirit of man; does more for the right attuning of his soul, than could the most exquisitely balanced theological discourse on the sacrifice of the altar.

Here, again, it seems to us that the conservative position, as the product of the slowly accumulated experience of multitudes and centuries, has probably more to say for itself than plain common sense can see at a glance or two.

(vi)

Again, under the alluring semblance of simplification and a return to the Spirit of a gospel preached to the poor and unlettered, puritanism seems to us in some way to be vitiated by a false simplicity—a simplicity of impoverishment, not a simplicity of comprehensive unification. God, the theologians say, is infinitely simple, and yet he is the plenitude of every sort of being and perfection. And our evolutionists tell us that the highest type of organism is that in which the greatest multiplicity of structure and function is most perfectly unified. Given equal richness of content, the simpler unity is the better; but not if the simplification be at the expense of content. The tendency of puritanism is to reduce Christianity to its lowest terms; to cast off all that has grown out of, or on to, its primitive expression; to bring it down to the level of the lowest and most universal spiritual capacity; to make it democratic in just what seems to us the wrong and popular sense of the term. For it is to favour one section of the Church at the expense of another; to starve the higher and rarer capacity in the interests of the lower and commoner; to assume that the spiritual equality of God's sons means an equality of gifts and graces; to forget that the Christian *demos* includes and needs every grade and kind of spirituality from the lowest to the highest.

For this reason as well as for its severe rationality puritanism, in spite of its studied abstract simplicity, has always been the religion of a certain class, and a certain temperament, and a certain culture. Whereas Catholicism, in spite of, or rather because of, its vast complexity, has been, as no other, a religion both of the crowds and masses, and also of the intellectual, the cultivated, the mystical, the aesthetic minority.

Seeing the intimate psychological bond that exists between the letter and the spirit, the body and the soul, the outer expression and the inner significance of a religion, we are not fanciful, but thoroughly philosophic in concluding that as a Catholic church (say St Etienne in Paris) is to a puritan conventicle, or as Catholic public worship is to the simplicity of prayer-meeting, so is the Catholic spirit to the puritan—both simple; one with the simplicity of an imperfectly harmonized fullness and multiplicity; the other, with that of an exclusive and rigorous parsimony. It is true that the religion of Christ is the religion of the poor and simple. But popular folk-religions have always been of the Catholic type in their untrimmed luxuriance; whereas Unitarianism, for all its abstract simplicity, has never been popular; and what commends Methodism or Salvationism to the crowd is really their departures from dryness and severity; their concessions to the experienced demands of the non-rational elements of human nature. The religion or Spirit of Christ has the simplicity of a principle of life and growth; but what grows out of it is an organized multitude of beliefs, precepts, observances, and institutions in which its potential fullness and fruitfulness is progressively and endlessly revealed. The Pantheon is at once an exceedingly simple and an exceedingly complex structure, the product of repeated applications of a single law. Complex as Catholicism is, it is governed by a few simple ideas. The whole church of St Etienne, with its altars and furniture, its ritual, its music, its cycle of fasts and feasts, is subordinated to and governed by the figure of the Crucified which surmounts the Tabernacle of his mystical presence. All is but the expansion of the meaning and significance of Christ crucified for humanity. "The Fatherhood of God, the brotherhood of man"—there is Christianity in a nutshell; the very kernel of the gospel. Yes; but Christianity in a nutshell is not enough. If it is to cover the needs of humanity; to spread its branches more widely, century after century; to reveal its latent possibilities; the kernel must be taken out of the nutshell and planted. The inexhaustible plenitude of all truth lies wrapped up in the innocent formula: "The Fatherhood of God, the brotherhood of man". As it stands it is not simple but "mysterious" in the deepest

L

sense. The complex doctrinal system of Catholicism is really an attempt to simplify and explain it.

(vii)

Moreover, we find in such a church as St Etienne the expression, not of an individual, but of a collective Spirit, world-wide and ancient, of which it is the product. Everything there speaks of communion with a great international religious organism; with the remote past of Catholicism; and, through Catholicism, with the past of those older religions out of which it has grown. It is a visualized and sensible expression of the religious experience of the best part of humanity, by means of which the religious sense of the individual is wakened, stimulated, and informed; and his consciousness of solidarity with the general life of mankind deepened and strengthened. Every such renewed consciousness of communion with Catholicism is a sacramental reinforcement of the spiritual and "over-individual" elements of his interior life—an inward grace mediated through an outward sign. It brings the soul into a more or less dimly understood, but sensibly felt, union, not only with the religious life of past centuries, but with the secular history of France, of Europe, of the world. For Catholicism means the leavening of every human interest with the leaven of the gospel, the Christianizing, not merely of the religious process, but of the whole process of civilization—of labour, science, art, of social and political institutions. The life of the Church has not been eremitical and aloof, but tangled—often far too much tangled—in that of the world around it. In her temples we are surrounded by the memorials, not only of saints, but of heroes and warriors and statesmen and poets and philosophers and writers; for these, too, contribute to the multitudinous elements unified in the spirit of Catholicism. To be a Catholic is to be historically related to them, to feel one's kinship with them as children of the same civilization which Catholicism has fostered and impregnated, and of which it has been a constituent factor.

As a complexus of feelings, judgments, and impulses, a "Spirit" necessarily tends to increase in complexity with every moment that brings new experiences to be drawn into its synthesis. Our life-task is one of unification, of building-in these accumulating experiences so skilfully as not to destroy, but rather to perfect the harmony of our multitudinous thoughts, desires, and sentiments. If our religion, our

Christianity, is alive and growing, it must necessarily be ever evolving a complex system of feelings, determined by and determining an equally complex system of judgments, fructifying in a correspondingly complex system of impulses. Simple as is the law of these developments, the product is not simple in content, but inexhaustible beyond all formulation.

And what holds for the individual Spirit, holds still more evidently for the collective Spirit—the Spirit of Catholicism—that resultant of the religious experience of whole nations and centuries, which is presented to us in the institutional Church, and which acts as an instrument of spiritual education in enabling us to feed on and appropriate, according to our several needs and capacities, the gathered riches of so vast and ancient a tradition.

While, then, condemning that superfluity and lavishness which fails to secure a good, or a truth, or a loveliness that may be attained more effectually by fewer and simpler means, we condemn no less heartily that impoverishing puritanism which values such simplicity absolutely, and not merely in proportion to the richness of the result secured. To use a thousand words in expressing what could be said better in a hundred is a sin against simplicity; but it is no less a sin to use a hundred when a thousand are necessary, and to sacrifice content and clearness to brevity. Religion aims at communicating God to man, at filling the soul with the inexhaustible riches of Divine truth and goodness and loveliness. It cannot put the infinite into a nutshell; it cannot put the whole truth into three words. Though it may—and often does—sin against simplicity, both by undue compression and undue diffusiveness, all the language and symbolism at its disposal is not enough for what it has got to convey.

Life on a desert island is simplified—and starved. To find everything for oneself; to be dependent on God alone—that is, on God as outside and transcendent, not as mediated through creation and humanity—means sterility in every department of life, inward and outward. Can religion be an exception? Is it not plain that its possibilities are increased in every dimension through our connection with a close-knit, world-wide, world-old communion?

Through Scylla and Charybdis, or; The New Theology and the Old,
pp. *20–39*

MEDIEVALISM AND MODERNISM

(i)

Medievalism is an absolute, Modernism a relative term. The former will always stand for the same ideas and institutions; the meaning of the latter slides on with the times. If we must have a sect-name, we might have a worse than one that stands for life and movement as against stagnation and death; for the Catholicism that is of every age as against the sectarianism that is of one.

A good deal of the force of the Encyclical[1] as an appeal to the Christian sense is due to its ambiguous use of the term Modernist.

It professes to be describing those Roman Catholics who believe in this principle of "Modernism", and who are confident that a synthesis between faith and the established results of criticism is possible without damage to either. But, in fact, it describes as Modernists those Catholics also who possess no such confidence; who consider that criticism is fatal to Catholicism and to its principal beliefs and institutions, who ridicule such syntheses as utopian, and who, in many cases, are among the most active opponents—official or unofficial—of "Modernism". In short, it describes as "Modernists" all those professed Roman Catholics who accept the results of criticism, however those results may tell upon their faith, whether disastrously or otherwise. Thus it cleverly lays every "Modernist" open to the suspicion of being an unitarian or an atheist or an agnostic; it brands them all alike as hypocrites and pretenders. Unfortunately there are, and there always have been, such men in the Church even on the Chair of Peter; and that, long before the days of criticism. Scepticism is not modern, nor is atheism, nor hypocrisy. Let us, then, keep the word "Modernist" to designate those who believe in the Roman Catholic Church as firmly as medievalists do; but whose deeper faith is not frightened but stimulated by the assured results of modern criticism. For, as it is belief in the living Christ that makes a Christian, and not any particular Christology, so what makes a Catholic is not this or that abstract theory of the Church, but a belief in the historical Catholic community as the living outgrowth of the apostolic mission. No one who has

[1] *Pascendi Dominici Gregis.* See below, Appendix (i).

lost faith in the mission and destiny of the Roman Church and in the advantage of being identified with it is a Roman Catholic.

To believe in the living historical Catholic community means to believe that by its corporate life and labour it is slowly realizing the ideas and ends in whose service it was founded; that through many fluctuations and errors and deviations and recoveries and reactions it is gradually shaping itself into a more efficient institution for the spiritual and moral development of individuals and societies; that by its continuity and extension it is the collective subject of a vast experience of good and evil, of truth and fallacy, and of a slow but sure process of reflection on the same; that if it advances laboriously and imperceptibly it is because its evolution, like that of nature, is the result of so vast, so costly and even so cruel an experience, and because the contributions of individual effort are opposed tooth and nail until their right to survive and conquer has overcome almost every conceivable objection. One's belief in the Church as the organ of religion is to some extent one's belief in the laws of collective psychology, which are the laws of nature, which are the laws of God. . . .

In this belief in the living organism of the Church, Modernist and Medievalist are at one. They are both Catholics whatever their theoretical analysis of Catholicism; both have a right to be in the Church. As far as one does not believe that the Church is slowly working out an ever truer and more fruitful religion; as far as he views the whole process as barren, idle, unmeaning, "a tale told by an idiot full of sound and fury but signifying nothing", he does not believe in the Church and is not a Catholic.

But the Modernist is a Catholic with a difference. What is this difference?

The difference is that whereas the Medievalist regards the expression of Catholicism, formed by the synthesis between faith and the general culture of the thirteenth century, as primitive and as practically final and exhaustive, the Modernist denies the possibility of such finality and holds that the task is unending just because the process of culture is unending.

Hence the new historico-scientific methods and their results, the new social and political ideas and institutions, being irreconcilable with the medieval synthesis, seem to the Medievalist irreconcilable with what he considers to be the primitive final and perfect expression of

Catholicism. The old synthesis has been perhaps modified at the Councils of Trent and the Vatican; but only along the same lines and categories, and by way of defining more closely its opposition to post-medieval culture. The Modernist is no blind worshipper of present culture. He knows it is a medley of good and evil, and needs careful criticism and discrimination. But he believes that, on the whole, it stands for gain rather than loss; and that its new and true values must be absorbed into the Catholic organism if the latter is to live.

If he believes in the Church as a Catholic, as a man he believes in humanity; he believes in the world. To regard the world outside the Church as God-forsaken; to deny that God works and reveals himself in human history, that he is in and with mankind in all its struggles against evil and ignorance and degradation, that he is the primary author of all intellectual, aesthetic, moral, social, and political progress, seems to the Modernist the most subtle and dangerous form of atheism.

Nay, of the two, his faith in the world is more fundamental than his faith in the Church—in the world of which it is written, "God so loved the world that he gave his only begotten Son". For he who sits at meat is greater than he who serves; and the Church, like her Master, is sent for the service of the world; to serve it, not to rule over it, or trample on it, or despise it. If she has something to teach it, she has much to learn from it. It is the living whole of which she is but an organic part; and the whole is greater than even its most vital organ. The Modernist loves the Church for the sake of the world and humanity which means that he loves humanity more, as the fuller and all-inclusive revelation of God. The Manichean dualism that opposes the Church to the world, as light to darkness, is to him a compendium of many heresies. Any barrier that hinders their free interchange of benefits is impoverishing to both alike. Each must absorb the quickening forces of the other under pain of a monstrous and lop-sided development.

Again, whereas the Medievalist, with his mechanical and static idea of ecclesiastical infallibility, canonizes the entire medieval synthesis indiscriminately; the Modernist, with his dynamical idea of a process that will infallibly work out right in the end; with his conception of our highest truth as ever alloyed with error, of our highest good as ever alloyed with evil, is one who discriminates and qualifies, who distrusts absolutism of every sort.

He does not view the essence of Christianity as consisting of one or two simple principles given from the first and abiding unchanged beneath a bewildering mass of meaningless and mischievous encrustations. Its essence is continually being built up by the expansion and application of these normative principles; by their combination with all that is good and true in the process of human development. It consists not merely in the leaven but in the whole mass that is leavened and Christianized, and that grows in bulk from age to age. So far he agrees with the Medievalist against the Protestant. But he does not believe that the process stopped with the thirteenth century, and is, therefore, truer to the Catholic principle.

For him, however, it is a double process of good and evil; of false and true. He recognizes, what the reformers could not recognize with their dim historical light, that the tares were sown almost contemporaneously with the wheat; and are always being sown; that if the wheat has grown, the tares have also grown even from the Apostolic age—from the first pious tamperings with the gospel text; that there has been a development not only of good but of evil principles, not only of truths but of errors, not only of the leaven of the gospel but of the leaven of hypocrisy. He sees that in every generation some tare or another ripens and betrays its true character and needs to be uprooted; that there are epochs when a perfect harvest of such tares demands a sort of revolution—a ruthless thrusting in of the sickle of criticism, a binding in bundles and burning of noxious weeds. He recognizes in the recent developments of the Roman-law conception of ecclesiastical authority on the one side, and on the other in the recent results of Biblical and historical criticism and of social and political developments, the signs of such a crisis in the life of the Church. His is no blind Philistinism that would raze the Church to the ground and run up a smart up-to-date structure on the old site. He holds firmly that nothing which has, on a large scale and for a long period, both lived and given life can be destroyed without irreparable loss and impoverishment. His sole effort is to separate the perishable from the imperishable elements in all such cases; to change as little, to preserve as much, as truth and truthfulness will permit.

Alive to all abuses and errors connected with dogmas and institutions, he is not less alive to the services they have rendered, to the principles they have imperfectly expressed. Christ-worship, saint-worship, miracles, sacraments, dogma, theology, uniformity, ritual, priesthood, sacrifice, papacy, infallibility, nay, Medievalism itself, all stand for so many attempts to satisfy the religious requirements of human nature.

Whatever is mechanical, gross, unhistorical, or decadent must be so removed as to save those values by which they have lived in spite of their evident limitations. If the marriage of Christian principles with the sane principles and elements of growing civilization has been fruitful of true developments of the Catholic idea, their marriage with the unhealthy and evil elements of the same has produced spurious developments, in which, however, the nobler strain must be recognized and purified. Even things so utterly evil as persecution and inquisition have been not merely approved by good men, but approved as right, because they were the perverse and stupid application of the undoubted truth that the destroyer of souls is a greater danger to the public than a murderer; that temporal death is a lesser evil than spiritual. No immorality could have lived and thriven unless it had perversely appealed to conscience under some appearance of morality. We must not empty out the baby with the bath. We must save the apparent morality if we would reveal the full deformity of what it covered and prevent its return in the same guise.

And so, for the Modernist, even the errors, sins, and follies of the past are valuable experiences which the Church is all the wiser and deeper and richer for having passed through and beyond. In this, the same law governs the formation of collective as of individual character. Virtues that have not been driven home by hard struggle lie light on the soul's surface; the storm that rocks the tree roots it.

It is by the experimental method that Nature gropes her way to what is more useful, more true to life's laws. Catholicism is a great experimentation in religion; a quest of the fullest and most perfect expression of Christianity. Medievalism, in the eyes of the Modernist, is a necessary experiment which must be worked out to its extremest and bitterest consequences if the Church is to realize inwardly and comprehensively a truer, deeper, richer notion of liberty and authority, of faith and orthodoxy, of revelation and theology, of growth and identity, than were possible otherwise. Thus it is that God in history is ever judging the world, gathering the wheat into his barn and burning the chaff with fire unquenchable. For ourselves, with omnipotence and omniscience at our disposal, we should have arranged things differently; we should have saved all the waste and woe of this tedious experimental process; we should have created an immutably perfect Church by the *fiat* of our will. But God's ways and thoughts are not as ours, nor can we wonder if he works as slowly and wastefully in the kingdom of Grace as in the kingdom of Nature. The argument from what we ourselves should have done to what God must therefore have done is the principal basis of the ultramontane Church-theory; but it is somewhat shaken by the consideration of what God has actually done and does daily.

Finally, the Modernist demands, not greater freedom, but absolute freedom for science in the widest sense of the term. He will not have it fettered except by its own laws and methods and by the experience which is its subject-matter. He will not allow even theology to be tied down to any revealed and stereotyped statements, but only to the religious experiences of which certain statements are the spontaneous self-chosen, but at most symbolic, expressions. Such experiences are the substance of revelation; the inspired statements are but its classical and primitive symbols, and cannot be treated as premisses for deduction.

Science for him is one general system dealing with all experience and trying to arrange it into a single synthesis of the understanding. As a theologian, he takes account of spiritual and supernatural experiences as part of the totality of experience; he considers the religions of mankind; the religion of Israel, the religion of Jesus and his apostles, the religion of the Catholic community—all, as so much experience. He considers the spiritual forces and tendencies and sentiments that have embodied themselves in the history, institutions and doctrines of the Roman Catholic Church and in the lives and actions of her children, and which are revealed in defeat as well as in victory, in false as well as in true developments. And from such consideration, he arrives progressively at a better idea of the essence and aim of Catholicism and at a truer criterion by which to shape the course of its future developments.

Modernism therefore has nothing to do with that sort of more educated and temporizing ultramontanism that shrinks from an inopportune pressing of principles which the world has unfortunately outgrown; that loves to rub shoulders cautiously with science and democracy; that strives to express itself moderately and grammatically; that would make a change of circumstances and opportunities pass for a more tolerant Spirit; and that is usually rewarded for its pains by finding itself between the hammer and the anvil.

Modernism does not seek to modify this or that tenet or institution. It is an all-pervading principle affecting the whole of Catholicism from end to end with its distinction between the Divine and the human element; the Spirit and the embodiment; the permanent and the variable. If it is a heresy at all, it is "the compendium of all heresies".

Medievalism: A Reply to Cardinal Mercier, pp. *144–153*

(ii)

The hope of a synthesis between the essentials of Christianity and the assured results of criticism is very widespread nowadays, and those who share it are commonly called Modernists or Liberals. There is a marked division of Modernists according as their tendency is to consider that alone to be essential to Christianity which agrees with their idea of the assured results of criticism, or to consider as the only assured results of criticism those that fit in with their conception of the essentials of Christianity. Both tendencies are vicious and, if unchecked, destroy the very idea of Modernism, which professes to consider each interest impartially, without respect to the other, in the belief and hope that the results will prove harmonious. Religion cannot be the criterion of scientific truth, nor science of religious truth. Each must be criticized by its own principles. . . .

To suppose . . . that . . . Modernism is a movement away from the Church and is converging towards Liberal Protestantism is to betray a complete ignorance of its meaning—as complete as that of the encyclical *Pascendi*. With all its accretions and perversions Catholicism is, for the Modernist, the only authentic Christianity. Whatever Jesus was, he was in no sense a Liberal Protestant. All that makes Catholicism most repugnant to present modes of thought derives from him. The difficulty is, not Catholicism, but Christ and Christianity. So far as other Christian bodies are true to Christ, they are faced by the same problems as are Modernists. If they escape them, it is because, in defiance of history, they have shaped Christ to their own image, and see in him no more than the Moslem sees in Mohammed.

The wisest men may be wrong, not only in detail, but in their whole scheme of things; yet they are not therefore fools. The Modernist's confidence in Christianity may be displaced, but it cannot be despatched in a smart article or encyclical. We may be sure that religion, the deepest and most universal exigency of man's nature, will survive. We cannot be so sure that any particular expression of the religious idea will survive. Nay, we may be sure that all must perish, that none can ever be perpetual and universal save that which shall at last recognize and conform to the law of the religious process, as they come to be established by reflection on wider experience. Should Christianity be unable, or unwilling, to conform to these laws, it must perish, like every other abortive attempt to discover an universal religion as catholic as science. Religion, however, will profit and learn by failure. Fragments of the ruin will be built into some new construction raised on the old site—just as the ethics of Jesus have been built into the structure of Liberal Protestantism.

But the Modernist hopes for better things and thinks that he sees the principles of a true Catholicism in Christ and Christianity. Theoretically it may be so. The difficulties, however, are mainly of the practical order, and men will differ in their estimate of their magnitude.

Christianity at the Cross-Roads,
pp. xv, xx-xxii

PART III

VON HÜGEL

THE HISTORICAL ELEMENT IN RELIGION

A . . . point on which men specially busy with the adaptation of the Christian doctrine and practice to what appears to be the best, or at least most abiding and most growing amongst the new conditions of mankind, are likely—especially, I think, in Latin countries—pretty readily to cease seeing things steadily and whole, is history. I mean, in particular, the difficulty, function, need within the religious life of Factual Happenings and of belief in their happenedness.

When, during the last nine years of Pope Leo XIII's life, I regularly spent half—more than half—of my existence in Rome, and the question of Biblical Criticism was beginning, increasingly, to occupy and to alarm the authorities, I used fairly often to visit Cardinal Rampolla, recently deceased, then Papal Secretary of State; and his Eminence would invite my impressions and opinion upon this great subject-matter. The Old Testament was then to the front; and I ventured to suggest how fortunate, upon the whole, was still, at that time, the position of the Roman Catholic Church in this field. For it could, with perfect truth, claim to have laid, through its priest, Richard Simon, and its layman, Jean Astruc,[1] the foundations of the criticism of the Pentateuch; and it could also assert that so far it had not committed itself to any solemn or final acts against it. Would it not be well, even in precise and solemn theological condemnations of the results of specialist studies, science or scholarship, to rest satisfied with the condemnation of Heliocentrism and Galileo, as the share, in such

---

[1] Richard Simon (1638–1712), French Oratorian and biblical scholar commonly regarded as the founder of Old Testament criticism. In his *Histoire critique du Vieux Testament* (1678) he denied the Mosaic authorship of the Pentateuch. He was afterwards expelled from his order. Jean Astruc (1684–1766), physician and student of the Pentateuch, who argued that *Genesis* is a composite work based on earlier documents. See below, p. 213 (Ed.).

acts, of the Roman Church? Why not leave to the Presbyterian Churches *their* share of such proceedings, in their solemn trials and condemnations of Pentateuchal criticism in the persons of my valiant friends, William Robertson Smith and Charles Augustus Briggs?[1] If the situation were left thus, a pretty fair division of praise, if not of blame, would remain apportioned between the Roman Catholic and the most anti-Roman of the Christian Churches.

Criticism moved on, especially after Pope Leo's death, from the Old Testament to the New; and a devotedly good, but quite differently tempered bishop came to sit in St Peter's Chair, fronted thus by questions of the deepest delicacy and difficulty, and of the widest range and alternatives. And, under the rapid succession of almost numberless condemnations and restrictions of every kind and of almost every degree of solemnity and precision, it is no wonder if (especially in cases where the critical, or even hypercritical, acumen and activity of men is greater than their philosophical training, self-discipline and insight, or, especially, than the depth, delicacy and urgency of the spiritual life within their souls) certain extreme effects are now traceable, within the Roman Catholic Church, as truly in the direction towards the left as in that towards the right.

I am not, here, thinking of M. Loisy, the dignity of whose life, the abiding fineness of so much of whose critical commentaries, whose admirable defence, in these last few years, of the original character and abiding worth of religion, as against Sir J. G. Frazer and M. Salomon Reinach, and of the historical reality of Jesus against Arthur Drews, and especially whose many troubles and sufferings added on to his immense laboriousness keep me still his devoted grateful friend, and hold me aloof from examination and criticism of the faults which doubtless cannot fail, here also, to limit and obscure his great lights and merits. But I am thinking of more than one other man known to me as, in intention and doubtless in the eyes of God, still active members

---

[1] W. Robertson Smith (*1846–1894*), professor of oriental languages and Old Testament exegesis at the Free Church College, Aberdeen, dismissed from his chair in *1881* as a result of severe criticism of his scholarly opinions voiced at the General Assembly of the Free Church. C. A. Briggs (*1841–1913*), appointed professor of Hebrew at Union Seminary, New York, in *1874*, was in *1891* tried for heresy. Although acquitted by the New York presbytery, he was suspended two years later from his clerical duties. In *1899* he was ordained in the Protestant Episcopal Church (Ed.).

of the Roman Catholic Church, and whom, again, I am not disposed to criticize as characters, but only in one of their ideas or convictions.

I find then, here, sometimes even a considerable conservatism as to the degree to which, *as a matter of fact*, historical happenings have become, or are becoming, untenable as such, or in this or that form of happenedness. But what has here disappeared, what indeed is recognized as having gone from out of these minds, is any belief in the abiding necessity, the irreplaceable function of historical happenings within the spiritual life. Such men may be, I believe they are, more conservative than M. Loisy was to what they hold to stand disproved; but they are fully, explicitly radical, in their negation as to any intrinsic necessity for the survival of any factual happenings whatsoever. They may still actually hold the Virgin Birth and the Bodily Resurrection in the ordinary sense and degree of factual happenings; but not only could these happenings, as such, but also the Sermon on the Mount and the Parables, the Cures and the Conversions, the Passion, indeed the very Person of Jesus, as so many actual happenednesses and at one time visible and audible facts, go, and nevertheless Christianity and Catholicism could and would remain. For that Christianity and Catholicism are essentially a system of principles and laws, for and in all the deeper and deepest human life and conduct, are ideals and incentives all the more operative because they take a visible, pictorial form. These things, these ideas, would remain true, even if every one of the alleged happenings and historical facts turned out to be pure creations of the imagination, incorporating, not what is nor what was, but what ought to be, and the deepest note in the human soul, this oughtness.

But this degree and kind of "safety", of emancipation from the complications and uncertainties of contingency, turns out, I submit, impossible and ruinous, under the combined pressure of general experience, whether individual or social, of psychology and epistemology, especially as applied to religion, and especially of the analysis of Christianity's deepest characteristics.

Certainly, in general psychology and epistemology, we have already found a great twin fact to be fundamental—the difference, indeed, between sense-stimulations and impressions on the one hand, and mental presentations and convictions on the other hand; and yet also the need we men have—yes, we men, not any abstract system, nor beings of a higher order than our own—of those sense-stimulations, for the awakening within our souls of these mental presentations and convictions. Thus, at the very basis and beginning of our rational, characteristically human life, lies this mysterious incommensuration between the apparent nature of its constituents and the close interconnection of their action; what seems the sheerest, the most fleeting of contingencies is strictly necessary for the awakening of even the simplest idea and assurance of something profoundly different, of persistent being, of space and time, of Eternity, of God himself. At the higher or profounder ethical level we find again a somewhat similar, but still richer and more wonderful twin fact: the deep difference between sense and soul, and yet the need that the soul has of sense, even, especially, for its purity; for the purity of man should ever be conceived with reference to his body, it is the virtue of the spiritualization of sense—you can no more have it without sense than you can have it without Spirit. And, above all, at the religious level and within religion's characteristic world, do we get, increasingly with the increasing richness, hence truth and vitality of the religion, an again similar twin fact of difference and dependence. Certainly Christianity stands for the deeply fruitful fact, conviction, practice and achievement—Incarnation, in the widest and most varied, as well as in the most precise and deepest, sense of the word. For Christianity, surely, is not simply a doctrine—however true—of certain laws and principles of the spiritual life, with vivid pictures of apparently historical scenes and personages, not one of which need have any factual, happened reality. But precisely the central conviction and doctrine of Christianity is the real prevenience and condescension of the real God—is the penetration of Spirit into sense, of the spaceless into space, of the eternal into time, of God into man. Here, again, incommensurables are in close relations of effect, of need. The lower is here the occasion—for us poor men, in this our little dispensation, the necessary occasion—is the nidus, springboard, material, vehicle of the higher and the highest. The higher bends down to, attracts, the lower; the lower rises on tip-toe towards, thirsts after, and finds and wills the higher.

This condescension and ascension, this union, is doubtless achieved in unspeakably different degrees, and even kinds, of fullness and perfection. Yet it is not a simple idea, but a solid fact; not something that so universally *ought* to happen, that in fact it never happens at all; not something, again, that we can, or even must, assume to have happened at some time, in some place, with profoundest fullness, but in this its happenedness is known to God alone. No: even though historical tradition everywhere brings with it certain difficulties and obscurities of its own, it can and does, still outside of our ethical or religious interpretations of it, also furnish us with a certain kind and degree of reasonable assurance that such and such scenes, words, persons—whatsoever their worth and meaning—have really happened. And psychology and epistemology, still more ethics, and, above all, religion, in particular Christianity, cannot really do without this most humble seeming assurance of sheer happenedness, even though they all—religion especially—rightly and promptly find on occasion of and in these happenings meanings, truths, realities, and motives, beyond what the non-philosophical, the non-ethical, particularly the non-religious man will discover in them.

The special difficulty here will, I believe, eventually turn out to lie, not in the apparent paradox of the general position—here Christianity is very certainly anchored in the imperishable reality of things and of man's essential position and make—but in the complexity and delicacy of the practical application and working of this general position and principle within the organized religions and for the average man. And this means, ultimately, the difficulty of creating, and still more of maintaining amongst more than a picked few, a sufficiently high level of intellectual patience, and of faith in God and in the fundamental position—the major premiss—of those organized religions themselves.

For it is evident that we can take this need, on the part of every full and popular religion, of historical happenednesses, of factualness, in one of two ways: a difficult and slow, but, in the long run, thoroughly safe and fruitful way, which specially affirms the major premiss of the position underlying the historical religions; or an easy and prompt, but, in the long run, unsafe and sterilizing or revolt-producing way, which specially affirms the minor premiss of that same position. In the first way, we mean that a nucleus of historically assured and histori-cally testable factual happenings is indeed necessary; and that, believing as we do in God, and in his slow and mysterious, yet most real, in the long run irresistible, working within man's struggles and labours, especially where these are sincere, sensitively docile to the teachings of their own science and of its history, and disinterested and costly,

M

we feel assured that, through and in this our human toil, he will see to the persistence of this nucleus; but that, just as he alone can sufficiently maintain this nucleus throughout and beyond our best endeavours, so also he alone knows with entire finality the precise delimitation of this range of happenedness. What we religionists thus affirm is much like what all spiritualists affirm concerning the reality of body and soul, and of their mutual relation and need: the body requires the soul, the soul requires the body; there is a real and necessary interdependence between the two, yet they are not simply co-extensive; the soul ranges further than the body. And this way would still leave considerable duties to the official Church authorities. They would have to discountenance all views that inculcate or imply the non-necessity of a factual nucleus; to exhort to, better still to help in the development of, cautious and courageous, deeply scholarly and sensitively spiritual veracity in such studies; and to keep carefully alive the sense and practice of the religious life, of the soul's relations to the great realities of God and of other souls, and of the creeds as standing for this great system of truth and reality, possessed also of a nucleus of historical happenedness. The creeds would thus remain true, even if this or that of their articles would have slowly, cautiously, to be re-interpreted as true in not a factual sense or in a factual sense somewhat different from the old one. In this way nothing would here conflict, on principle and in the long run, with the reasonable claims of historical criticism, or with the major premiss of the Church's fundamental position itself— that her religion is in part based upon historical facts ascertainable by the usual historical methods, and is emphatically not a simple intuitionism or *fideism* of any kind.

But if the question be answered the other way—which assuredly is the more obvious, the more clear, the more consonant with, and comforting to, human impatience—the Church authorities, and, indeed, the ordinary believer with them, are called upon to defend (and this quite finally, as the last ditch in the protection of the Christian citadel) not only the major premiss, but the minor as well; indeed not so much the major as the minor. Here the anxiety is not to keep the Church from fideism—to retain history as history—that is to allow, indeed to encourage, historical tests and conclusions to be applied and to obtain as regards the historical happenings, real or apparent, present within the Christian tradition and creed. The anxiety here is to retain at any cost, even at the cost of the ruin of this major premiss, the minor premiss in exactly the extension, detailed applications, and kind and degree of meaning in which it has for very long been held. Not only, thus, does the creed possess an abiding nucleus of happenedness, not only does it remain abidingly true, in the traditional sense of this truth, if the creed be taken as a whole, and not only can even its several articles all continue to be held true in very real senses of the word "truth"; but each article, in so far as ever held to state an historical happenedness at all, is taken as of strictest necessity abidingly true and binding in that precise kind and degree of happenedness. Taken thus the claim to history, to happenedness, cannot fail, more or less, sooner or later, to find itself in conflict with the historical workers and their conclusions. For even though the Christian faith arose on occasion of, and around, and concerning certain factual happenings, which it penetrated and interpreted, but has transmitted to us also as so many happenings credible even by those who do not thus penetrate and interpret them; yet this same faith also early developed certain fact-like pictures and symbols of this its belief; it is impossible carefully and sincerely now to study the Pentateuch or the Johannine writings, without the admission of this much. Such pictures and symbols are not necessarily false, but their truth will be not that of happenedness.

Now it is doubtless because of the strong insistence by the official authorities upon taking factualness in this second very wide extension and absolutely fixed application, that so appreciable a number of the finer minds even amongst men sincerely anxious to be, sincerely believing themselves to remain, sincere Christians, indeed Catholics, have allowed themselves to fly to the other extreme—to the denial of any and all necessary, abiding connection between factual happenings in general and religious faith. Yet this latter negation is even more "simple", *i.e.* less adequate to life and the real situation, than is the affirmation of those who have occasioned it. And this "simple" negation then reacts back upon the "simple" affirmation, not all the scholarship, good faith and sufferings of such doctrinaire reformers can prevent their "simple" negative from still further confirming their official opponents in the conviction that only in their own extension and precision of absolute factualness can the health and security of religious faith be found.

Essays and Addresses on the Philosophy of Religion (Second Series), pp.

103-111: "On Certain Central Needs of Religion, and the Difficulties of Liberal Movements in Face of the Needs; as Experienced within the Roman Catholic Church during the last Forty Years".

FREEDOM IN THE CHURCH

How engrossingly interesting are the facts and conceptions of liberty and equality as these have grown under the stress of the richness of the human life and destiny, especially as these have been revealed, and immensely enhanced, by Christianity in the most various ways and stages! And how especially instructive is this study if taken in comparison with those "simplifications", abstract theories and doctrinaire battle-cries produced, in these matters, by the abuses of human institutions civil and clerical, and by the impatience and counter-injustice of the sufferers from them!

The chief upshot for our fourth complex here is that liberty especially yet also equality, has received its profoundest growth and propagation in the world of thought and emotion at the hands of Christianity, and that Christianity promptly utilized and deepened certain Greek philosophical, especially Stoic, conceptions for the articulation of these its convictions; but that certain parts and tendencies of these same Stoic conceptions were and are unassimilable by Christianity, and that it is precisely these parts and tendencies which the doctrinaires of the Enlightenment and of the French Revolution developed into a difference and recalcitrance of the most far-reaching importance and effect.

According to the characteristically Christian conception, we start with human society as an organism—a body composing, and composed of, its members, each various although constituting only one body; each powerful, but powerful to give because also powerful to get, because actually first receiving much and very much; each necessary with a certain uniqueness, but this within an organism larger than itself. Already here, at the start, each individual member is necessary, is various, is unique; their liberty is not *in vacuo* or without aim or end; and their equality is not atomistic or interchangeable. All have duties, all have rights, all have service within and for the one body. And of such organic bodies there is not only one, but there are many: the family, the commune, the Church, human society at large, the State; these are all organic, all give to the individual as well as they receive from him; they are none simply the sumtotal of their constituent parts. And the individuals composing these complexes are themselves organic, a little world within themselves; and they can and do grow from relatively unarticulated or chaotic entities into being richly articulated, harmonious persons. A body with its members, not a sand-heap with its grains of sand. And further, in the Christian conception and conviction, the individual is indeed not merely a part of a whole, in the sense that he has no worth in himself; he, the individual soul, has an infinite worth; yet—let us mark it carefully—upon *three conditions*, which indeed are each equivalent to the other. The individual here, prized thus infinitely, is not the empirical, unspiritualized, predominantly animal individual, as we find him on the street or in many of our own moments—in and as predominant in all except the saints of God; but the individual here meant is the person, the spiritualized, the God-seeking, the God-sought soul. And if even those individuals on the street and in our own many moments can also be treated as thus precious, this is only because, and in so far as, they are capable of becoming such a person and moments in such a personality. Again, the individual thus prized develops into a person within one, or rather several wider complexes, the family, society, the State, and (religiously) within, and through service for, the kingdom of God. None of these complexes are simply the sum-total of the individuals who enter them, or even of the persons who become persons within them; they all are more and other than such a bare sum; they all give as well as get: they all possess a quasi—Personal spirit, influence, formative power. And, finally, the individual thus personalized is solicited, sustained, completed and crowned by God, the great prevenient Spirit who works within and through this his kingdom of spirits, yet who is not (any more than the created spirits composing this kingdom) simply a part of, or even simply the totality of, this spirit-complex. This last condition must stand over for our last complex. Now against this apprehension, rich, concrete, organic, various in unity—where the individual gets before he gives, and where he becomes a person, no doubt in conflict as well as in conformity with his environment, itself never simply perfect since composed of fellowmortals—yet, still, becomes a person never simply through and by himself, and never as a unit interchangeable with other units—stands the thin, abstract, atomic conception of the doctrinaire Enlightenment.

Here there is, strictly, no complex, for there is no whole consisting of differing, mutually supplementary, mutually necessary parts. And, strictly, there is only one legitimate sum-total—the State. And this State is the clearly understood and deliberately willed contractual creation of the originally independent individuals; they were equal, and they remain equal, and the contract aimed, and aims, above all, at securing this equality. The individual thus is here before the totality and the individual no more becomes a person that the sum-total becomes an organism. The types of the body, of the family, of the kingdom of God have here no place.

It appears fairly clear, too, that this inorganic, repetitive, uncompensatory, monotonously equalitarian system readily suggests an equality—an interchangeableness of quality and worth—also between different stages of society, and different contemporaneous bodies, schools, Churches: an equality really abstract, unreal, doctrinaire. And here, again, through an impatient forcing of facts, and a violent clarifying of the rich obscurities of life, we end, not in levelling up as far as may be, but in levelling down as ought not to be. We want to be equally just, and we become uniformly undiscriminating, incapable of loving, hence of understanding any one thing, from sheer determination not to allow it to be, in its degree and kind, unique, irreplaceable.

Now it is plain, not only that the abstract, atomistic conception of liberty and equality, and the forcing of life into these moulds, is the easier view, at least for abstractly thinking races and movements, such as the Latin mostly are, but also that religious reformers will everywhere pretty readily sink from the organic to the atomic conception, at least as regards the Churches, or the particular Church to which they belong. For such reforming movements are inevitably the work of individuals, or at least of small groups of men, in conflict with the average and the routine of the general body, the Church complex to which they belong. Hence, even simply to preserve the sense of the need of such a complex, whilst working hard, and amidst often violent opposition from the *hic et nunc* mouthpieces and organs of this complex, for its reform is of necessity both difficult and rare.

I take it that, in the recent movements within the Roman Catholic Church, there has been less lost in the way of a diminution of the sense that a religious organism, a Church, is needed, than in the way of a diminution of the sense that the various religious bodies and Churches are of most diverse idiosyncrasies, strength and weakness, of very different stages of spirituality and experience, resourcefulness of help, degree of truth, life, love, reality. And yet, if these differences are facts, they should be remembered, should they not? After all, amongst animals the ox is strong in his neck and horns: do not deprive him of these "mere accidents", these "non-essentials". Insects fly at random and drop down helpless if you deprive them of even one of their feelers—those small, insignificant-looking etceteras of their structure. The union of the Lutheran and Calvinist Churches of Germany has largely helped on the dreary non-Church-going, the vague religiosity in place of definite religion, of the greater part of Protestant Germany.

The recognition of these differences will be able to become both vivid and elastic, patient and articulate, in proportion as Christians of all sorts and degrees come to recognize—as, if they grow in the historic sense, they inevitably will—the two great ranges of variety, successive and simultaneous, to be found in those great collections of classical religious writings, the Old and the New Testaments, which still feed and stimulate them all. For there is the divinely permitted, the divinely willed variety and growing worth of the Old Testament on to the New: what a blessing, what a ferment of wide and wise ideas concerning God's education of our race is thus the Christian Church's splendid breadth of action when it solemnly included the Old Testament in the Christian Canon of Scripture! This inclusion, and again the presence in the New Testament of a strong Church current—I am thinking especially of one great element in St Paul, and of the presuppositions of the Johannine writings—a current which does not prevent the Synoptists representing more the smaller groups of Christians all bent upon heroic holiness, and St Paul and the Johannine writings containing also a strongly mystical, enthusiastic current: all this remains, amongst every Church, Sect and isolated individual of an at all Christian type, an admirable ferment and incentive to the conception and conviction of Giveness, Prevenience, Objectivity, Universality, the Church; those of Initiative, subjective striving, small groups of heroic souls, the "Sect"; and those of the Circle, the dimmer yearnings, the immediacies too, of thought and of feelings, of the mystics. We thus see that these latter two movements and dispositions have also their deep roots already in the New Testament itself; and that the first—the Church movement—is no more, in its essence, a corruption of, or a deflection from the other two movements, than are the second two movements, in their essence, a corruption or deflection from the first. All three movements are, in their essence, legitimate and ineradicable. But the Church movement is the more massive, and the one most capable of the breadth, patience, sympathy necessary for the inclusion, the encouragement of the other two. And certainly only in proportion as it can, and actually does so, is the Church type justified, theoretically and practically, in claiming a strictly sole rule. This type, in such a case, becomes so inclusive as to deserve, in this its inclusiveness, to be recognized as all-sufficing.   *Ibid.*, pp. *103–117*

THE MODERNIST CRISIS

It seems to me that there are two, really (in substance) distinct, subject-matters which could be described under the term "Modernism". The one is a permanent, never quite finished, always sooner or later, more or less, re-beginning set of attempts to express the old Faith and its permanent truths and helps—to interpret it according to what appears the best and most abiding elements in the philosophy and the scholarship and the science of the later and latest times. Such work never ceases for long, and to it I still try to contribute my little share, with such improvements as the experiences of the Pontificate of Pius X have—in part only very slowly—come to show me to be desirable or even necessary. The other "Modernism" is a strictly circumscribed affair, one that is really over and done—the series or groups of specific attempts, good, bad, indifferent, or variously mixed, that were made towards similar expressions or interpretations, during the Pontificate of Pius X—beginning, no doubt, during the later years of Leo XIII, but ending with the death of Fr T[yrrell] and with Loisy's alienation from the positive content that had been fought for— also from the suppression of *Rinnovamento*[1] onwards, and the resolution of so much of the very substance of the movement, not only, or even chiefly, under the stress of the official Church condemnations, but from within the ranks of scepticism dominating what remained of organs claiming to be "Modernist".

[1] See Introduction, p. *60* (Ed.).

Now I take it that you are certainly not attempting the fine, but gigantic task, of even a sketch of "Modernism" in the first sense, but only a sketch of "Modernism" in the second sense.[1] And I do not really see what my own, or indeed any one else's, writings, since that definitely closed period or crisis, have to do with your subject-matter. And the point is not a purely academic one, for my mind; nor does it, I believe, spring from cowardice. It arises forcibly in my mind—as far as I know myself—from a strong desire not to appear (it would be contrary to the facts, and indeed contrary to my ideals and convictions) *as though all that action of the Church authorities had, in no way or degree, been interiorly accepted by me.* Certainly that action was, very largely, violent and unjust; equally certainly, if one had been required definitely to subscribe to this or that document without express reservations, one could not, with any self-respect left, have done so. Yet it is not cowardice or policy, it is in simplest sincerity, that I have come to see, more clearly than I used to do, how much of serious unsatisfactoriness and of danger there was especially in many of the philosophical (strongly subjectivist) theories really held which *Pascendi* lumped together. And Troeltsch[2] has taught me vividly how profoundly important is Church appurtenance, yet how much appurtenance never, even at best, can be had without some sacrifices—even of (otherwise) fine or desirable liberties or unhamperednesses. These two things—the actual fact of a very real, though certainly not unlimited submission, and the duty of such submission—I care much should not be left uncertain on occasion, in my own case. And a list of my own, or any one else's work, since that crisis, given without comment, could hardly fail, I should think, to look thus "superior" and defiant. Having said my little say, I will leave it to yourself to act as your knowledge of your book, and of what I want, will appear to you to be best.

Baron Friedrich von Hügel: Selected Letters (1896–1924), edited with a Memoir by Bernard Holland, pp. *248–249*

[1] Miss Petre, to whom this letter was addressed (March *13, 1918*), had asked von Hügel to furnish her with a list of such of his published writings (after *1914*) as he might think appropriate for inclusion in a forthcoming book of her own on Catholic Modernism. The baron complied with her request, but also with a certain reluctance, which he proceeds to explain (Ed.).

[2] Ernst Troeltsch (*1865-1923*), a liberal Protestant theologian whose writings von Hügel much admired (Ed.).

PART IV

BLONDEL, LABERTHONNIÈRE AND LE ROY

MAURICE BLONDEL

THE PROBLEM OF APOLOGETICS

1. Natural and Supernatural

Since philosophy considers the supernatural only in so far as the idea of it is immanent in us, and since it considers natural reality as transcending the knowledge which we have of it, it prepares us to understand better and better we cannot disregard Nature nor confine ourselves to it; that the human order has its share in everything but finds its sufficiency in nothing; that our natural being, although incapable of achieving itself and despite the devastating claims made upon it by the supernatural which it has failed to recognize, is nevertheless indestructible; and that, in its radical insufficiency, man's action remains co-extensive with that of God, according to the theological doctrine so rigorously summed up by St Bernard: *Non partim gratia, partim liberum arbitrium, sed totum singula opere individuo peragunt; ut mixtim, non singillatim; simul, non vicissim per singulos profectus operentur. Totum quidem hoc et totum illa; sed ut totum in illo, sic totum ex illa.*[1]

So philosophy shows us that man can never legitimately or in reality confine himself to the human level, that, even when he appears to do so, this appearance conceals, if he is sincere, a real participation in what he fails to recognize, and that, in a word, no natural solution is a solution at all; but it also makes us realize that the rejection or systematic disregard of what is found to be implied by human action is not simply the privation of a higher and supererogatory state, but a positive failure, and that the human order is not only sufficiently

---

[1] *Tractatus de gratia et libero arbitrio*, ch. XIV, § 47.

solid and subsistent to be the foundation for all divine projects but also remains indestructibly itself even beneath the weight of eternal responsibilities. Thus, it seems, fresh light is shed upon a question which is a source of scandal and distress to our contemporaries, the question of damnation. And thus again the much misunderstood doctrine of "vicarious satisfaction" is clarified: in view of the providential plan and the unity of the Divine purpose, which is free in principle but bound up together in all its parts, man's supernatural vocation implies that sin is deicide; that man should be what he is, and from the moment when he became a sinner, it was therefore a matter of strict necessity that Christ should suffer and die; and it was further necessary, in order that sin should be pardoned and effaced in man, that this necessary death should be at the same time willingly and lovingly accepted; it was necessary, again, for this necessary and freely redemptive oblation to be efficacious in each of us, that each of us should consent to it and should co-operate in the saving expiation, which, though sufficient and superabundant in itself, is incomplete in us unless we do our part.

Thus we discover man's natural incapacity not only to reach his supernatural end but also to enclose himself in his own natural order and to find an end of a kind in that; but we discover, too, the astonishing power which this same man has, despite his dependence, since he can not only lose his soul without abolishing himself but also rise up against God and lead him to death—or follow him in life; and this shows, more than anything else could do, the consistency and the dignity of man in his greatest weakness, the divine cost of his life, the extent of his human duty, and the solidity of fundamental human nature, since God, who can be content with the fulfilment of these natural human obligations, cannot dispense man from them.

Man, thrown back upon himself and cut off from the higher life, whose source is not in himself, is condemned simply because he has not changed: and this shows, from the point of view of the concepts which philosophy can only study in their relationships with one another, the absolute distinction between the natural and the supernatural: the opposite results of the alternative are not symmetrical, and "yes" provides a superabundance infinitely greater than the positive declension which is brought about by "no". So, beyond the Divine drama which is at work in the consciences of all men, there is now, for souls who believe and are alive, a new mystery of grace which Revelation alone can disclose to us and only to some extent. While the distinction between the two orders remains complete and unplumbable, we gain a deeper insight into their connection and their harmony. Since man has his share in everything and his sufficiency in nothing, none of his thoughts or acts, despite their indestructibility, can validate itself, or, if one may so put it, be adequate to itself unaided. If in the study of sensible reality and even of the lowest forms of existence, we find, in so far as we try to disengage some objective element, that our thought loses itself in an endless flight and continually goes beyond itself without ever being able to pin down this sensible or scientific or metaphysical phenomenology, it is perhaps because we can never touch being at any point without encountering at least implicitly the source and bond of all being, the universal Realizer. Neither sensation, not science, nor philosophy terminate absolutely in themselves οὐ τελευτῶσιν. Yet they cannot leave in mid-air or suppress these appearances which give them life, χαίρειν ἐᾶν τὰ φαινόμενα ἀδύνατον. It would be a fine thing for philosophy to prepare or encourage one of the dogmatic definitions with which the future will perhaps enrich the ever-increasing treasury of the faith. There are two theological opinions, either of which we are at present free to choose: according to one, the Incarnation of the Word has as its motive simply original sin in view of the Redemption upon the Cross; according to the other, the original plan of creation embraces the mystery of the Man-God in such sort that the fall of man determined only the sorrowful and humiliating conditions which Christ accepted together with the superabundance of grace and dignity which is the fruit of this superabundance of love. It is possible that the Church will decide between these one day, and in favour of the second. For if it is true that the least of sensible phenomena and the most elementary of corporeal existences cannot be conceived as real unless we see an element impled in it which cannot be accounted for by the merely creative decree of the First Cause; if it is true that we cannot bring our action to completion or remedy our faults or even have a real and living idea of God himself without appealing to this mediator; if it is true, as St Theresa teaches, that it is an illusion to think that we can detach ourselves better from material things and have a purer knowledge of God if we leave aside the humanity of Christ, whereas in fact this sacred humanity, "which ought not to be put in that class",[1] remains the only Way as well as the Supreme Truth, so that without it nothing in heaven or earth is intimately known, then it seems that philosophy, by demanding an element distinct both from Nature and also from the author of Nature himself in order to conceive the effective realization of the whole order of things, would clarify and justify, from its own point of view, what is perhaps an implicit dogma, Emmanuel as the final cause of the creative plan.[2] So, after having first put aside, in order to define the notion of the supernatural, all questions of fact or of particular individuals, we should be led in the end by this unique route, and in a manner which is at once discreet and imperious, to suggest in its most precise form the need for the concrete reality of the Word, to prepare at this point alone, which alone the philosopher can touch, for the insertion of historical apologetics, and to justify the necessity of studying, acknowledging and bringing alive for one's own mind the fact of all facts, the divine fact of Christianity. And then this sublime postulate of philosophical reason would be in harmony, without any confusion of roles, with the most human of the sciences, the science of history, as well as with the loftist teaching of theology.

[1] That is, not a humanity like any other humanity. The rather baffling notion of Christ's mediation as the final *explanation* of objective knowledge was entertained by Blondel throughout his career. It must not be taken to deny that our knowledge of reality is objective in itself (*Translator's note*).

[2] Not, of course, that God is to be made passive, by reaction, to the activity of things or made subject to the necessity of perceiving or submitting to them in order really to produce them. But if we enter upon the labyrinth of sensible existence, if we consider that knowledge and being on this level form the first solid link in the whole chain of our representations and realize that the consistency and fixity of all the rest depends on it, and if finally we try to conceive the conditions on which all the realization of phenomena depends, including those which we call secondary or subjective qualities, those, in short, which manifestly presuppose, in order to exist, rational perception in a corporeal organism, then it will certainly seem that this reality must be inevitably conceived as bound up with the organic and rational activity of a mediator capable of attaching this form, inconsistent in itself, to the existence of the absolute being, who alone, in seeing, brings what he sees into existence, but who sees it *aliter per divinitatem, aliter per carnem*, whether one must find this mediating flesh in man united to the Word who enlightens every mind, and whose part would thus be to act as the universal bond of being throughout all history, or whether one must, in fact, have recourse to Christ's Incarnation itself.

2. Philosophy and Christianity

From what has been said it is perhaps legitimate to conclude that the conflict between rationalism and Catholicism can be resolved to the material advantage both of philosophy and of the Christian conscience. So we should like to say to unbelievers and believers alike: "There is only one religion which carries with it and demands Philosophy". And it would be necessary to add: "There is only one philosophy which leads to and calls for Religion". But the relationships between religion and philosophy have been so misunderstood that friends have been taken for enemies and enemies for friends. And I have desired above all to put on their guard against these misunderstandings so many men of good will who unwittingly frustrate their own intentions.

In the secular duel, which party succumbs and at whose expense is reconciliation achieved? What remains dead upon the battlefield, as the one deplorable cause of the misunderstandings and as a sort of pledge of a final agreement, is (among all the elements which scholasticism has put together) neither the Christian idea nor the philosophical idea but the middle term by which they had been united—the ancient conception of the divinity of reason, the realism, both ontological and intellectual, of a thought which controls everything, the doctrine of the self-sufficiency of metaphysics, the belief in the intrinsic consistency of objects apart from any mediating activity and simply as they are apprehended by the mind; in short, a false philosophy which sought to persuade us *a priori* that the rational order contains all the rest in an eminent degree. It appeared victorious, but hardly seems so now except to some who should have rejoiced in its defeat. For its victims still insist in trying to restore it because they wrongly think it the loyal servant of a theological rationalism which, itself legitimate, fundamentally condemns it. Let us at least learn the lesson that by bringing everything back to thought we are inevitably led to suggest that thought, in ourselves, is sufficient for everything. What is it, then, that triumphs? It is philosophy itself, thanks to the gentle and secret influence of the Christian Spirit which it seemed to combat and which seems to resist it, the philosophy which springs from the evolution of human thought not as a passing phase but as an acquisition justified in itself. For it is supremely instructive to see how, left to itself, exclusive rationalism or the bastard form of philosophy comes to limit itself in the way which is most in conformity with the fundamental requirements of Christianity. In fact, to be opposed to the recent transformations is to work against those who are working for us and to deny to them what they are offering to give us in large measure. It has needed the whole of a slow and laborious evolution of thought to reveal the true perspective, to bring to birth the only method which allows the constitution of an integral philosophy in integral Christianity, to lay the only foundations on which a new "School" can be built—let us not lose, then, in the future, the advantages offered to both sides by the position which has now been reached. To insist on restoring what is dead in the old school, killed by a dead rationalism, is to fall inevitably under the assaults of the double critique which has destroyed the Christian pseudo-philosophy by the metaphysics of transcendence and the rationalist pseudo-philosophy by the doctrine of immanence, and is now itself outdated.

No doubt, whatever one does to justify this total transposition of philosophical questions, even if one shows its necessity and its advantages by a detailed account of it, it will not be possible to make contact at once with the majority even of reflective minds, precisely because of the value and the novelty of the points of view laid open: too many conventions and interests are at stake. Many perhaps, finding that a good deal of trouble has to be taken in order to reach conclusions which seem not very different from those familar to them, will prefer, through mere habit or human respect or fear of effort, to make charges against what I have written or cast suspicion on it instead of considering it, without troubling to argue and without saying whether they take their stand on a defined dogma or a supposed philosophical orthodoxy. And here I must remark that if I have confined myself to questions of method it is because the way in which one reaches conclusions helps not only to make them valid, but also to define them, to renew them, and to enrich them. Above all, so long as Catholicism does not take this road, it will remain outside the pale in the world of philosophical thought and will not be able to encounter thinking men or to be encountered by them. And here is a fresh source of mutual recriminations. For those who are perhaps already disposed to approve the method or capable of grasping the necessity of it will reject the conclusions, and those whom the conclusions might attract will reject the method. However, if there are always in Christianity latent virtualities which each age discovers in proportion to its needs, one may hope that from the great movement of thought in our time there will emerge, little by little, the philosophical form which is in keeping with its religious requirements. Protestantism, swept on by the current of its logic, has not been able to stand up against its own principles: its prompt and facile agreement with an ephemeral pseudo-philosophy has been so far only a superficial crisis. After so many transient experiments and hasty improvisations the time has come perhaps for the truly Catholic idea to show its power and to promote a philosophy which is the more appropriate to it the more autonomous it is, a philosophy which only gives proof of its solidity by being more difficult to constitute and more impersonal. We must not complain of having to make a greater effort if it leads to a greater result: on the contrary, we must rejoice to see that easygoing hopes are disappointed, that egoistical pessimism is condemned, that an attachment to our own way of thinking has become impossible, that the demands of an impatient or interested zeal have been rejected and disallowed by events. France, which has been accused of lacking the philosophical spirit by reason of its Catholic formation, is perhaps the more capable of sustaining trials and troubles because it is the more capable of finding truth and goodness. It is time to realize these disregarded potentialities. Looking, then, to the future, let us descry in these present conflicts the ultimate triumph of the Christ who was humble and hidden in his life and is still humble and hidden in his progress through human history, even leaving to his temporary opponents the apparent initiative for those great inspirations of justice and of reason which have their secret origin in himself.

Perhaps this philosophy which boldly claims that it cannot leave aside the problem of the supernatural, which is more closely bound up at all points heretofore and which at the same time goes further in the critique of the very notion of religion, which lays bare the neuralgic points and faces perilous paths by going beyond doctrines of the most advanced kind which have been most justly condemned[1]—

---

[1] What Blondel presumably means is that these doctrines confused the supernatural with the natural by failing to tackle the problem on the profoundest level (*Translator's note*).

N

perhaps this philosophy will seem temerarious to some. But the danger does not lie there. Two hundred and fifty years ago Pascal was forced to touch on burning topics with a frankness which seemed to him to violate certain reticences of the Christian soul, and he uttered this cry of indignation in his private notes: "The wretches who have obliged me to speak about the heart of religion!" For of course, with his Jansenist and fideist tendencies, he feared to lay a sacrilegious hand upon that mystical foundation of all authority which he found in custom and even in mere outward show;[1] but perhaps, with the perspicacity of genius, he realized that reason was not yet armed to face, in the full light of day and in the spirit of criticism, the terrible combat which Bossuet too saw to be in store for Christianity. That combat is now ours, and we have still to sustain it without disguise and without reserve. In its boldest effort to close the door to faith, reason has gathered strength to open it. After all its endeavours we have nothing to compromise by frank speaking. The only danger now lies in abandoning the strict rules of a discussion which must go on relentlessly to the end. To obey these rules, in a matter in which silence or lack of interest are supremely injurious, is the greatest claim to intellectual respect and the only bond—but one most close and strong—between souls who are apparently sundered by an abyss of positive beliefs but who should be fraternally united in their anxious search. For this search, which precedes and can even substitute for possession, must always accompany it and vivify it; it is the human response to grace and the intellectual condition of charity. And the more frank and unyielding it is as between discordant minds, the more salutary it is through the esteem which it engenders at the price of a radical sincerity. Let us say, then, contradicting Pascal's remark in a spirit of peace and truth, that we are "happy to be able to speak, to be obliged to speak, to see so many constrained and eager to speak, about the very heart of religion".

*Lettre sur les exigences de la pensée
contemporaine en matière d'apologétique*
(trans. by Illtyd Trethowan), pp. *199–208*.

---

[1] "*Même dans le grimace*"—Blondel seems to be referring to Pascal's advice to take holy water even if one feels a distaste for it. This passage must not be taken as implying a general depreciation of Pascal, with whom Blondel had much in common (*Translator's note*). See Introduction, p. *53*.

CONCERNING *L'ACTION*

My original intention was to establish a philosophy which was autonomous but which from a rational point of view nevertheless complied with the most minute and rigorous demands of Catholicism. I was amazed to discover that, both in the development of doctrine and in the outlook of those around me, philosophical speculation proceeded as though man's true state was a purely natural one, upon which, like a wig, Christianity could be thrust—though a Christianity which would not succeed in gaining a hold even in the minds of those still faithful to their baptismal vows, and still less in the minds of those who, although steeped in the Christian religion, benefit from it only by breaking with it or even opposing it. The former showed only an artificial sort of harmony, and the latter an indifference or even hostility which their way of regarding the religious problem prevented them from overcoming.

Christian philosophy seemed to me to have been treated too much as a compromise or patchwork. It seemed to me that now one should start again, whether by taking from the ancients or from "secular" philosophers those seeds which prepare the ground and provide the sap for Christianity, or from the Christian philosophers themselves a preoccupation with homogeneity which has sometimes been integrated, often misunderstood, and occasionally exaggerated, as it was by St Bonaventure and Malebranche. . . . It seemed to me that one could do more than simply draw up a rationalistic, self-sufficient doctrine—a closed system which would leave no openings for religious scruples; and from then on my primary aim was to discover by studying human activity and thought the points of intersection which not only render it possible for Christianity to strike roots deep in our consciences, but also for it to make demands in the name of inner integrity as well as of Divine authority and of the outward manifestations which authenticate revealed truths and prescriptions.

I came to the conclusion, when seeking the cause of that disease of speculation for which I wished to find a cure, that our habit of confining philosophy to the field of ideas and abstract theories was the reason for the abuse of the differences between instinct and thought and action, and even between action and faith and inquiry. I became intent on locating the exact spot at which these things meet; it was no doubt right to distinguish and discriminate between them, but it was wrong to separate, isolate and even set them in opposition to one another. In fact, human action seemed to me to be the point on which the powers of Nature, the light of the understanding, the strength of the will and even the benefits of grace converge—not indeed to merge into one another, as still less to fight and destroy each other, but to combine their efforts and bring about the magnificent unity of our destiny. . . .

In order to protect myself from dangerous incriminations I have been led at too great length into controversies that have diverted my originally exclusively philosophical aim into the sphere of apologetics. For the present it had become necessary to establish that, without venturing into the theological field, without aspiring to take part in historical and exegetical arguments, without the least assumption that conscience was capable of discerning grace or that reason could call on, recognize or grasp the supernatural, philosophy poses certain questions, specifies certain attitudes and a certain kind of concern, and lays down certain fundamental premises which religious teaching could profitably use as a basis for its authority and for introducing its invigorating activity into the innermost depths of man's soul.

"Lettre-préface pour une réédition de *L'Action*",
in *Études blondéliennes*, i, pp. *16–18*.

LUCIEN LABERTHONNIÈRE

KNOWLEDGE OF BEING AND KNOWLEDGE OF THE SELF

Knowledge of being does not come to us from without. In order to know being as it is outside one must begin by knowing it in oneself. It is from the knowledge of being within us that we can attain the knowledge of being external to us. The knowledge we have of what is without is relative to the knowledge we have of ourselves; and the knowledge we have of ourselves is relative to what we are. And what we are is what we will to be.

Not that this should be understood to mean that we create ourselves. Strictly speaking we create nothing at all. And to suppose that we can will *not* to be is no whit the less to submit to being. Howsoever, what we are depends on us, because it is for us to choose the end that gives meaning to our existence. Actually, in life as it is willed and thought about, what we are comes from what we cleave to, from what we love. It is what we love that determines us; that constitutes us, I would venture even to say, in our own eyes. It is necessary for this to be so, for otherwise the diversity of the ideas which we form of our own nature would be inexplicable. If, as the philosophical idealists of our century have supposed, we know ourselves in the fixity of a given nature, no opposing views on this point would arise and there would be neither materialists nor sceptics nor phenomenalists.

When, then, we say that knowledge of being is relative to what we are, it is not a question of what we are independently of ourselves, at our primary and unconscious roots, but of what we are by our will and in the freedom of our moral life. Were it not from ourselves that we derive the concept we have relative to being, from whence, as Leibniz says, could we derive it? But from this point of view is it not plainly evident that metaphysical concepts are, first and essentially, states of the mind? How important it is no longer to misunderstand this! Yet unhappily it is what always is misunderstood, when these concepts are considered in the abstract, as things which subsist in themselves and which the reason finds ready-made.

No one better than St Augustine has understood and signalized the relation we are trying to establish. It is in a sense the whole purpose of the *Confessions*—that unique book whose thought remains always full of light and vitality. In it one sees how knowledge transforms itself and discovers being, according as the will is purified by disengagement from the love of vain appearances. To the period of his attachment to pleasure corresponds a materialistic outlook. "I could not," says the saint, "conceive a reality other than what presented itself to the eyes." God was for him a human form, or a substance filling space. "I was ignorant of myself," he says again, and he conceived himself too as of something possessing extension. Then came the critical period, one of fluctuating opinions and uncertainties. That which he had loved, that which he had believed, that by which he had sought to constitute himself in being now at last seemed empty and inconsistent. He then applied himself to look for something else, something which, no doubt, he had already to some degree found, but which at the outset he was in no condition to recognize inasmuch as he still remained attached to the vanities that had seduced him. Little by little he transformed himself, with the help of his natural largeness of mind. From the matter that he was he became in his own eyes Spirit, at the same time that God, equally, became himself. And his knowledge of himself and of God is fully luminous and reassuring when he himself reaches the point of seeing himself inwardly in God and God in himself. *Noverim te, noverim me.*

Essais de Philosophie religieuse, pp. *40–42*

THE GOD OF THE GREEKS AND THE GOD OF THE CHRISTIAN

God for the Christian is no longer the idea of ideas or an "essence" whence other essences proceed by logical participation. He is the Being of beings and the Life of their life. He is he who *is*, who has life in himself and by whom other beings are and live. He is not a supreme concept, but a supreme action, as also an immanent action. He is not an unmoving First Mover, wholly at rest above all movement and all living; he is the movement of life itself, as its principle and end. He is a purposive becoming, at the very point where the Greeks set only a blind fate. He is in the very chaos of reality, justly imparting to it his own character of infinity and presenting himself to it from within, in an immediate encounter, in order to enable it to find, organize and establish itself in him.

Whereas the Greeks were intent on conceiving the world *sub specie aeternitatis*, in Christianity, it could be said, God is conceived *sub specie temporis*. Whereas also the idealist deification of the world by abstract thought brings about no change in the unhappy condition of a reality given over to fate, the realist humanization of God, on the other hand, brings to this same condition a principle of genuine divinization and a seed of eternity. For by being present in time and participating in the development of humanity and of each individual within humanity, God is not the less eternal nor does he any the less possess in himself the plenitude of being and of life.

His eternity however is not time as it were arrested, in which life would be no more. On the contrary, it is the maximum of life; and it is towards this maximum of life that we are advancing, across the vicissitudes of time. It is not given to us to share in it merely by thought and transitorily, as though by a fleeting glance directed towards some enchanting abode whilst below an unpitying fate sweeps us away into the night. We share in it by our action and by our very being. Eternity is not outside time, as that which was before time and will be after it. Conceived thus it would never be other than time. It is within time itself, as that which impels and sustains time's process. Time is but the form which it assumes in us and in relation to us, in order to render itself accessible. And of this form we gradually divest ourselves as more and more we share in eternity, and in the act of living concentrate our being in God.

If Greek philosophy is in the most rigorous sense of the term an Idealism, then Christian doctrine may with equal rigour be described as a Realism.

Le Réalisme chrétien et l'Idéalisme grec (5th ed.), pp. *73–75*

ÉDOUARD LE ROY

WHAT IS A DOGMA?

At the outset I would say that a dogma cannot be assimilated to a theorem known only as a statement without proof, the truth of which is guaranteed simply by the affirmation of a master.

Such however, I realize, is the ordinary conception. God is represented, in the act of revelation, as a very learned professor who must be taken at his word when he communicates to his audience results the proofs of which it is not capable of understanding. But this scarcely appears satisfactory to me. . . .[1]

Let us take a few examples, to make clear what I mean.

"God is personal." We have here a dogma. Let us consider it as a statement having predominantly an intellectual meaning and a speculative content, a proposition belonging primarily to the order of theoretical knowledge. I leave aside the difficulties raised by the name "God" and concentrate on the word "personal". How ought it to be understood?

[1] God has spoken, one is told. But what does the word "speak" mean in this context? Obviously it is a metaphor. What exactly does it connote? Therein lies the whole difficulty.

If one allows that in using this word we are to think of the Divine personality according to the image presented by our psychological experience, on the model of what common sense refers to by the same name—that is, as an idealized and perfected human personality— we are left with complete anthropomorphism, and Catholics certainly are at one with their opponents in rejecting any such notion as this. Taken to its limits it is a mere crudity productive either of error or else of sheer verbiage—in any case capable of nothing more than vague metaphors and in the end, perhaps, self-contradiction.

Must we say then that the divine personality is essentially transcendent and beyond all comparison? It could well be; but in that event the term is very ill-chosen and seems calculated to create illusion. For as we declare that the divine personality resembles nothing that we know, what right have we to call it "personality"? Logically it should be denoted by a word that applies only to God and could be used with no other reference. Such a word however would be inherently indefinable. Picture to yourself a concatenation of syllables void of all positive significance and call it x. On this hypothesis the expression "God is personal" has no meaning other than that "God is x". But does this convey any *idea*?

For those who look for an intellectualist interpretation of the dogma "God is personal" there is an inescapable dilemma. Either you define the word "personality" and thus immediately fall into anthropomorphism, or else you do not, and slip no less surely into agnosticism. You are in a cleft stick.[1]

Take another example, the resurrection of Jesus. If the purpose of this dogma—whatever its ulterior and practical consequences—is primarily to add to our knowledge by guaranteeing the authenticity of a particular fact, if it constitutes above all a statement in the intellectual order, the question it at once raises is this: What precise meaning are we expected to attach to the word "resurrection"? Jesus, having undergone death, is come alive again. What, theoretically considered, does this signify? Not, surely, that after three days Jesus appeared again in a state identical with that prior to his crucifixion. The gospel itself informs us expressly to the contrary. The risen Jesus was no longer subject to the ordinary physical or physiological laws, his

---

[1] The same difficulty applies to propositions like "God is self-conscious", "God loves, wills, thinks", and so forth.

"glorified" body no longer perceptible under the same conditions as formerly, and so forth. What does this tell us? That the idea of "life" has a different content according to whether one applies it to the period before the crucifixion or to that which followed it. Well, then, what does it stand for as regards this second period? Nothing that can be expressed conceptually. It is simply a metaphor incapable of restatement in literal terms. Here again it would be necessary, strictly speaking, to coin another word, one confined to this single instance and therefore impossible to define in any normal way.

As a final example let us take the dogma of the real presence. Here it is the term "presence" which calls for interpretation. What does it usually mean? A being is said to be present when it is perceptible, or when, whilst remaining in itself beyond perception, it manifests itself by its perceptible effects. Now according to dogmatism itself neither of these two conditions is realized in this particular case. The presence in question is a mysterious presence—ineffable, unique and having no analogy with anything that one commonly understands by the word. I next ask what this means for us. Something that one can neither analyse nor even define can be called an "idea" only by an abuse of words. A dogma is interpreted as a statement in the intellectual order. But what does it state? It is impossible to say with precision. Does this not condemn the hypothesis?

In short, the supposition that dogmas are statements whose primary function is to communicate theoretical knowledge of a certain kind, meets everywhere, as it seems, with insurmountable obstacles. It appears to have the fatal effect of turning dogmas into nonsense. So perhaps we should resolutely abandon it. Let us consider, then, what other sort of meaning would alone remain possible and legitimate.

First of all—unless I am mistaken—a dogma has a *negative* sense. It excludes and condemns certain errors rather than determines truth in any positive way. Let us go back to our examples again, taking up the dogma that "God is personal". Nowhere here do I see a definition of the Divine personality. It teaches me nothing about that personality; it does not reveal its nature; it affords me no explicit idea of it whatever. But I do see very clearly that it says "God is not impersonal"; that is, that God is not a bare law, a formal category, an ideal principle, an abstract entity, any more than he is a universal substance or some undefined cosmic force diffused throughout all things. Briefly, then, the dogma "God is personal" furnishes me with no new, positive conception, nor again does it guarantee the truth of any particular system among those which in the history of philosophy have been successively propounded. But it does warn me that such and such forms of pantheism are false and ought to be rejected.

I could say as much of the real presence. The dogma in no way sets out a theory of that presence; it does not even inform me as to what it consists in. But it does tell me very clearly that it ought not to be understood in one or another of certain ways formerly proposed; for instance, it tells me that the consecrated host must not be taken for a mere symbol or figure of Jesus.

Christ's resurrection provides occasion for similar comments. In no wise does the dogma instruct me as to the mechanism of this singular fact, nor does it say what Jesus' new life was like. In a word, it presents me with no *conception*. On the other hand, however, it excludes certain conceptions that I might be tempted to fashion. Death did not set a term to Jesus' action relative to the things of this world. He still intervenes and lives amongst us, though not simply in the manner of a thinker now gone from us whose influence nevertheless remains fertile and long-lived and whose work goes on yielding results. He literally is our contemporary; for death, in sum, was not for him, as for ordinary men, the definitive cessation of practical activity. This is what the dogma of the resurrection teaches us.

Is it necessary to insist on this further? For the moment it does not seem to me useful to do so. The foregoing examples are enough to show the principle of interpretation that I have in view. No doubt considerable development would be necessary, did one wish to detail the full consequences of this principle and all its possible applications; in which case an ordered study of the different dogmas would be indispensable. But this is not the point I desire to make. My intention is simply to present an idea. That is why I am not concerned either to multiply examples or even to develop any one of them fully.

For the rest, the idea in question is not new. It belongs to the most authentic tradition. Indeed is it not the classical teaching of the theologians and doctors that, in the supernatural order, the surest method of investigation is the *via negationis*? I may recall, in this regard, a well-known text of St Thomas: *Est autem via remotionis utendum, praecipue in consideratione divinae substantiae. Nam divina substantia omnem formam, quam intellectus noster attingit, sua immensitate excedit; et sic ipsam apprehendere non possumus cognoscendo quid est, sed aliqualem eius habemus notitiam cognoscendo quod non est.*[1]

I should, however, mention an objection that could come to mind. It will readily be agreed that the dogmatic codification promulgated by the Church in the course of history has a mainly negative character, at all events when observed from the intellectual standpoint, as is the case with us at the moment. The Church herself declares, in fact, that it is no part of her mission to proclaim new revelations but only to safeguard a deposit. And to this mission the negative method, as adopted, is appropriate. All the same, in what does the deposit itself consist if not in a particular body of fundamental affirmations? Take the primary expression of the Christian faith, the *Credo*. What could be more positive? Here now is the basis of doctrine—that which characterizes and constitutes it. Moreover, whoever says *revelation* undoubtedly says *affirmation*, not *negation*.

Assuredly, I deny nothing of all this. But one must distinguish. The Symbol of Nicaea and Constantinople already shows signs of negative elaboration—on the divinity of Jesus Christ as against the heresy of Arius, or the procession of the Holy Spirit as against the Macedonians, and so on. From this angle, therefore, there is nothing to contradict our conclusions; it is the grammatical form alone that is affirmative, and basically it is a matter of excluding errors rather than of formulating theories. But let us take the Apostles' Creed. Here indeed there is nothing negative, but nothing also that is properly intellectual and theoretic; nothing that properly belongs to the order of speculative knowledge; nothing, in a word, that approximates to the statements of theorems. It is a profession of faith, a declaration of attitude. By and by we shall examine some dogmas from this practical standpoint, which—let me hasten to say—is in my sight the main one. However, let us for a moment longer keep to the intellectual view. The apostolic

---

[1] *Contra Gentiles,* I. xiv. ("Now in treating of the Divine essence the principal method to be followed is that of remotion. For the Divine essence by its immensity surpasses every form to which our intellect reaches; and thus we cannot apprehend it by knowing what it is. But we have some knowledge thereof by knowing *what it is not.*" Ed.)

Credo, in its primary aspect, affirms the existence of realities whereof it affords no sort of representative theory, even rudimentary. Thus its role in regard to abstract and reflective knowledge is this: *To pose objects and, in consequence, problems*. Finally, as one sees, the proposed objection has no weight and we can maintain our theses until further orders.

Hence, as statements of a theoretical order, dogmas have first and foremost a negative sense. History demonstrates this clearly, in showing us their successive hatchings out in the form of heresies.[1] The genesis of any dogma whatever has always followed the same course, always presented the same phases. At the outset we have purely human speculations, explanatory systems in every way similar to other philosophical schemes; in short, theoretical essays relative to the actual facts of religion, to the mysterious realities lived out by the Christian community in its practical beliefs. Only after this do we get dogmas, in order to condemn certain of these tentatives, to charge certain of these conceptions with error, to rule out certain of these intellectual representations. Whence it comes that dogmatic formulas often borrow expressions from diverse philosophies without going to the trouble of fusing and unifying these heterogeneous languages.... As also that dogmatic formularies are able to give the law in respect of the incomparable and transcendent and yet avoid falling into the contradictions either of anthropomorphism or of agnosticism. It is man who, with his opinions, his theories, his systems, supplies the dogmas with their intelligible material. The latter limit themselves to an occasional *veto*, or to a declaration that "this opinion, this theory, this system will not do", without ever indicating further why they are unacceptable or what should replace them. Thus negative dogmatic definitions do not limit knowledge or impede its progress. They merely close the gate to wrong routes.

From the strictly intellectual standpoint, dogmas it seems to me, have only the negative and prohibitive sense of which I have just spoken. Were they to formulate absolute truth in adequate terms— supposing such a fiction to have any meaning—they would be unintelligible to us. Were they to convey only an imperfect truth, relative and changing, they could not rightly command unconditional acceptance. The only radical way of meeting all objections of principle

---

[1] Note the habitual formula in conciliar decrees: "*Si quis dixerit . . . anathema sit*".

is to conceive them, in the way we have done, as definable—in their speculative aspect, that is—simply in respect of earlier doctrines upon which they pronounce an unbiassed judgment. Moreover, is it not the teaching of the theologians, even the most intellectualist among them, that in a dogmatic statement the reasons which can be incorporated in the text are not in themselves objects of faith imposed upon belief?

From the foregoing an important consequence already follows. It is that from the intellectual standpoint the true method of studying dogmas is the historical one. The science known as *positive theology*, or better, *history of dogma*, seeks to perform this task. Far more than so many purely dialectical treatises, it has an effective apologetic value. In any case it is impossible to understand dogmatic statements, as, still more, to justify them, unless one begins by putting them firmly back into their proper historical setting, outside of which their authentic meaning gradually becomes vague and may even at times end up by disappearing altogether.

However, dogmas do not have only a negative sense; and even this negative sense, which they present when viewed from a particular angle, does not constitute their essential and primordial significance. That derives from the fact that they are not simply propositions of a theoretical character and that they should not be considered from the intellectual standpoint alone or from that of pure knowledge. It is this which we must now make quite clear. . . .

A dogma has above all a *practical* sense. It states, before ought else, a *prescription of the practical order*. It formulates, beyond all else, a *rule of practical conduct*. Therein is its principal value, its positive significance. This is not to say, moreover, that it has no relation to thought, since (1) there are also duties in regard to the act of thinking, and (2) dogma itself involves the implicit affirmation that ultimate reality is such as to justify the conduct prescribed as reasonable and sound.

Here I gladly quote the following passage from Fr Laberthonnière: "Dogmas are not simply enigmatic and obscure formulas promulgated by God in the name of his own omnipotence in order to chasten our pride of spirit. They have a moral and practical import, a vital meaning more or less open to us according to the degree of spirituality to which we have attained."[1]

[1] *Essais de philosophie religieuse* p. *272.*

Let us keep to the examples already given, since they also clearly reveal the different types of dogma. "God is personal" means "Behave in your relations with God as you would in your relations with a human person". Similarly, "Jesus is risen" means "Be in relation to him as you would have been before his death, or as you would be if confronted by a contemporary". Again, the dogma of the real presence means "Act in relation to the host as you would in relation to Jesus himself visibly present". And so on. It would be easy to multiply examples, as to develop any one of them further.

That dogmas can and should be interpreted in this way is not in doubt, and doubtless no one will contest it. Christianity indeed—as it cannot too often be repeated—is not a scheme of speculative philosophy but a source and a rule of life, a discipline of moral and religious action—in short, a body of practical means for gaining salvation. Why, then, should there be anything very surprising in saying that dogmas relate primarily to conduct rather than to purely reflective knowledge?

Dogme et Critique, pp. *16–26*

PART V

BUONAIUTI AND OTHERS

WHAT MODERNISTS WANT

For us, profoundly Christian souls, religion, far from being a vague, mystical feeling which soothes the spirit and isolates it in a barren egoism, is a Divine reality, which kindles into and exalts the souls of men, and, knitting them together in a bond of brotherhood, directs their life towards a supreme and common goal. For us Christianity is the highest expression of religion thus conceived, and of Christianity in its turn we consider Roman Catholicism to be the amplest realization. With the affirmation of Christianity as life, we affirm also that it cannot be a mere intellectual abstraction, and, therefore, "the pure Gospel" of which you speak, "stripped of the explanations of theology", is not for us a reality, since, if it wishes to be reality and life, it must become externalized in forms derived from similar expressions of ordinary human activity. As Christians, we accept the authority of the Church, as the careful dispenser of the deposit of eternal truth inherited from Christ, to regulate and govern our religious life, and to interpret and supply its living needs and claims. We accept, further, the dogmas and rites by which all souls, in the communion of faith, hope, and charity, may participate in the life of the living Christ. . . .

Some have already announced the death of Catholicism, others have bemoaned its miserable condition. We do neither. It is not every crisis that brings death. At times an organism, when once the crisis is past and it has been purified of those elements which are alien and hostile to its nature, emerges to a more vigorous life. And we, who still feel all the riches and the inexhaustible power of Christianity in virtue of an intimate experience which overcomes every human argument to the contrary, have, in answer to your paternal call, girt ourselves with confidence to the task of imparting to the minds of others, and helping them to feel, this ineffable experience.

But today men exhibit a spirit of distrust and suspicion with regard to us. They are inclined beforehand to reject our invitation. This it is which makes the crisis more acute. Our work would be in vain if we did not retrace the causes of the crisis with objectivity and clearness of vision, just as the work of the physician is vain if he does not seek, before prescribing the remedy, an accurate knowledge of the disease. A frank and loyal sincerity must be the guide of all our research; for all our work which was not guided by the desire of objective truth would be contrary to the Divine Spirit, which is *the* Spirit of truth. . . .

Christianity of itself transcends every political party as it transcends every current metaphysic whatsoever. In order that it may live it needs to assimilate, through both the one and the other, the civilization that surrounds it. But this civilization is in a continuous process of transformation. To philosophical systems, other philosophical systems succeed; to the social, political, and economic needs of a particular period other needs succeed. These systems and needs repeat themselves, with alternating authority, in the course of the centuries, provoking that slow, tortuous movement in a generally upward direction which we call progress. In this upward movement Christianity ought to be the centripetal force, spurring on and leading forward humanity in the course of the various stages of its evolution, penetrating with its Spirit and moulding with its Divine forms the manifestations peculiar to each of them, yet not wholly identifying itself with any of them. And he who regards as definite forms of Christianity what are only expressions peculiar to the civilization which at a given moment it has made its own, is inevitably co-operating towards its ruin.

Christianity exists in the world as a law of Love and of Truth. It is love and truth that inspire those two factors of modern civilization—science and democracy. That we may make it Christian we have welcomed them, seeking to make them our own, without reserve, without fear, without excessive concern for the past.

But science and democracy, if they are to move forward securely, must submit to the control of criticism which is based, not on the force of authority, but on the value of things objectively established. From this point of view, their acceptance and the task of assimilating them demand of the Church many sacrifices. We know well how the Church, succeeding in Rome to the world-wide dominion which the Emperors abandoned to it, inheriting their authority and fusing it with that of the new races, inaugurated in the Pontificate an authority of its own by which it might reign supreme over all civil powers, an authority which was still further reinforced by that spiritual dominion its right to which no one disputed. And, further, the Church of the Middle Ages, having completed the fusion of Christian dogma with the Aristotelian philosophy by means of that scholasticism which then included all the knowable, became the arbiter of knowledge and of the minds who knew. This position, even though the events of these late centuries have weakened its force, is still strong enough to render the work of adaptation to the new character of civilization a difficult one for the Church.

The democracy demands of the Church, not only an attitude less conservative and less intent upon favouring the last remnants of the privileged nobility, but also a transformation and purification of forms and persons in her own government, still as tenaciously monarchical and absolute as when she adopted it at the end of the third century and consolidated it in the Middle Ages. To this end those old coercive methods must be abandoned or relaxed; a certain measure of autonomy in their own provinces must be restored to the bishops; a more liberal consideration shown towards the religious activity of the laity; sounder tests established in the choice of persons appointed to the supreme direction of her affairs; and in this directing body a wider representation of foreign nations provided for, whereby each may be governed by rules suited to its genius and local requirements.

On the other hand, the demands of science are much more serious. As has already been stated, a change has been wrought in modern intellectual conditions. Our habit of mind is at the opposite pole from that out of which our apologetic was built up. Religion, if it is to be accepted, cannot impose itself by means of a syllogism. It presupposes the *rationabile obsequium* without which it has no moral value for those who profess it. God, revelation, the Church, dogma, cannot be imposed from without by reasoned arguments. The soul must first seek them through its own free action, must find their reasons and learn their worth under the stimulus of its own religious experience, and bring this experience into relation with the religious experience of the human spirit throughout the ages.

God is not an intellectual abstraction, much less a physical reality

o

offering itself as an object of our sensible experience. He reveals himself to man by working in the intimate recesses of his personal *ego*, manifesting himself at first through a confused and inarticulate feeling of infinite, transcendental, incomprehensible Reality. Little by little this feeling, becoming more intense, invites to the act of adoration, till at last the soul feels the urgent need of entering into relations with this invisible Reality, and is led, not only to return upon itself in an act of reflection in order to investigate the origin and seek for the value of this experience, but also to review the whole history of the past and examine in it the origin and development of the relations of humanity with the supernatural world. To this end the student will not be able to limit himself to the study of the Bible only, as a unique source of the history of religion. For him the Bible is *as yet* a book having the same value as all other books, sacred or profane, which record the history of antiquity. Only after these have been confronted by him with one another, and all alike subjected to the control of critical science; only when the superiority of the religious sentiment, as it germinated and advanced to maturity among a people which had to traverse supreme difficulties and to exist under conditions which were often unfavourable to the rapid growth of a civilization developing in the same way as that of the surrounding nations, has asserted itself in his mind; only when he is able to establish the fact that the religious experience of Israel corresponds with a more perfect and complete synthesis of the spiritual attitudes and requirements of the ancient world: then, and only then, will he accept the Old Testament.

But he has still something further to accomplish. To us the religion of Israel belongs but indirectly. Today we are Christians, and our civilization is Christian; but, before we were so, we belonged to the Graeco-Roman civilization. And if Christianity is the fulfilment of the religion of Israel, it had, in order to become ours, to make itself Graeco-Roman by assimilating Western civilization to itself. Thus, even when the Old Testament has been accepted, there still remains an immense work to be accomplished. It is necessary not only to submit to criticism all the books of the New Testament, but to study their intimate relations, both those which they may have with the books of the Old Testament and those with Graeco-Roman civilization. Thus the student will be able to ascertain what was the original Spirit of the Christian revelation, what were its primitive and genuine elements, what were those which it derived from the religion of Israel, and what from the Hellenic civilization. Afterwards he will study the progress and rapid diffusion of the Christian religion by means of the Church, whether and how the Church continued the mission of Christ, whether and how it answers to the spiritual requirements of different peoples, whether and how it co-operates with their advance in civilization.

And if from all these researches he is able to show that the religious sentiment appeared in humanity at first under superstitious and imperfect forms—as all manifestations of physical, intellectual and moral life were imperfect and primitive—and then, with the slow and gradual evolution of civilization, instead of being eclipsed and disappearing, rose to higher forms and attained to a reflex knowledge of itself, until it took concrete form in the Christian religion; and if it in turn, considered under the forms of Catholicism, can show that it contains within itself energies which the human spirit will find it useful to assimilate, energies which will help that spirit forward along the path traced by high modern ideals; then alone will the student be able freely to accept the Catholic religion with its authority, its theology, its Sacraments, and its discipline.

For us, this necessity of submitting everything that is the object of our living and profound faith to the control of criticism on the same terms as all the beliefs and expressions of the religious life of various peoples involves an intense, a fatiguing, and even a painful labour. But nothing has prevented us from undertaking it. If we are truly convinced of our faith, not only ought we to have no fear of science, which, when it is true and certain, is itself also an emanation of the Divine Truth, but we ought also to hope from such control for an ever more living light upon the truths which form the pivot of our religious life.

Quello che vogliamo (*What We Want*), an Open Letter to Pius X from a Group of Priests (trans. by A. L. Lilley), pp. *5–7, 10 f., 21–31*

THE PROGRAMME OF MODERNISM

1. The True Presupposition of Modernism

First of all we must lay bare an equivocation by which inexpert readers of the Encyclical[1] might easily be misled. That document

---

[1] *Pascendi Dominici Gregis.* See below, Appendix (i).

starts with the assumption that there lies at the root of Modernism a certain philosophical system from which we deduce our critical methods, whether Biblical or historical; in other words, that our zeal to reconcile the doctrines of Catholic tradition with the conclusions of positive science springs really from some theoretical apriorism which we defend through our ignorance of scholasticism and the rebellious pride of our reason. Now the assertion is false, and since it is the basis on which the Encyclical arranges its various arguments we cannot in our reply follow the order of that fallacious arrangement; but we must first of all show the utter emptiness of this allegation, and then discuss the theories which the Encyclical imputes to us.

In truth, the historical development, the methods and programme of so-called Modernism are very different from what they are said to be by the compilers of *Pascendi Gregis*.

So far from our philosophy dictating our critical method, it is the critical method that has, of its own accord, forced us to a very tentative and uncertain formulation of various philosophical conclusions, or better still, to a clearer exposition of certain ways of thinking to which Catholic apologetic has never been wholly a stranger. This independence of our criticism in respect to our purely tentative philosophy is evident in many ways.

First of all, of their own nature, textual criticism, as well as the so-called Higher Criticism (that is, the internal analysis of Biblical documents with a view to establishing their origin and value), prescind entirely from philosophical assumptions. A single luminous example will suffice—that furnished by the question of the *Comma Johanneum*— now settled for ever. In past days when theologians wanted to prove the doctrine of the Trinity they never omitted to quote from the Vulgate: "There are three that bear record *in Heaven, the Father, the World and the Holy Ghost.*"[1] Now the italicized words are lacking in all the Greek mss of today, cursive or uncial, and in all the Greek epistolaries and lectionaries, and in all the ancient translations, except the Vulgate, in the works of the Greek Fathers and of other Greek writers prior to the twelfth century, in those of all the ancient Syrian and Armenian writers, and in those of a great number of the Latin Fathers. This silence of East and West is all the more remarkable as the passage would have been of priceless value in the Arian controversy. That it

[1] I John v. 7.

was not then appealed to, proves that it did not exist at the beginning of the fourth century. Moreover, a collation of mss and their comparison with the works of the heretic Priscillian, discovered a few years ago, makes it clear that the verse in question comes from Spain, and was fabricated by that heretic (A.D. 384) in favour of his trinitarian views, of which Peregrinus made himself the propagandist. Now it is plain that in order to arrive at such a conclusion and to study a literary problem critically, no sort of philosophical doctrine or presupposition is required. The same can be said of a whole host of Biblical and historical problems whose impartial solutions, leading to results so different from those of traditional Catholic criticism, are the true cause of that revolution in religious apologetic which we find forced upon us by sheer necessity. Does one really need any special philosophical preparation to trace a diversity of sources in the Pentateuch, or to convince oneself, by the most superficial comparison of texts, that the Fourth Gospel is a substantially different kind of work from the synoptics, or that the Nicene Creed is essentially a development of the Apostles' Creed?

But besides these intrinsic reasons, we can invoke indisputable facts in proof of the independence of our criticism in relation to our philosophical tendencies.

First of all, this criticism is far more ancient than the philosophy with which we are credited. Nothing had been heard of "agnosticism" or "immanentism" when between *1670* and *1690* Richard Simon published his marvellous *Histoires Critiques* of the Old and New Testament, which represents the first really serious application of scientific methods to the study of the documentary records of Catholic Revelation. The first of the two volumes, in particular, is at once a splendid scientific reconstruction of the literary history of the Israelites founded on a minute examination of the state of the texts that have gone to the compilation of the Bible and also an admirable treatise on the critical classification of the versions of the Hebrew text, with a list of the varieties of interpretations which it has received at different periods.

Nothing had been heard of "symbolism" or of historical "transfiguration" when Dr J. Astruc, in an anonymous work published at Brussels *1753*, "Conjectures sur les mémoires originaux dont il paraît que Moïse s'est servi pour composer le livre de la Genèse", tried for the first time to systematize the theory of the most ancient sources used in that part of the Pentateuch.

Since the time of those great men, criticism, without the slightest vestige of philosophic preoccupation, has applied to the Bible and to the history of Christianity those very same scientific principles which indeed are not susceptive of any change or perversion for the simple reason that they are the principles of historical science as such. We are not to blame if, arriving on the scene after centuries of critical study, we find all those positions destroyed which traditional theology had assumed without discussing the texts or making sure of their documentary value; on the contrary, we think we deserve well of religious apologetic if we honestly strive to transfer the rational defence of faith from the tottering basis of what has proved to be an anticritical exegesis, to the solid, because unassailable, basis offered by the deepest exigencies of the human soul and by those spiritual life-needs which have given birth to the whole process of Christianity.

Furthermore, the independence and priority of criticism in relation to philosophy in our intellectual movement can be established clearly in the case of more than one of our representative students. It was his long critical researches as to the Old and New Testament that led Abbé Loisy, whose former work had been exclusively critical, to write his celebrated studies (in *1900* and *1901*) on *Revelation* and on *The Religion of Israel*, which were the beginning of his apologetic labours. It has been a prolonged documentary study of the gospel narratives that has led so many of us to revise the traditional opinions about the foundation of the Church and the institution of the Sacraments.

Finally, it has been long years passed in the patient comparison of the various stages that mark the development of Catholic thought that have almost unconsciously driven us to adopt a new theory as to the development of dogma from the teaching of Christ, preferring to see everywhere the continual and secret working of a Divine indwelling Spirit rather than contradict plain facts by admitting an abrupt and complete revelation of the *Credo* which never took place. This is so true that some of us, who are constitutionally averse to synthetic efforts and impatient of every attempt at apologetic conciliation, avow ourselves critics pure and simple, ignoring, if not actually opposing, any tentative hypothesis to harmonize an unchanging faith with a progressive critical science.

We seem to have said enough to show that it is not an impartial estimate of facts but a clever polemical stratagem that leads the authors of the Encyclical to strike at what they suppose to be certain philosophical presuppositions of our system, but what are in any case the conclusions of long critical efforts and not the premisses nor the directing principles of the research by which those conclusions were reached. Hence we cannot, still less should we desire to, follow the Encyclical on to a ground so treacherous and insecure. No doubt it was a very convenient artifice to present our movement to the public as hingeing on a few abstract principles (how sorely distorted we shall presently see) whose designed paradoxical form makes them glaringly incompatible with the fundamental positions of Catholic theology. But it would be folly on our part to let such an equivocation pass without protest. We must rather vindicate before all things the critical basis and fundamental facts on which our whole system rests; we must show that if Modernism is not merely an empty or ambiguous term it stands for a method, or rather for *the* critical method, applied conscientiously to the religious forms of humanity in general, and to Catholicism in particular. And if such a faithful application leads to a complete revision of the positive bases on which the scholastic interpretation of Catholicism was raised, and so provokes the need of a new apology for our faith, this is not due to a freakish caprice of our reason, proudly contemptuous of scholasticism, whose principles, on the contrary, we understand very well and whose historical function we appreciate. It is due to a manifest exigence of the religious sense which seeks to preserve its power over men in ever new forms of thought. It was inevitable that medieval scholasticism (*i.e.*, the fusion of Aristotelian thought with Catholic teaching such as it was up to the end of the twelfth century) springing into existence in a period void of the least vestige of historic sense and of the remotest suspicion as to what had been the actual facts of the evolution of Christianity—it was inevitable that such a system should fall to pieces as soon as its presupposition of a mechanical revelation, petrified in the moment of its instantaneous completion, was found to be based on Biblical and patristic texts accepted without any sense of critical discernment. Add to this, the criticism to which the logical realism of Aristotle has been subjected by the more recent philosophical tradition, and it is easy to imagine the disastrous crisis which has arisen for the scholastic interpretation of Catholicism. Modernism has been born and matured by the need of meeting this lamentable crisis, and it will continue to bear this party-name till the day when, after having created and propagated this new interpretation of Catholicism by force of its tenacious devotedness, it will mingle with, and become one and the same thing as, Catholicism.

The reasons are clear, then, why we do not think fit to follow the Encyclical line by line in the deceptive picture it draws of the Modernist as philosopher, believer, theologian, critic, apologist, reformer, and to set over against each head of its accusation the sincere explanation of our modest aims and our true ideas. To us it seems a strange pretension to present Modernism as a synthesis, since we are the first to declare openly and emphatically that we have as yet no definite synthesis and are only groping our way laboriously, and with much hesitation, from the now assured results of criticism to some sort of apologetic, whose aim is not to subvert tradition but solely to make use of the eternal postulates of religion familiar to the most authentic conception of Catholicism.

We shall therefore put together briefly the results of Biblical and historical criticism; we shall show how they have simply necessitated a change in our conception of inspiration and of revelation, and the introduction of the conception of religious evolution; how, as regards the New Testament, they have necessitated a distinction between the outward history and the inward history, between the historical Christ and the mystical Christ, the Christ of reason and the Christ of faith; we shall call attention to the undeniable fact that the Catholic tradition (that is, the living transmission of the religious Spirit liberated by the gospel) has undergone profound revolutions in respect to its theoretic formulation, beginning with the Messianic preachings of Christ and going on to the Hellenistic Fathers of the second century; thence, to the anti-Gnostic controversialists; thence, to the definitions of the first ecumenical councils, to the medieval doctors, to the scholastic systematization, to the Tridentine formulas. And from this we shall show how the honest recognition of such an evolution has led us to justify our faith by the notion of the permanence of something Divine in the life of the Church, in virtue whereof every new doctrinal formulation, every new juridical institution (in so far as it more or less consciously tends to the preservation of the gospel Spirit) can claim a Divine origin and a Divine maintenance.

No one can evade the results of scientific history, and so we shall start from them. Modern criticism has revolutionized the historical outlook; its method has become a most delicate and complex instrument on which alone we can depend if our evocation of the buried past is not to be mere fiction or romance. In applying this method to religious documents and tradition we are only logically consistent. Besides, we are thus only obeying an orthodox postulate of theology which puts the sacred Scriptures first among the *loci theologici* (that is, the source from which the teachings of faith can be drawn), and which demands that the Scriptures be so seriously and carefully studied that the structure reared upon them may not rest upon sand. When it is objected that Catholics prove the authority of the Church from Scripture, and the authority of Scripture from the Church, our approved apologists answer rightly that, in the former case, we argue from Scripture not as Divinely inspired but as from a human document subject to the same canons of criticism as the Koran or the Homeric poems.

As St Thomas[1] says, faith and reason cannot be in conflict. We should therefore courageously apply our criticism to the study of religion, confident that whatever is destroyed by the process can in no way belong to the substance of our religious faith.

Then when we come to discuss the philosophical principles for which the Encyclical rebukes us, we shall make it clear that some of the charges are simply false, and that if others are partly true they are nowise contrary to Catholic tradition, which, be it remembered, reaches back further than the *Summa* of St Thomas, let alone the Council of Trent. Christianity had lived long before one or the other, and there is no reason why we should not uphold an interpretation of Catholicism older than either, if the circumstances that called for it were in some way analogous to those of the modern religious world.

2. Criticism and the Development of Christianity

The critical method applied to the history of Christianity has yielded results no less decisive.

The traditional apologists have been wont to view the Church

[1] *Contra Gentiles*, i. 7. *The Programme of Modernism*, Buonaiuti, (trans. by A. L. Lilley), pp. 15–27.

as an institution leading a life apart from the surrounding social and political world, growing and shaping itself according to peculiar laws of development, whose largely miraculous character forbids their verification. This ancient conception of the Church as the work of the *Logos*, and as a domain closed to the influence of those laws which govern the growth of human societies, having once obtained footing in the great historical construction of Eusebius, has for long ages been the postulate of all Catholic ecclesiastical history.

A prepossession of this kind, joined with the notion of revelation as being, before all, a communication of unchangeable abstract propositions, led to another assumption, namely, that the dogmatic affirmations, which gradually became part of the inherited intellectual explanation of faith, as well as the external forms progressively assumed by the ecclesiastical organization, existed, at least implicitly from the very beginning in the preaching of Jesus, in the faith of the first Christians, and in the teaching of the Fathers.

Historical criticism has purged our minds inexorably of these prepossessions. For criticism, Christianity is a fact like any other, subject to the same laws of development, permeated by the same political, juridical and economic influences, liable to the same variations. Its quality of religious fact does not rob it of those other qualities which belong to every historical fact in which man's spiritual activity has found expression.

And therefore criticism, without any preoccupation, has studied the fact of Christianity in its historical context both as to its origin and its universal propagation. Studying and comparing the New Testament documents, considering the date of their composition and the practical scope of their several authors, it has, as we have seen, put it beyond doubt that their narrative shows traces of an elaboration of the person and teaching of Christ accomplished in the religious consciousness of the first two or three generations of believers. And then setting itself to discern, through these incrustations formed round them by an exalted faith, the authentic words of the Master and the simple theme of his discourses, it has been driven to the conclusion that the Gospel of Jesus was a persistent and enthusiastic proclamation of a coming kingdom of God; that it was free from all admixture of a materialistic eschatology; that at bottom it was an earnest and authoritative call to purity of heart. All the rest, that is, the wondrous affirmations as to the personal relations between Christ and the Father (so far as they exceed the then common identification of the Messiah with the Son of God), the ever more inward and spiritual conception of the Messianic kingdom, the special description of the Church or community of the faithful as the earthly equivalent of the heavenly kingdom—all this represents the formulation of new ideas evoked by Christian experience, especially in the more intellectual and cultivated followers of the gospel, and notably in St Paul. Such a criticism of the historical substance of Christ's teaching does away with the possibility of finding in it even the embryonic form of the Church's later theological teaching. So too an impartial study of the patristic tradition (preceded by a careful study of the authenticity of the documents to be used, and accompanied by a constant resolve not to read earlier witnesses in the light of later theological conceptions) has proved how idle it is to look there for the fundamental lines of Catholic theology as systematized by the scholastics and adopted in the definitions of Trent. What, without prepossession, must be admitted is, a progressive development of Catholic theology springing from the ineradicable need of supplying an intellectual embodiment and expression for that religious experience which, once evoked by the preaching of Christ, has remained substantially the same thing under all its successive embodiments.

An ancient legend told by Rufinus in the fourth century relates how "after the Lord's ascension the Apostles received orders to separate and spread over the world to preach the word of God. Before separating they took counsel and agreed on a common rule of belief lest they should be found teaching different doctrines. Full of the Holy Ghost they composed the creed." Thus in the fourth century the belief had gained ground that the principal dogmas of Christianity had been formulated by the Apostles, fresh from the teaching of their Master and filled with the Holy Ghost. Modern criticism has not only shown this legend to be false but has striven to show, positively, that it is arbitrary and aprioristic to hold that the dogmas of faith go back, in their present expression, to the primitive teaching of Christ and his immediate followers. Every day brings new successes in the endeavour to mark, by means of a critical analysis of documents, the slow, and at times imperceptible, evolution of Christian psychological experience towards the reflex formulation of dogma—an evolution guided by the necessity of finding theological formulas to foster and direct the original religion of the gospel, which consists in the expectation of a kingdom of Heaven upon earth, in the felt solidarity of all souls in relation to their common good, and in trust and confidence in the Heavenly Father.

The Encyclical, it is true, upbraids our criticism with starting from the assumption "that everything in Church history is to be explained by 'vital emanation', and that every event is the outcome of some want and should therefore be considered as historically later than that want". Herein it seems to reproach us with an assertion whose contrary is simply historically unthinkable and theologically erroneous. As we have already said, the history of the Church as a living is, in fact, governed by the same laws as other social institutions. Now it is an elementary law of life, in all its manifestations, that every organ answers to some vital need and that every output of energy is determined by some deep exigency of the subject. Moreover, it seems to us as theologically incorrect to suppose that ecclesiastical history is a triumph of caprice and lawlessness, as it is thoroughly orthodox to believe in a Divine Providence whose rule admits nothing superfluous, and which takes care that the course of events and the development of religious ideas in the Church are reached according to the varying but normal exigencies of the faithful. Nor are these mere aprioristic assumptions which vitiate the impartiality of historical research. History is within its province in seeking to determine the immanent reasons of facts and to trace the impalpable but very real exigencies whence the events recorded flow by logical necessity. History which fails to do this does not merit the name.

The conclusions of such a method, applied to the history of Catholicism, are simply disastrous to the old theological positions. Instead of finding from the first at least the germs of those dogmatic affirmations formulated by Church authority in the course of ages, we have found a sort of religion which was originally formless and undogmatic, and which came gradually to develop in the direction of definite forms of thought and ritual owing to the requirements of general intercourse and to the need of giving abstract expression to the principles which should shape the religious activity of the faithful. And this was effected partly by the efforts of Christian thinkers and partly by the negation of the positions adopted by heretics. The gospel message could never have lived and spread abroad in its primitive spiritual simplicity. When it passed the borders of Palestine and was found to be of universal import, in order to evoke, in other peoples, the same religious experiences—unselfishness, inward purification, hope in a supernatural reward of righteousness, reliance on Jesus the Christ and Redeemer—it had to adapt itself to their mentality and to present Christ, with his message of redemption, in a different garb from that which he assumed in his Jewish surroundings and in the popular prophetic tradition.

Wonderfully flexible in its psychological simplicity, like every religious revival, primitive Christianity spread over the Roman world, that is, over the countries bordering the basin of the Mediterranean, adapting itself to the mentality and spiritual education of every region and borrowing from each the elements most suited for its own further development. This work of adaptation (accompanied by the spontaneous accommodation of the gospel message to the ever more inexplicable delay of the Advent, whose nearness Christ had predicted) was completed in a relatively short time and, thanks to the influence of so great a religious thinker as St Paul, has left its traces in the narratives of the life of Jesus which were primarily rather doctrinal and hortatory than strictly historical. Such elaborations affected most especially those doctrines that afterwards became fundamental for Catholicism—the Trinitarian and Christological dogmas, and the organization of the Church.

This Church, which lay beyond the horizon of Christ's outlook, bounded by the Parousia, grew up naturally among his followers and quickly passed from the charismatic hierarchy of its first days, arranged according to personal graces and gifts of the Spirit, to the official and monarchic hierarchy arranged according to measures of jurisdiction and sacramental power.

As to Trinitarian and Christological dogma, criticism has marked the various stages of its progress on its way to the lucid affirmations of the second Council of Nicea. The continual exaltation of Christ in the esteem and affection of his followers, the various formulas invented to express his supernatural dignity according to the philosophical and theological language of the converted nations, combined with the sudden elaboration of certain Hebrew conceptions recast and catholicized by St Paul, all evoked a rapid development of the intellectual elements latent in that spiritual movement set going by the gospel message. The Acts (ii. *22*), echoing the primitive Christian teaching, speak of Jesus as "A man to whom God has borne witness by miracles and wonders and signs wrought by his means". He is the Messiah upon whom an ignominious death has conferred heavenly glory, and who must soon return to inaugurate his kingdom. Such was the simple and deep faith of the first disciples. But Christ has called all the members of the human family to be sons of God, and has presented himself as their archetype. He is, therefore, himself pre-eminently the Son of God, according to the prophetic tradition which attributes that dignity to the Messiah.

Side by side with this profound elaboration of the simple gospel ideas of Christ's personality there was a development of the idea of the Holy Spirit. As is usual at the beginning of any new religious upheaval, extraordinary phenomena, startling manifestations of a supernatural energy, took place in the little communities excited by the eager expectation of a universal renewal of all things. This energy or power, which took possession of the souls of men saturated with Biblical lessons and narratives, was spontaneously identified with the Spirit of Javeh, to which the Old Testament usually ascribed any action that seemed to exceed the normal faculties of man. A natural relationship soon came to be established between the Father (to whom was directed the filial devotion of the faithful), the Son (who was the giver of the Spirit, that is, of power to become sons of God) and the Spirit (who was the cause of the more striking manifestations of the new faith). And since it was especially at baptism that these surprising and mysterious effects of conversion were more manifestly displayed, it was in connection with this initiatory rite that Christians first formulated the invocation of the Trinity—a formula unknown to St Paul. From baptism the Trinitarian formula passed, as Justin teaches us, into the liturgy.

Upon these elementary data, the still timid and hesitating expressions of the latent intellectual and dogmatic implications of Christian religious experience, there came to be based a vast theological structure whose beginnings and developments are not difficult to trace. St Paul had already speculated as to the pre-existence of Christ, as to Christ's identity with the Holy Spirit, as to the effects of the said Spirit, which did not merely (like the Spirit of Javeh in the Old Testament) augment man's physical and natural energies, but transformed man's inner life, raising it to a higher level of existence and operation. And by such speculations he led the way in that sort of reflection which tends to express in precise philosophic categories the relations existing between those realities which feed and foster the Christian life.

The translation of the Hebrew conception of the Messiah into the Platonic idea of the *Logos* marks a culminating point in this theological elaboration. Here the Messiah dreamt of by souls anxiously awaiting the redemption of Israel was identified with the abstract notion, essentially Hellenic, of a cosmic intermediary between the world and the Supreme Being. A Hebrew conception possessing certain moral and religious values, but otherwise unmeaning for the Hellenic mind, was translated into Alexandrine terminology in such a way as to retain those values in another and more metaphysical setting. To us today the lines pursued by this rapid evolution of ideas give the impression of a cold, aprioristic system. But in reality this progress of Christian life towards a better formulation of itself was the collective work of multitudes who "lived" their faith in thought as well as in word, action and feeling.

Christology, so closely bound up with Trinitarian theology, naturally underwent in its turn a parallel and dependent development. The Messianic notion of the Son of David, and the apocalyptic notion of One who was to appear in the clouds, and the title "Son of God", which in Hebrew was synonymous with the Messiah, once transferred to Greek soil, where parentage between gods and heroes was a common belief, opened the road to the notion of a unique relation between Christ and the Father, and even of an identity of nature.

Finally, as regards the organization of the Christian communities, they had come by the beginning of the second century to adopt the monarchic episcopate as the result of taking over certain offices and titles, partly from the synagogue, partly from the Hellenistic confraternities and societies.

The display of so vigorous a development, accomplished in the bosom of the communities at a time when the empire was doing its best to stifle the gospel, is one of the most remarkable features of early Christian history. Not only was persecution unable to crush the nascent religion; it could not even arrest that healthy effort of the experience originated by Christ to evolve from itself a dogmatic formulation and an authoritative organization by which to feed and foster the new Christian conscience, and to enable the Church to provide her ministers with a creed and an authority for the furtherance of her spiritual conquests. As soon as the last persecution had proved a lamentable fiasco, and the astute Constantine had perceived the wisdom of attaching his fortunes to those of Christianity by making it a state religion, the Church was all ready for that first impressive display of her material and moral force, which took place at Nicea, where the Trinitarian dogma and the consubstantiality of the Word with the Father were solemnly defined. Thus at Nicea were definitively laid the bases of that structure of orthodox thought raised up in succeeding centuries.

Theological conflicts recommenced, however, very soon, and this time the disputes were mainly Christological. Apart from the short-lived Macedonian controversy (settled at Constantinople) about the relation of the Holy Ghost to the other Divine Persons, the war was waged over the relation of the human and Divine elements united in the person of Christ. It is remarkable to notice the jealous watchfulness of the Christian conscience, lest in this search for a formula to express a fact beyond the ordinary range of human comprehension any sacrifice should be made of the religious experience of Christ's immanence in the soul or of his redeeming efficacy. Nestorianism with its sharp distinction of two persons in Christ, human and Divine, implicitly imperilled the infinite value of his acts and so was condemned by the Council of Ephesus. Eutyches went to the opposite extreme, insisting on unity of person to the prejudice of duality of Nature, thus putting the imposing figure of the Redeemer outside the ranks of humanity, and so was condemned at Chalcedon. Thus has Catholic dogma threaded its way between the extremes of error, being the intellectual expression of the deepest needs of the Christian conscience, which seeks in Christ at once the man who has suffered for us and the God who has merited for us.

But the Church, pushed by historical events into the office of guide and controller of the peoples of the West, so strangely intermixed after the barbaric invasion, soon felt a need of new methods of propaganda and government. The strife with Monothelitism (the last disguised remnant of the Monophysite heresy) is only a secondary episode of Oriental character in comparison with the grave problem facing the

Church in the midst of a society reduced to intellectual chaos and looking to her not only for religious instruction but also for the rudiments of philosophical and scientific education. Henceforth the arena of intellectual conflict is not theology, properly so called, but philosophy, or rather, philosophical apologetic. In the Middle Ages, in a society she had moulded with her own hands and inspired with her own Spirit, the Church's most urgent task was to shape or to adopt a philosophy which might serve as a preparation for dogma, as an instrument of intellectual and even moral discipline in every department of life. And this is just why the Church, at the beginning of the medieval philosophical controversies, turned with sympathy to the realistic logic—although rejecting the metaphysic—of Aristotle, finding therein the most effectual formulation of a mental attitude towards reality in harmony with the requirements of the absolutist conception of religion and those of a theocratic use of moral and political power. Modern criticism has sought, as yet without full success, to call up from the past the various attempts made before arriving at that blend of Aristotle and Christian dogma which characterizes the golden age of scholasticism. The problem of "Universals", contained in a text of Porphyry, which has reached us through Boethius, was the nucleus of philosophic inquiry. The first essays at a philosophical apologetic were made in the Carlovingian schools, but with a result contrary to the Church's desire. Scotus Erigena was a solitary thinker far too deeply saturated with a mystical individualism to be able to provide the society, sheltered under the wings of the papacy and the Empire, with the impersonal and absolute formulas of a satisfactory metaphysic. But the attempt which failed once was renewed with that courage which is inspired by the needs of a new age. Yet how many failures were necessary before arriving at a harmonious synthesis! The nominalism of Roscelyn, the conceptualism of Abelard, the realism of Bernard, the intuitionism of the St Victors represent so many currents that strove to prevail in a conflict of ideas which but reflected those real conflicts between papal and imperial power by which society was torn asunder. Finally, coinciding in time with that great papal theocracy which was the fruit of centuries of political effort, came the imposing construction of scholasticism, in which philosophy and dogma seemed to be harmonized, and whose mission it was apparently to bind intelligences in the bonds of a metaphysic

P

which was in reality the most potent instrument of moral domination that the age of Innocent III could have possibly desired.

It is in the fact that scholasticism was begotten by the practical needs of that age—that is, by the need of providing a philosophic and religious synthesis which should tie down man's spirit in a posture of humble submission in matters of reason and conduct—it is in this fact that criticism finds the chief reason of the slight historical consciousness of which scholasticism gives evidence. All the patristic sources, all the expressions of Christian experience fashioned by previous generations, are noticed and used by the scholastic divines only so far as they serve to support their intellectual positions. Nowhere do we find signs of an impartial inquiry as to what the primitive Christian fact was in reality; nowhere a docile acceptance of the genuine data of patristic tradition whenever these were opposed to their Aristotelian prepossessions. Scholasticism is precisely the intellectual expression of the Christian experience as adapted to the spiritual needs of the early Middle Ages. And this is why the papacy has clung to it with a tenacity worthy of a better cause, and brought about its canonization at the Council of Trent. It recognizes instinctively (though not avowedly) in scholasticism the most effectual defence of that age in which its own authority reached a fullness of splendour soon afterwards lost irreparably. Even today it would fain rehabilitate scholasticism. But how is it possible to revive such a mode of apologetic now that criticism has, without any sort of prepossessions, reconstructed the whole story of the evolution of Christianity with all its successive stages and varieties of expression? Criticism has made us see how Catholic dogma has sprung entirely from the need of setting experience in harmony with the mind of the age, and the unchanging Spirit of religion with the ever-varying expressions of thought. How can we refuse to accept these conclusions which are not the result of hare-brained speculation but of a most painstaking analysis of Christian documents? If the Church needed to oppose them uncritically with the assumptions of the Middle Ages, she would have to face disaster and bankruptcy. But there is no such need. Providentially the Church has not yet defined the relations between her immutability and her flexibility. And, therefore, we who believe in the harmony of faith and science, and who therefore accept the results of criticism as well as that measure of immutability required by the inherent truth of Christianity, have had recourse to certain new apologetic considerations which seem to us to possess an abundant persuasiveness in the eyes of our contemporaries. We have been able to show how spontaneous the evolution of Christianity has been, and yet how indispensable it has seemed at every historical crisis for the preservation of Christian piety, and how, without it, religion would have been perverted, weakened and perhaps destroyed. Whence it follows that we cannot possibly deny the evolution of Catholicism.

As we cannot refuse the results (ever more or less imperfect) of social evolution, so, too, the whole process of Christian development, wrought by the Christian consciousness upon the religious experience of the gospel, strikes us as something legitimate in itself which we are not free to accept or refuse, since in refusing it we should dry up the deepest roots of our spiritual life. And even if certain modes of thought, and certain conceptions of authority, transmitted to the Church from the Middle Ages, seem to us to have now grown to be encumbrances, we do not believe that we have, as individuals, any right to oppose them, but only to spread abroad among the masses of the faithful a consciousness of their inutility and obstructiveness. For a higher experience and expression of Catholicism must be the fruits of a more enlightened, more cultivated, more spiritual collective conscience. It is from this point of view that a conciliation of the rights of criticism with the deepest needs of faith seems possible to us. Everything in the history of Christianity has changed—doctrine, hierarchy, worship; but all these changes have been providential means for the preservation of the gospel-spirit, which has remained unchanged through the ages. Of course the scholastics and the Fathers at Trent came into a much richer theological heritage than the Christians of the first century; but the religious experience, that in virtue of which they were Christians, was the same for them all. And for us today it is likewise the same, although it moves but slowly towards a new self-formulation, owing to the sway, no longer intellectual but simply juridical, of scholasticism, which has won the surely anomalous position of an "official" philosophy. The formulations of the past and of the future have been, and will be, equally legitimate, provided they faithfully respect the growing needs of evangelical piety, ever eager to find in reflex thought a better instrument for its own preservation and utterance.

Reasoning thus, we find ourselves undoubtedly in harmony with one of the fundamental tendencies of contemporary philosophy, and which is even considered the very condition of the possibility of a philosophy—the immanental tendency. According to this principle, nothing can enter into and get hold of man's spirit that does not spring from it and in some way correspond to its need of self-expansion. For it there is no fixed truth, no unalterable precept, that is not in some way self-imposed and innate. Applied to the history of Christianity this immanental principle provides the best defence for those positions which the Church has arrived at in obedience to the constant instigation of the collective conscience.

Il programma dei modernisti (trans. by G. Tyrrell),
pp. *87–109*

3. Agnosticism and Immanentism

Discussing the philosophy of the Modernists, the Encyclical reprehends its agnostic principles, its immanental method, its agnostic application to history of the postulates of the "transfiguration" and "disfiguration" of phenomena.

Let us speak, first of all, of our supposed agnosticism. It is based on the idea, says the Encyclical, "that human reason is wholly confined to the region of phenomena, that is, to what appears, and to the manner of its appearance. Beyond that it has no right, no natural power, to go." We hope to make clear the contradiction into which the Encyclical falls in its desire to prove us agnostics. Indeed, in the very same paragraph it credits us with opinions flatly incompatible with agnosticism. For it says that "they" [the Modernists] "have settled and determined that science and history must be atheistical"; and a little later it adds that, according to Modernists, "religion, whether natural or supernatural, must, like every other fact, admit of an explanation". With what consistency can the Encyclical reproach us in the same breath with an agnostic prepossession which forbids any affirmations of reason about the super-phenomenal, and also with an atheistic postulate in science and history, and with the principle that the origin and nature of religion admit of an explanation?

But let us overlook these little slips which the compiler of the document has made in the embarrassing task of squeezing Modernism into the antiquated categories of his own philosophy, and let us examine seriously if there be aught of agnosticism in our system. And let us begin from the definition of agnosticism formulated by its great leader, Herbert Spencer. His conclusion, expounded and defended in *First Principles*, is as follows: "If we look into the nature and value of religion and science we find in the former certain primary ideas and universally present elements, and in the latter certain truths not deducible from other truths, and therefore inexplicable. So that at the basis both of religion and science we come on a sort of neutral ground which evades our mental analysis—on a bundle of ideas and sentiments which we cannot account for. On this ground, faith and science may and should be reconciled. We should acknowledge this domain of the 'Unknowable'; but as being such we should carefully refrain from every sort of irreverent desire to penetrate its nature or to determine its attributes and modes of action by our puny metaphysical speculations."

Now this agnostic confession of impotence in the face of the mystery of the universe is radically opposed to our mind. Our apologetic is precisely an attempt to escape from this agnostic knowledge-theory by rising above it; just as agnosticism stands for an attempt to rise above materialistic positivism. The agnostic, saturated with rational-istic principles, can imagine no other forms of knowledge than the sense-experience of phenomena and the dialectical reason invoked to dissipate the formal arguments of religious philosophy in defence of certain theories about the origin of the universe and its dependence on a Supreme Being. As Kant had revealed the antinomies of the cosmological, the psychological and the theological ideas, so Spencer, by means of pure argument, has tried to point out the arbitrary and aprioristic elements that enter into all our metaphysical and religious explanations of the real; concluding that there is a basis of reality impervious to our cognitive faculties, and on which we must not trespass.

Our own attitude with regard to knowledge and its value is radically different, and not only coincides with that more generally assumed by the philosophy of today, but is also in continuity with the general results of the criticism of science.

First of all we distinguish different orders of knowledge—pheno-menal, scientific, philosophic, religious. Phenomenal knowledge embraces all sense-objects in their particularity; scientific knowledge

applies its calculations to the various groupings of perceived phenomena, and gives expression to the constant laws of their changes;
philosophical knowledge is the interpretation of the universe according
to certain inborn categories of the human mind, and having regard
to the deep-seated, unchanging demands of life and action; religious
knowledge, in fine, is our actual experience of the Divine which works
in ourselves and in the whole world.

Naturally this does away with the old definitions, inherited by
scholasticism from certain classical sources, by which science was
conceived as "the knowledge of an object according to its causes—
efficient, final, material and formal", and philosophy as "the knowledge
of things human and divine in their ultimate causes". But it is not our
fault that the philosophy of science has, on its part, demonstrated
how much pure convention there is in every science; or if psychological
analysis, in its turn, has shown the subjective and personal elements
which contribute to the formation of abstract knowledge. So that
today it is no longer possible to speak of a cognitive faculty which
functions in complete independence of our subjective needs and
interests, and arrives at a certainty and a truth which is "an equation
of thought to thing" (*adaequatio rei et intellectus*). Today speculation
is recognized to be a sort of *action*, in the more general sense of the
term, and to be subservient to action. The act of knowledge is
the result of a laborious effort of the spirit to dominate reality and
turn it to its own service by aid of certain mental *schemata*, or
plans, in which it represents the useful relations and connections of
objects.

Such a conception is liberating in the broadest sense. Considering
the cognitive faculty as a function of man's whole inward life; always
remembering the relation of strict solidarity between abstract thought
and action; breaking down the fictitious barriers raised between thought
and will by scholastic psychology, we contrive to give an enormous
expansion to the region of "the knowable", and to show that man is
able, although by forms of knowledge hitherto little appreciated, to
attain to those higher realities, the intimate apprehension of which
augments the value of life and enriches it with new possibilities. Just
as science, by its combination of experiment with the laws of the
calculus, extends our dominion over the physical world, and as
metaphysics corresponds to the necessity of guiding our action by a

fixed conception of the universe, so the needs of our moral life, and that experience of the Divine which we possess in the hidden depths of our consciousness, issue in a special sense of spiritual realities which dominates the whole of our ethical existence.

For us it matters little to attain to God through the demonstrations of medieval metaphysics or through arguments from miracles and prophecies, which offend rather than impress the modern mind, and evade the control of experience. We recognize in ourselves other powers of Divine knowledge; we find in ourselves that inferential sense, of which Newman speaks, by which we can be assured of the presence of higher and ineffably mysterious powers with which we are in direct contact. Compared with this knowledge-theory of ours, agnosticism seems, as in fact it is, a cold, rationalistic system. We accept that criticism of pure reason which Kant and Spencer have made; but far from falling back, like Kant, on the aprioristic witness of the practical reason, or from ending, like Spencer, in the affirmation of an "Unknowable", we maintain the existence of other powers in the human spirit, every bit as reliable as the argumentative reason, for attaining to truth. It cannot be denied that our postulates are inspired by the principles of immanentism, for they all assume that the subject is not purely passive in its processes of knowledge and in its religious experiences, but brings forth from its own spiritual nature both the witness to a higher reality intuitively perceived and the abstract formulation of the same.

But is this principle of vital immanence so dangerous as the Encyclical seems to believe?

"Since—according to the Modernists—religion is nothing but a form of life, its explanation is to be found precisely in the life of man. Hence their principle of religious immanence. Furthermore, the first movement of every vital phenomenon, such as religion is said to be, is always to be ascribed to a certain need or impulse; speaking, then, more especially of the life of religion, its beginnings are to be ascribed to a certain sentiment or stirring of the heart." Even allowing for the unavoidable travesty to which our thought is subjected, owing to the attempt to express it in the categories of scholasticism, we recognize that these are, in substance, our ideals upon the origin of religion. Religion is shown to be the spontaneous result of irrepressible needs of man's spirit, which find satisfaction in the inward and emotional experience of the presence of God within us. In maintaining this are we in conflict with tradition? Let us see.

We must recognize, first of all, that the arguments for the existence of God, drawn by scholastic metaphysic from change and movement, from the finite and contingent nature of things, from the degrees of perfection, and from the design and purpose of the world, have lost all value nowadays. The conceptions on which these arguments rest have now, owing to the post-Kantian criticism both of abstract and empirical sciences and of philosophical language, lost that character of absoluteness which they possessed for the medieval Aristotelians. Since the mere conventionality of every abstract representation of reality has been demonstrated, it is clear not only that such arguments fall to pieces but that it is idle to construct others of the same class. Hence it was natural to have recourse to the testimony of conscience in order to demonstrate the existence of God, or rather, to justify our faith in the Divine. Thus an appeal was made to man's moral impulses, which, for the rest, are the most authorized witnesses in this matter, since the origin of religion is a fact of conscience and should be investigated accordingly. Such a mode of procedure is not only fully justified in itself, but has been held legitimate by the most illustrious representatives of Catholic teaching.

The judgment, "God exists", is, like every other judgment, either analytic or synthetic; or, to speak not with Kant but with the scholastics, is either necessary or contingent. But an affirmation of existence cannot be an analytical judgment; that is, the notion expressed by the predicate ("exists") cannot, of itself, form part of the notion expressed by the subject. It must, therefore, be a synthetic judgment; and since the Catholic philosophy does not admit judgments called synthetic *a priori*, we must conclude that it is synthetic *a posteriori*, that is, a judgment to be proved by experience and not by mere reflection. And since, in this case, there can plainly be no question of laboratory experiments, we must conclude that God's existence can be proved only by conscience and in the experiences of conscience. We are therefore perfectly logical in seeking to ground our affirmation of a transcendent divinity on the immanent needs of man's conscience, and in striving to follow up the deep aspirations and ever-recurring necessities which spur the will to raise itself with all its might towards God, who, as St Augustine says, already works in us creating this desire to seek him. So reasoning we are in perfect harmony with the scholastic as well as with the patristic tradition. The latter, more especially, considering Aristotelianism fatal to the profession of Christian orthodoxy, considered faith quite sufficient for itself and independent of philosophy. The former, although characterized by the predominance of realistic logic over mystical intuition, never forgot the moral argument when it wanted to prove the existence, the value, the purpose of spiritual realities. . . .

Thus we can maintain that our position as regards the proof of God is perfectly coherent with the best Christian tradition. Led as we are by the theory of sciences to a revision of all our empirical notions; enlightened as we have been by descriptive psychology as to the origin and value of abstract ideas in a way diametrically opposite to the scholastic theory of the *intellectus agens* and the *intellectus possibilis*; persuaded henceforth beyond doubt as to the natural conventions that enter into all our metaphysical conceptions of the real, we can no longer accept a demonstration of God supported by those "idols of the tribe"—the Aristotelian conceptions of motion, of causality, of contingency, of finality. We believe, moreover, it is better for the Christian conscience to allow explicitly that if the demonstration of God is essentially bound up with these conceptions then indeed criticism has definitively paved the way to atheism, but at the same time to affirm with the fullest conviction that there is another method of demonstrating that truth, the chief argument of all—older than scholasticism—the argument of the living and acting Spirit which, amid all the contingencies of its surface life, bears in itself a restless hunger for the Divine, and comes to live a more noble life only on condition of recognizing this hunger and satisfying it with the religious experience that its surroundings and historical setting naturally impose upon it.

Ibid., pp. *110–121*

THE FUTURE OF CATHOLICISM

The Modernist programme was composite and multiform. This is what explains the difficulty of the enterprise, its apparent lack of success, and the necessity of being armed with patience and possessed of tenacity when one still seeks to work for its slow and painful realization.

Those who, on the morrow of the encyclical *Pascendi* and the new disciplinary regime which in practice it installed in the Church, lowered their flag and retired discouraged from a fruitless struggle, did not have a sufficiently precise view of the heavy responsibilities which circumstances imposed. They did not know how to prepare their arms for the inevitable return. The encyclical did not proclaim the death of Modernism; it was able only to terminate violently its naïve and simple adolescence. The brutal blow that the Church gave it imposed upon it a revision of its programme, a transformation of its tactics, a new appreciation of the accessory circumstances and of the concrete possibilities of its work.

Modernism should and ought to be essentially an effort conscious and obstinate, to rediscover, through critical exploration of the revealed sources and history of Christianity, certain central values of the New Testament preaching whose efficacy the dogmatic tradition seemed to have made useless; values of which, to the contrary, contemporary spirituality seemed to have the deepest and most urgent need. Those who have reproached Modernism with being an inadmissible collection of scientific objectives and edifying ends, have not succeeded in penetrating to the heart of a movement which is destined to realize a vast and arduous programme.

Religious criticism such as the Modernists intended was only a means, but it was an indispensable means. A sure instinct warned the Modernist consciousness that conflict between the exercise of the reason on the one hand, and the drive towards the Divine Reality in religious history on the other, would be an insane denial of the providential laws of life and by consequence an absurdity and a blasphemy. So Modernism wished to take as its point of departure the unrestricted questioning of the nature of the actual appearance of the first forms of religiosity in general and then of the Christian fact in particular, as a way to the peaceful solution of the painful conflict which arises when the modern Spirit scrutinizes the early Christian tradition, seeking there the way to a new ascendancy of that message.

The evidence which was thus invoked was not refused us. Like parents whose familiar inflections we carry unconsciously in us, our fathers in the faith were enabled by such patient criticism of the texts to let us hear the accents of their ardent hope. Those who heard that echo through their scientific training, have demonstrated both its

fascinating attraction and its ineffable comfort. They came to believe
that if we continue in that same way, making known to others the
response whispered in our ears by this Spirit of our distant ancestors,
making known to the slumbering mass of believers the primitive
continuity of the faith, too often held by the fetters of an overly
rationalized dogmatic and an externalized and pharisaic discipline,
the revolutionary truth of the gospel may rise again from the wreck of
desiccated tradition and awaken men to the universal nature of man's
moral environment, however that may have been corrupted by
materialistic interests and preoccupations.

Critical history has been a superb effort of the contemporary mind,
which the timid and lazy mistreat. It is today the unique and indispensable instrument for a religious renaissance. It is this which the
Modernist consciousness stated and still states, not only because of its
own experience, but also because it has learned the nature of the spontaneous process of growth which the most advanced cultures reveal.
In those places where religious studies are pursued over a long time
and with the greatest wealth of material, we see the Modernist programme in its largest sense, indicative of the true goal of all modern
spiritual evolution: the pre-dialectical value of religiosity, the moral
and eschatological content of the Christian message, the continuity of
Christian evolution in history, the return to the elementary *givens*
of the gospel, with a view to the universal renewal of men's spirits
through the numinous categories of moral salvation.

We can understand from this how logical and how unequivocal
was the instinctive reaction of the official Catholic world, petrified
as it was with pharisaism, when in seeking to place an immovable
barrier on the road of the Modernist reform, it struck first of all at the
scientific movement which constitutes the preparatory stage for
spiritual renewal. . . .

Rome, by its intemperate and nefarious gesture, whose import the
future alone can rightly measure, has disdained and rejected the
assistance of Modernism. But despite this, Modernism must not
abandon any point of its programme, any article of its "profession of
faith". It well knows that the supreme manifestation of the Divine in
history—that is to say, the union of morality and religion, of the transitory and the eternal, of heaven and earth, of the kingdom of man and
the kingdom of God, as proclaimed in the preaching of Christ—

lives on and flourishes in the ideal and in the disciplinary structure of Catholicism in spite of innumerable deformations and contaminations.

Today this union runs a terrible danger. The spirit of paganism has spread its shadow over the world as it has not done for twenty centuries; it has advanced to the very threshold of the sacred dwelling-place of the Son of Man. Modernism lifted its voice, to warn and to counsel: "Enlarge the place of thy tent, stretch forth the curtains of thy habitation; spare not; lengthen thy cords and strengthen thy stakes; for thou shalt spread on the right hand and on the left; and thy seed shall people the deserted cities and have the nations as an heritage" (*Isaiah* liv. *2–3*).

That counsel and the warning still resound. God is with them. For wherever there is unanimous desire for brotherly concord in the heart of men, there is God, there is his act, there is his providence. Rome can choose. All depends on her, and on her alone. The new house for the spiritual solidarity of men *will* be raised, consolidated by Rome's blessing; or without fear the new house will defy Rome's anathemas, knowing that from henceforth those anathemas are powerless.

Le Modernisme catholique, quoted in C. Nelson and N. Pittenger,
Pilgrim of Rome, pp. *102–104*

THE PAPAL CONDEMNATION

(i)

Pascendi Dominici Gregis: September *8, 1907*[1]

One of the primary obligations assigned by Christ to the office divinely committed to Us of feeding the Lord's flock is that of guarding with the greatest vigilance the deposit of the faith delivered to the saints, rejecting the profane novelties of words and the gainsaying of knowledge falsely so called. There has never been a time when this watchfulness of the supreme pastor was not necessary to the Catholic body, for, owing to the efforts of the enemy of the human race, there have never been lacking "men speaking perverse things" (Acts xx. *30*), "vain talkers and seducers" (Tit. i. *10*), "erring and driving into error" (*2* Tim. iii. *13*). It must, however, be confessed that these latter days have witnessed a notable increase in the number of the enemies of the Cross of Christ, who, by arts entirely new and full of deceit, are striving to destroy the vital energy of the Church, and, as far as in them lies, utterly to subvert the very Kingdom of Christ. Wherefore We may no longer keep silence, lest We should seem to fail in Our most sacred duty, and lest the kindness that, in the hope of wiser counsels, We have hitherto shown them, should be set down to lack of diligence in the discharge of Our office.

That We should act without delay in this matter is made imperative especially by the fact that the partisans of error are to be sought not only among the Church's open enemies; but, what is to be most dreaded and deplored, in her very bosom, and are the more mischievous the less they keep in the open. We allude, Venerable Brethren, to many who belong to the Catholic laity, and, what is much more sad, to the ranks of the priesthood itself, who, animated by a false zeal for the Church, lacking the solid safeguards of philosophy and theology, nay more, thoroughly imbued with the poisonous doctrines taught

[1] Addressed to "the Patriarchs, Primates, Archbishops, and other Local Ordinaries in Peace and Communion with the Apostolic See".

by the enemies of the Church, and lost to all sense of modesty, put themselves forward as reformers of the Church; and, forming more boldly into line of attack, assail all that is most sacred in the work of Christ, not sparing even the Person of the Divine Redeemer, Whom, with sacrilegious audacity, they degrade to the condition of a simple and ordinary man. . . .

It is one of the cleverest devices of the Modernists (as they are commonly and rightly called) to present their doctrines without order and systematic arrangement, in a scattered and disjointed manner, so as to make it appear as if their minds were in doubt or hesitation, whereas in reality they are quite fixed and steadfast. . . .

To proceed in an orderly manner in this somewhat abstruse subject, it must first of all be noted that the Modernist sustains and includes within himself a manifold personality; he is a philosopher, a believer, a theologian, an historian, a critic, an apologist, a reformer. These roles must be clearly distinguished one from another by all who would accurately understand their system and thoroughly grasp the principles and the outcome of their doctrines.

We begin, then, with the philosopher. Modernists place the foundation of religious philosophy in that doctrine which is commonly called *Agnosticism*. According to this teaching human reason is confined entirely within the field of *phenomena*, that is to say, to things that appear, and in the manner in which they appear: it has neither the right nor the power to overstep these limits. Hence it is incapable of lifting itself up to God, and of recognizing his existence, even by means of visible things. From this it is inferred that God can never be the direct object of science, and that, as regards history, He must not be considered as an historical subject. Given these premisses, every one will at once perceive what becomes of *Natural Theology*, of the *motives of credibility*, of *external revelation*. The Modernists simply sweep them entirely aside; they include them in *Intellectualism* which they denounce as a system which is ridiculous and long since defunct. Nor does the fact that the Church has formally condemned these portentous errors exercise the slightest restraint upon them. . . . Yet it is a fixed and established principle among them that both science and history must be atheistic: and within their boundaries there is room for nothing but *phenomena;* God and all that is Divine are utterly excluded. . . .

However, this *Agnosticism* is only the negative part of the system of the Modernists: the positive part consists in what they call *vital immanence*. Thus they advance from one to the other. Religion, whether natural or supernatural, must, like every other fact, admit of some explanation. But when natural theology has been destroyed, and the road to revelation closed by the rejection of the arguments of credibility, and all external revelation absolutely denied, it is clear that this explanation will be sought in vain outside of man himself. It must, therefore, be looked for in man; and since religion is a form of life, the explanation must certainly be found in the life of man. In this way is formulated the principle of *religious immanence*. Moreover, the first actuation, so to speak, of every vital phenomenon—and religion, as noted above, belongs to this category—is due to a certain need or impulsion; but speaking more particularly of life, it has its origin in a movement of the heart, which movement is called a *sense*. Therefore, as God is the object of religion, we must conclude that faith, which is the basis and foundation of all religion, must consist in a certain interior sense, originating in a need of the Divine. This need of the Divine, which is experienced only in special and favourable circumstances, cannot, of itself, appertain to the domain of consciousness, but is first latent beneath consciousness, or, to borrow a term from modern philosophy, in the *subconsciousness*, where also its root lies hidden and undetected.

It may perhaps be asked how it is that this need of the Divine which man experiences within himself resolves itself into religion? To this question the Modernist reply would be as follows: Science and history are confined within two boundaries, the one external, namely, the visible world, the other internal, which is consciousness. When one or other of these limits has been reached, there can be no further progress, for beyond is the *unknowable*. In presence of this *unknowable*, whether it is outside man and beyond the visible world of Nature, or lies hidden within the *subconsciousness*, the need of the Divine in a soul which is prone to religion, excites—according to the principles of *Fideism*, without any previous advertence of the mind—a certain special *sense*, and this sense possesses, implied within itself both as its own object and as its intrinsic cause, the Divine *reality* itself, and in a way unites man with God. It is this *sense* to which Modernists give the name of faith, and this is what they hold to be the beginning of religion.

But we have not yet reached the end of their philosophizing, or, to speak more accurately, of their folly. Modernists find in this *sense*, not only faith, but in and with faith, as they understand it, they affirm that there is also to be found *revelation*. For, indeed, what more is needed to constitute a revelation? Is not that religious *sense* which is perceptible in the conscience, revelation, or at least the beginning of revelation? Nay, is it not God himself manifesting himself, indistinctly it is true, in this same religious *sense*, to the soul? And they add: Since God is both the object and the cause of faith, this revelation is at the same time *of* God and *from* God, that is to say, God is both the Revealer and the Revealed.

From this, Venerable Brethren, springs that most absurd tenet of the Modernists, that every religion, according to the different aspect under which it is viewed, must be considered as both natural and supernatural. It is thus that they make consciousness and revelation synonymous. From this they derive the law laid down as the universal standard, according to which *religious consciousness* is to be put on an equal footing with revelation, and that to it all must submit, even the supreme authority of the Church, whether in the capacity of teacher, or in that of legislator in the province of sacred liturgy or discipline. . . .

It is thus that the *religious sense*, which through the agency of *vital immanence* emerges from the lurking-places of the *subconsciousness*, is the germ of all religion, and the explanation of everything that has been or ever will be in any religion. This *sense*, which was at first only rudimentary and almost formless, under the influence of that mysterious principle from which it originated, gradually matured with the progress of human life, of which, as has been said, it is a certain form. This, then, is the origin of all, even of supernatural religion. For religions are mere developments of this *religious sense*. Nor is the Catholic religion an exception; it is quite on a level with the rest; for it was engendered, by the process of *vital immanence*, and by no other way, in the consciousness of Christ, who was a man of the choicest nature, whose like has never been, nor will be. In hearing these things we shudder indeed at so great an audacity of assertion and so great a sacrilege. And yet, Venerable Brethren, these are not merely the foolish babblings of unbelievers. There are Catholics, yea, and priests too, who say these things openly; and they boast that they are going to reform the Church by these ravings!

. . . In their writings and addresses they seem not unfrequently to advocate doctrines which are contrary one to the other, so that one would be disposed to regard their attitude as double and doubtful. But this is done deliberately and advisedly, and the reason of it is to be found in their opinion as to the mutual separation of science and faith. Thus in their books one finds some things which might well be approved by a Catholic, but on turning over the page one is confronted by other things which might well have been dictated by a rationalist. When they write history they make no mention of the divinity of Christ, but when they are in the pulpit they profess it clearly; again, when they are dealing with history they take no account of the Fathers and the Councils, but when they catechize the people, they cite them respectfully. In the same way they draw their distinctions between exegesis which is theological and pastoral and exegesis which is scientific and historical. So, too, when they treat of philosophy, history, and criticism, acting on the principle that science in no way depends upon faith, they feel no especial horror in treading in the footsteps of Luther and are wont to display a manifold contempt for Catholic doctrines, for the Holy Fathers, for the Oecumenical Councils, for the ecclesiastical Magisterium; and should they be taken to task for this, they complain that they are being deprived of their liberty. Lastly, maintaining the theory that faith must be subject to science, they continuously and openly rebuke the Church on the ground that she resolutely refuses to submit and accommodate her dogmas to the opinions of philosophy; while they, on their side, having for this purpose blotted out the old theology, endeavour to introduce a new theology which shall support the aberrations of philosophers. . . .

But it is not only within her own household that the Church must come to terms. Besides her relations with those within, she has others with those who are outside. The Church does not occupy the world all by herself; there are other societies in the world, with which she must necessarily have dealings and contact. The rights and duties of the Church towards civil societies must, therefore, be determined, and determined, of course, by her own nature, that to wit, which the Modernists have already described to us. The rules to be applied in this matter are clearly those which have been laid down for science and faith, though in the latter case the question turned upon the *object*,

Q

while in the present case we have one of *ends*. In the same way, then, as faith and science are alien to each other by reason of the diversity of their *objects*, Church and State are strangers by reason of the diversity of their ends, that of the Church being spiritual while that of the State is temporal. . . .

. . . The State must, therefore, be separated from the Church, and the Catholic from the citizen. Every Catholic, from the fact that he is also a citizen, has the right and the duty to work for the common good in the way he thinks best, without troubling himself about the authority of the Church, without paying any heed to its wishes, its counsels, its orders—nay, even in spite of its rebukes. For the Church to trace out and prescribe for the citizen any line of action, on any pretext whatsoever, is to be guilty of an abuse of authority, against which one is bound to protest with all one's might. Venerable Brethren, the principles from which these doctrines spring have been solemnly condemned by Our Predecessor, Pius VI, in his Apostolic Constitution *Auctorem fidei*.

(ii)

Lamentabili Sane Exitu: July 3, 1907

With truly lamentable results, our age, casting aside all restraint in its search for the ultimate causes of things, frequently pursues novelties so ardently that it rejects the legacy of the human race. Thus it falls into very serious errors, which are even more serious when they concern sacred authority, the interpretation of Sacred Scripture, and the principal mysteries of Faith. The fact that many Catholic writers also go beyond the limits determined by the Fathers and the Church herself is extremely regrettable. In the name of higher knowledge and historical research (they say), they are looking for that progress of dogmas which is, in reality, nothing but the corruption of dogmas.

These errors are being daily spread among the faithful. Lest they captivate the faithful's minds and corrupt the purity of their faith, His Holiness, Pius X, by Divine Providence, Pope, has decided that the chief errors should be noted and condemned by the Office of this Holy Roman and Universal Inquisition.

Therefore, after a very diligent investigation and consultation with the Reverend Consultors, the Most Eminent and Reverend Lord Cardinal, the General Inquisitors in matters of faith and morals have judged the following propositions to be condemned and proscribed. In fact, by this general decree they are condemned and proscribed.

·   ·   ·   ·   ·

1. The ecclesiastical law which prescribes that books concerning the Divine Scriptures are subject to previous examination does not apply to critical scholars and students of scientific exegesis of the Old and New Testament.

2. The Church's interpretation of the Sacred Books is by no means to be rejected; nevertheless, it is subject to the more accurate judgment and correction of the exegetes.

3. From the ecclesiastical judgments and censures passed against free and more scientific exegesis, one can conclude that the Faith the Church proposes contradicts history and that Catholic teaching cannot really be reconciled with the true origins of the Christian religion.

4. Even by dogmatic definitions the Church's magisterium cannot determine the genuine sense of the Sacred Scriptures.

5. Since the deposit of Faith contains only revealed truths, the Church has no right to pass judgment on the assertions of the human sciences.

6. The "Church learning" and the "Church teaching" collaborate in such a way in defining truths that it only remains for the "Church teaching" to sanction the opinions of the "Church learning".

7. In proscribing errors, the Church cannot demand any internal assent from the faithful by which the judgments she issues are to be embraced.

8. They are free from all blame who treat lightly the condemnations passed by the Sacred Congregation of the Index or by the Roman Congregations.

9. They display excessive simplicity or ignorance who believe that God is really the author of the Sacred Scriptures.

10. The inspiration of the books of the Old Testament consists in this: The Israelite writers handed down religious doctrines under a peculiar aspect which was either little or not at all known to the Gentiles.

11. Divine inspiration does not extend to all of Sacred Scriptures so that it renders its parts, each and every one, free from every error.

12. If he wishes to apply himself usefully to Biblical studies, the exegete must first put aside all preconceived opinions about the supernatural origin of Sacred Scripture and interpret it the same as any other merely human document.

13. The Evangelists themselves, as well as the Christians of the second and third generation, artificially arranged the evangelical parables. In such a way they explained the scanty fruit of the preaching of Christ among the Jews.

14. In many narrations the Evangelists recorded, not so much things that are true, as things which, even though false, they judged to be more profitable for their readers.

15. Until the time the canon was defined and constituted, the Gospels were increased by additions and corrections. Therefore there remained in them only a faint and uncertain trace of the doctrine of Christ.

16. The narrations of John are not properly history, but a mystical contemplation of the Gospel. The discourses contained in his Gospel are theological meditations, lacking historical truth concerning the mystery of salvation.

17. The fourth Gospel exaggerated miracles not only in order that the extraordinary might stand out but also in order that it might become more suitable for showing forth the work and glory of the Word Incarnate.

18. John claims for himself the quality of witness concerning Christ. In reality, however, he is only a distinguished witness of the Christian life, or of the life of Christ in the Church at the close of the first century.

19. Heterodox exegetes have expressed the true sense of the Scriptures more faithfully than Catholic exegetes.

20. Revelation could be nothing else than the consciousness man acquired of his relation to God.

21. Revelation, constituting the object of the Catholic faith, was not completed with the Apostles.

22. The dogmas the Church holds out as revealed are not truths which have fallen from heaven. They are an interpretation of religious facts which the human mind has acquired by laborious effort.

23. Opposition may, and actually does, exist between the facts narrated in Sacred Scripture and the Church's dogmas which rest on them. Thus the critic may reject as false, facts the Church holds as most certain.

24. The exegete who constructs premisses from which it follows that dogmas are historically false or doubtful is not to be reproved as long as he does not directly deny the dogmas themselves.

25. The assent of faith ultimately rests on a mass of probabilities.

26. The dogmas of the Faith are to be held only according to their practical sense; that is to say, as preceptive norms of conduct and not as norms of believing.

27. The divinity of Jesus Christ is not proved from the Gospels. It is a dogma which the Christian conscience has derived from the notion of the Messias.

28. While He was exercising His ministry, Jesus did not speak with the object of teaching He was Messias, nor did his miracles tend to prove it.

29. It is permissible to grant that the Christ of history is far inferior to the Christ Who is the object of faith.

30. In all the evangelical texts the name "Son of God" is equivalent only to that of "Messias". It does not in the least way signify that Christ is the true and natural Son of God.

31. The doctrine concerning Christ taught by Paul, John, and the Councils of Nicaea, Ephesus and Chalcedon is not that which Jesus taught but that which the Christian conscience conceived concerning Jesus.

32. It is impossible to reconcile the natural sense of the gospel texts with the sense taught by our theologians concerning the conscience and the infallible knowledge of Jesus Christ.

33. Everyone who is not led by preconceived opinions can readily see that either Jesus professed an error concerning the immediate Messianic coming or the greater part of his doctrine as contained in the Gospels is destitute of authenticism.

34. The critics can ascribe to Christ a knowledge without limits only on a hypothesis which cannot be historically conceived and which is repugnant to the moral sense. That hypothesis is that Christ as man possessed the knowledge of God and yet was unwilling to communicate the knowledge of a great many things to His disciples and posterity.

35. Christ did not always possess the consciousness of His Messianic dignity.

36. The Resurrection of the Saviour is not properly a fact of the

historical order. It is a fact of merely the supernatural order (neither demonstrated nor demonstrable) which the Christian conscience gradually derived from other facts.

37. In the beginning, faith in the Resurrection of Christ was not so much in the fact itself of the Resurrection as in the immortal life of Christ with God.

38. The doctrine of the expiatory death of Christ is Pauline and not evangelical.

39. The opinions concerning the origin of the Sacraments which the Fathers of Trent held and which certainly influenced their dogmatic canons are very different from those which now rightly exist among historians who examine Christianity.

40. The Sacraments had their origin in the fact that the Apostles and their successors, swayed and moved by circumstances and events, interpreted some idea and intention of Christ.

41. The Sacraments are intended merely to recall to man's mind the ever-beneficent presence of the Creator.

42. The Christian community imposed the necessity of Baptism, adopted it as a necessary rite, and added to it the obligation of the Christian profession.

43. The practice of administering Baptism to infants was a disciplinary evolution, which became one of the causes why the Sacrament was divided into two, namely, Baptism and Penance.

44. There is nothing to prove that the rite of the Sacrament of Confirmation was employed by the Apostles. The formal distinction of the two Sacraments of Baptism and Confirmation does not pertain to the history of primitive Christianity.

45. Not everything which Paul narrates concerning the institution of the Eucharist (I Cor. xi. *23–25*) is to be taken historically.

46. In the primitive Church the concept of the Christian sinner reconciled by the authority of the Church did not exist. Only very slowly did the Church accustom herself to this concept. As a matter of fact, even after Penance was recognized as an institution of the Church, it was not called a Sacrament since it would be held as a disgraceful Sacrament.

47. The words of the Lord, "Receive the Holy Spirit; whose sins you shall forgive, they are forgiven them; and whose sins you shall retain, they are retained" (John xx. *22–23*), in no way refer to the

Sacrament of Penance, in spite of what it pleased the Fathers of Trent to say.

48. In his Epistle (v. *14–15*) James did not intend to promulgate a Sacrament of Christ but only commend a pious custom. If in this custom he happens to distinguish a means of grace, it is not in that rigorous manner in which it was taken by the theologians who laid down the notion and number of the Sacraments.

49. When the Christian supper gradually assumed the nature of a liturgical action those who customarily presided over the supper acquired the sacerdotal character.

50. The elders who fulfilled the office of watching over the gatherings of the faithful were instituted by the Apostles as priests or bishops to provide for the necessary ordering of the increasing communities and not properly for the perpetuation of the Apostolic mission and power.

51. It is impossible that Matrimony could have become a Sacrament of the new law until later in the Church since it was necessary that a full theological explication of the doctrine of grace and the Sacraments should first take place before Matrimony should be held as a Sacrament.

52. It was far from the mind of Christ to found a Church as a society which would continue on earth for a long course of centuries. On the contrary, in the mind of Christ the kingdom of Heaven together with the end of the world was about to come immediately.

53. The organic constitution of the Church is not immutable. Like human society, Christian society is subject to a perpetual evolution.

54. Dogmas, Sacraments and hierarchy, both their notion and reality, are only interpretations and evolutions of the Christian intelligence which have increased and perfected by an external series of additions the little germ latent in the gospel.

55. Simon Peter never even suspected that Christ entrusted the primacy in the Church to him.

56. The Roman Church became the head of all the churches, not through the ordinance of Divine Providence, but merely through political conditions.

57. The Church has shown that she is hostile to the progress of the natural theological sciences.

58. Truth is no more immutable than man himself, since it evolved with him, in him, and through him.

59. Christ did not teach a determined body of doctrine applicable to all times and all men, but rather inaugurated a religious movement adapted or to be adapted to different times and places.

60. Christian Doctrine was originally Judaic. Through successive evolutions it became first Pauline, then Johannine, finally Hellenic and universal.

61. It may be said without paradox that there is no chapter of Scripture, from the first of Genesis to the last of the Apocalypse, which contains a doctrine absolutely identical with that which the Church teaches on the same matter. For the same reason, therefore, no chapter of Scripture has the same sense for the critic and the theologian.

62. The chief articles of the Apostles' Creed did not have the same sense for the Christian of the first ages as they have for the Christians of our time.

63. The Church shows that she is incapable of effectively maintaining evangelical ethics since she obstinately clings to immutable doctrines which cannot be reconciled with modern progress.

64. Scientific progress demands that the concepts of Christian doctrine concerning God, creation, revelation, the Person of the Incarnate Word, and Redemption be readjusted.

65. Modern Catholicism can be reconciled with true science only if it is transformed into a non-dogmatic Christianity; that is to say, into a broad and liberal Protestantism.

INDEX OF PERSONS

Abelard, 225
Acton, Lord, 13
Aquinas, St T., 203, 217
Arnold, M., 43 n
Astruc, J., 173, 213
Augustine, St, 197, 232

Batiffol, P., 32, 33, 64
Benigni, Mgr, 64
Bernard, St, 187, 225
Billot, L., 63
Blondel, M., 15, 32, 38, 50, 52–56,
    65 n
Bonaventure, St, 195
Bourne, Cardinal, 41
Braithwaite, R. B., 59 n
Bremond, H., 43 n
Briggs, C. A., 174
Buonaiuti, E., 59, 63, 65
Butler, Abbot C., 33

D'Hulst, Mgr, 19, 20
Dolling, R., 37
Drews, A., 174
Duchesne, L., 18, 64

Erigena, Scotus, 225
Eutyches, 224

Fawkes, A., 11
Ferrari, Cardinal, 62
Fogazzaro, A., 12, 60, 61
Frazer, J. G., 25, 174

Galileo, 173

Harnack, A. von, 27, 28, 29 n, 30, 32,
    33, 70–75, 78, 79, 81, 93, 97
Hügel, F. von, 10, 11, 12, 14 n, 15,
    21, 22, 26, 32, 38, 50–52, 53, 54

Inge, W. R., 49 n

James, W., 43

Kant, 229, 232
Kierkegaard, 149
Kraus, F.-X., 12

Laberthonnière, L., 38, 50, 52, 55–57,
    205
Lagrange, M.-J., 64
Lemius, J., 63 n
Leo XIII, Pope, 10, 13, 14, 35, 64,
    101, 104, 184
Lerins, Vincent of, 83
Le Roy, É., 12, 52, 57–59, 63
Lilley, A. L., 11 n
Loisy, A., 10, 15, 16–36, 37, 43, 52,
    63, 65, 66, 174, 214

Malebranche, 195
Mercier, Cardinal, 48, 170
Mignot, Archbishop, 12, 32, 33, 63
Möhler, J. A., 15
Montalembert, 15
Murri, R., 60, 63

Newman, Cardinal, 15, 22, 39, 54,
    83, 231

Ollé-Laprune, L., 15

Pascal, 53, 194
Peirce, C. S., 43
Perraud, Cardinal, 34
Petre, M., 38, 39, 43 n, 65, 185 n
Pius X, Pope, 10, 13, 32, 35, 63, 184,
    242
Priscillian, 213

Rampolla, Cardinal, 64, 173
Reinach, S., 174
Renan, E., 15, 17, 36
Richard, Cardinal, 25, 33, 99
Roscelyn, 225
Rosmini, A., 60
Rufinus, 219

Sabatier, A., 23, 28
Sabatier, P., 51
Schell, H., 12
Semeria, G., 60
Simon, R., 173, 213
Smith, W. R., 174
Spencer, H., 229, 231

Stewart, H. L., 9 n
Sullivan, W. L., 12 n

Temple, W., 51
Theresa, St, 189
Tolstoy, 60
Troeltsch, E., 185
Tyrrell, G., 10, 11, 17, 36–50, 63, 65, 67

Vidler, A. R., 43 n, 49, 63

Ward, W., 14, 32, 39
Wernle, P., 15

INDEX OF SUBJECTS

Action, philosophy of, 52–55, 195, 196
Agnosticism, 228, 229, 239
Apologetics, problem of, 53, 187–190
Apostles' creed, 203, 204
Authority, ecclesiastical, 80, 81

Being, knowledge of, 196–198

Catholicism, nature of, 150–163, 233–236
Christianity, criticism and origins of, 98–107
—, history of, critically viewed, 217–228
—, in the modern world, 207–211
—, the essence of, 69–75
Church, Catholic, 61, 75–82, 180–184

Dogma and development, 82–89, 145–150, 217–228
—, meaning of, 57–59, 199–206
—, practical sense of, 205, 206

Episcopate, 79

God, arguments for existence of, 232, 233
—, belief in, 121–126

History and religious belief, 133–136, 173–179

Immanentism, 228–233, 238–240
Incarnation, 126–133

Modernism, errors of, condemned, 63–65, 243–248
—, meaning of, 1, 12, 13, 107–109, 164–170, 184, 185, 207–211
—, significance of, 65–67, 170, 171
—, varieties of, 2
Modernism and medievalism, 164–170

Organization in religion, need of, 97, 98

Religion as "natural", 150–153
Revelation and theology, 111–119

Sacramentalism, 90–93
Saints, cult of, 93–97

Worship, Catholic, 89–98

DATE DUE